NEW STUDIES IN BIBLICAL THEOLOGY 62

T0324552

ANSWERING THE
PSALMIST'S PERPLEXITY

'Creative, thoughtful and attuned to the interconnectedness of Scripture . . . Pastors preaching on the Psalms will glean from Hely Hutchinson's work, and students and scholars will reap a bountiful harvest.'
D. A. Carson and **Benjamin L. Gladd**

'Here is an up-to-date, broad-sweeping engagement with the book of Psalms and its contribution to the question of the relationship between the different biblical covenants. The reader finds here innovative interaction between Psalm 89 and the Psalter in its totality, set in the context of biblical theology and working with sound exegesis. Building on his previous work in Psalms studies, Hely Hutchinson tackles a difficult question: "What is new about the new covenant, according to the book of Psalms?"

'Many studies dealing with editorial criticism on the Psalter have been published in the past few decades. This one not only carefully locates the discussion in the Psalter itself, but also includes insights from the different covenants progressively revealed in Scripture. *Answering the Psalmist's Perplexity* is a refreshing and challenging study, but also a model of biblical theology.'
Pierre Constant, Chair of New Testament Studies, Toronto Baptist Seminary

'James Hely Hutchinson carefully traces the place of the biblical covenants within the book of Psalms, demonstrating both their importance for the canonical shape of the book and also why this matters for us today. Widely read and closely attentive to the text, this is a vital treatment of this important topic.'
David G. Firth, Trinity College Bristol

'My resonance with this book is deep and wide, methodological and exegetical. James Hely Hutchinson serves as a sure-footed guide (in English! at your desk!) through the highest mountain passes of the Psalter: its editorial arrangement, its contribution to our understanding of the covenants and its typological presentation of the coming King. Here is a book whose author has meditatively studied the Psalms, and reading this book is the next best thing to undertaking exegesis through the Psalter with him in class. So if you can't get to Belgium to take his class in French, avail yourself of what he has provided for you in this book.'
James M. Hamilton, Professor of Biblical Theology, Southern Baptist Theological Seminary, Louisville, Kentucky

'James Hely Hutchinson has dared to address some large, perpetually debated questions about the relationships between the biblical covenants through a new lens: the book of Psalms. In a creative interweaving of the messages of the different parts of the Psalter, understanding the Psalter as a unified collection in its final form, he shows how the major covenants – Adamic, Noahic, Abrahamic, Mosaic, Levitical, Davidic and new covenants – are addressed in the book of Psalms. He also highlights the continuities, discontinuities and complementary elements among them. An intriguing read that I recommend with pleasure.'

David M. Howard Jr, Professor of Old Testament, Bethlehem College and Seminary, Minneapolis, Minnesota

'In this book, James Hely Hutchinson offers an outstanding model for studies on biblical theology, exemplifying careful biblical exegesis and showing awareness of relevant scholarly issues involved, but also keeping in view the whole storyline of the Bible. He carefully traces from the book of Psalms how, even in the Old Testament, all the biblical covenants point beyond themselves to something new, bigger and better in fulfilment of the new covenant. Both pastors and students will benefit from the perceptively laid-out argument of this book. It will be an invaluable source of information for years to come on covenant theology discussions and Psalms study.'

Ma'afu Palu, Director of Graphe Bible College, Sydney, and Senior Pastor, Tongan Evangelical Wesleyan Church

'James Hely Hutchinson has spent more than two decades studying the arrangement of the psalms in the Psalter. His book provides a compelling account of the way in which this arrangement reflects God's salvation plan. By analysing the relationships between the different covenants mentioned across the Psalter, Hely Hutchinson provides fascinating insights into the way that the psalms work as a collection to give hope for the future ideal Davidic king who will bless and be blessed by a new-covenant people from all nations. He also explains and evaluates a spectrum of seven different positions on covenant relationships and irenically charts a way forward in the light of his findings in the Psalter. His book richly rewards careful reading.'

Anthony R. Petterson, Lecturer in Old Testament and Biblical Hebrew, Morling College, Sydney

'*Answering the Psalmist's Perplexity* stands as an indispensable resource for scholars delving into the Psalter, providing clarity on its relationship with biblical covenants, particularly the new covenant. Dr James Hely Hutchinson's meticulous analysis of the psalms' composition unravels the enigma that the psalmist ponders, shedding light on God's unwavering covenant faithfulness. In this scholarly work, Hely Hutchinson's insights not only enhance our understanding of the Psalter but also contribute to a deeper grasp of its pivotal role within the broader scope of redemptive history.'

Angie Velasquez Thornton, Director of Women's Ministry, SOLA (The Gospel Coalition, Quebec)

'In this fascinating study, Hely Hutchinson deftly and meticulously explores several key issues within a single volume. Not only does he present a robust, holistic interpretation of the Psalter, but he also demonstrates how the relationship between various divine–human covenants informs and is informed by the Psalter's arrangement. As such, this is a must read for all those interested in the Psalter's biblical-theological significance and/or contrasting theological systems in which the relationship between various divine covenants is of key importance.'

Paul R. Williamson, Lecturer in Old Testament, Hebrew and Aramaic, Moore College, Sydney

NEW STUDIES IN BIBLICAL THEOLOGY 62

Series editors: D. A. Carson and Benjamin L. Gladd

ANSWERING THE PSALMIST'S PERPLEXITY

New-covenant newness in the book of Psalms

James Hely Hutchinson

APOLLOS

Academic
An imprint of InterVarsity Press
Downers Grove, Illinois

APOLLOS (an imprint of Inter-Varsity Press, England)
c/o SPCK, Studio 101, The Record Hall, 16–16A Baldwin's Gardens, London EC1N 7RJ, England
Website: www.ivpbooks.com
Email: ivp@ivpbooks.com

InterVarsity Press, USA
P. O. Box 1400, Downers Grove, IL 60515, USA
Website: www.ivpress.com
Email: email@ivpress.com

Inter-Varsity Press, England, publishes Christian books that are true to the Bible and that
communicate the gospel, develop discipleship and strengthen the church for its mission in the world.

IVP originated within the Inter-Varsity Fellowship, now the Universities and Colleges Christian
Fellowship, a student movement connecting Christian Unions in universities and colleges
throughout Great Britain, and a member movement of the International Fellowship
of Evangelical Students. That historic association is maintained, and all senior IVP staff and
committee members subscribe to the UCCF Basis of Faith. Website: www.uccf.org.uk.

InterVarsity Press®, USA, is the book-publishing division of InterVarsity Christian Fellowship/USA®
and a member movement of the International Fellowship of Evangelical Students.
Website: www.intervarsity.org.

Unless otherwise noted, Scripture quotations are the author's own translation.
Translations from other languages are those of the author.

First published 2023

Set in 10/13.25pt Minion Pro and Gill Sans Nova
Typeset in Great Britain by CRB Associates, Potterhanworth, Lincolnshire
Printed and bound by CPI Group (UK) Ltd, Croydon, CR0 4YY

Produced on paper from sustainable sources

UK ISBN: 978-1-78974-098-1 (print)
UK ISBN: 978-1-78974-099-8 (digital)

US ISBN: 978-1-5140-0886-7 (print)
US ISBN: 978-1-5140-0887-4 (digital)

British Library Cataloguing-in-Publication Data
A catalogue record for this book is available from the British Library.

Library of Congress Cataloging-in-Publication Data
A catalog record for this book is available from the Library of Congress.

For Myriam,
wonderfully 'suitable helper' (Gen. 2:18, 20) in a tough ministry context.

Contents

Illustrations

Figures

Tables

Series preface

New Studies in Biblical Theology is a series of monographs that address key issues in the discipline of biblical theology. Contributions to the series focus on one or more of three areas: (1) the nature and status of biblical theology, including its relations with other disciplines (e.g. historical theology, exegesis, systematic theology, historical criticism, narrative theology); (2) the articulation and exposition of the structure of thought of a particular biblical writer or corpus; and (3) the delineation of a biblical theme across all or part of the biblical corpora.

Above all, these monographs are creative attempts to help thinking Christians understand their Bibles better. The series aims simultaneously to instruct and to edify, to interact with the current literature and to point the way ahead. In God's universe, mind and heart should not be divorced: in this series we will try not to separate what God has joined together. While the notes interact with the best of scholarly literature, the text is uncluttered with untransliterated Greek and Hebrew, and tries to avoid too much technical jargon. The volumes are written within the framework of confessional evangelicalism, but there is always an attempt at thoughtful engagement with the sweep of the relevant literature.

Hely Hutchinson's project is creative, thoughtful and attuned to the interconnectedness of Scripture – how the Psalms allude to critical sections of antecedent revelation. He rightly sees the Psalms as assembling the building blocks of a robust understanding of the new covenant, founded on the Noahic, Abrahamic, Levitical and Davidic covenants. Pastors preaching on the Psalms will glean from Hely Hutchinson's work, and students and scholars will reap a bountiful harvest.

D. A. Carson
Trinity Evangelical Divinity School

Benjamin L. Gladd
Reformed Theological Seminary

Author's preface

This book reflects over three decades of gestation. It was perhaps in 1990 that a friend asked me what was new about the new covenant, and I came to be exposed to some teaching on the 'big picture' of the Scriptures (this was a rare privilege back then!). Soon afterwards, in 1991, I began teaching biblical theology at church level. A year or so later, I became convicted that my ignorance of the book of Psalms needed to be put right, and that came to be translated into annual study retreats with groups of friends (1995–2000). As I embarked on formal theological training at Moore Theological College in Sydney in 1996, I became aware that Psalms scholarship was beginning to focus on questions relating to the arrangement of the Psalter, and this became an area of interest.

The 'new-covenant newness' stream and the 'Psalter shape' stream merged in 2002 for doctoral research under Émile Nicole at the Faculté Libre de Théologie Evangélique at Vaux-sur-Seine (in France) which was defended in 2006.[1] A large proportion of that material remained unpublished until it arrived in a recent (2022) book on new-covenant newness[2] and (especially) in its present form. Some of it, though, has fetched up in articles[3] or has featured in the lecture room: I have been teaching courses on the Psalms since 2003 and on biblical theology since 2005, first at Vaux-sur-Seine (plus, in the case of the Psalms, at the Institut Biblique de Nogent-sur-Marne) and, since 2007, at the Institut Biblique Belge in Brussels (renamed Institut Biblique de Bruxelles in 2019). At a more popular level, I have provided, most years since 2002, input related to the content of this book to Bible-study groups of St Helen's Church, Bishopsgate (London), which meet for the most intensive weekends of teaching that I ever give or experience. Several other church/training/conference/symposium groupings – from/in Spokane (Washington), Paris, Vaux-sur-Seine, Sainte-Foi-lès-Lyon, Toulon, Étupes, St Albans, London (Cornhill Training Course; St Helen's), Durham and (online)

---

[1] Hely Hutchinson 2006.
[2] Hely Hutchinson 2022.
[3] Notably Hely Hutchinson 2005a; 2015a (and, to some extent, 2013b).

Northern Ireland – have been exposed to parts of this material. So I would not be able to begin to evaluate how much of a debt I owe to others for their (often 'Berean'-like)[4] interaction, challenging me to show my working, sharpening my thinking, requiring that my assertions be refined ... While remaining shortcomings are, of course, my own, it is appropriate that my gratitude be expressed.

But there are parts of this book that are relatively 'untested' by such settings, and, until delivering the Annual Moore College Lectures of 2018,[5] I had never set out to teach directly on new-covenant newness as arising from Psalter shape. Further, the material in this book is fresh inasmuch as it amounts to an updating of my doctorate, for an English-speaking audience and readership, that takes account of recent developments in the debates regarding both covenant relationships and the configuration of the book of Psalms. It may be considered an attempt to take up the first part of the challenge that I issued in 2005:

> questions of degrees of continuity and discontinuity between the new covenant and covenants set up before the exile – which remain a source of division among Christians, especially between (Reformed) covenant-theologians on the one hand and dispensa-tionalists on the other – may be fruitfully studied in the books of Psalms and Chronicles ... certainly, in both books the question of the status of the Davidic covenant following the exile is given considerable prominence.[6]

In the providence of God, there is more of a 'market' for a study of this kind than there was at the time of my carrying out the doctoral research. With the recent rise of progressive covenantalism and 1689 federalism as recognizable movements within the evangelical landscape, questions of how covenants relate have been more and more on the agenda. In the area of Psalter shape, although some of the debates continue apace, 'editorial criticism' is now sufficiently mature that it is possible to speak of a broad

---

[4] See Acts 17:11.

[5] The material of this book has essentially been available online since 2018. See <https://www.youtube.com/watch?v=s6HrlyAzxpM&list=PLQ20r982e5fCICPGZ8JW2glX5oNOgClCX> (accessed 26 July 2023).

[6] 2005a: 120. Hensley has also taken up this challenge – though in a somewhat different direction, contending that 'editors royalized the premonarchic covenants and their associated promises and obligations' (2018: 267).

consensus on a number of key insights, and the time is ripe for building on them.

I do not consider the writing of this book to be a private venture. Quite apart from the time spent seeking God's face (cf. Ps. 27:8) and interacting with others, the original impulse for preparing this publication did not lie with myself. When I was approached, four years in advance, to consider delivering the Annual Moore College Lectures of 2018, my instinctive reaction was to decline the invitation. The decision to go ahead was made only with encouragement from the Board of Governors and Academic Board[7] of the Institut Biblique Belge (IBB, now Institut Biblique de Bruxelles). Also, members of churches who support our work at the IBB and other friends have kindly accompanied this project in prayer along the way.

I would like to say a particular word of thanks to my wife Myriam and daughter Clara, who have backed me in the challenge of finding time to produce the material in this form; to Mark Thompson, Principal of Moore College, for the invitation to deliver the 2018 Lectures; to his wife Kathryn who, along with the four Thompson daughters, displayed amazing kindness towards us as a family during our stay; to Peter Orr, for his constant encouragement, prayers and handling of the logistics in relation to the Lectures; to Émile Nicole, for his patient and helpful supervising of my doctorate alongside his carrying out of so many other responsibilities as Doyen of the Faculté de Vaux-sur-Seine; to Henri Blocher, for providing important help with my understanding of Psalm 89 when (during my doctoral research) I was taking a wrong turn, and also for his subsequent careful reading of my doctoral dissertation and judicious comments on it; to Greg Strain, for his friendship and encouragement to go ahead with this project; to Don Carson, not only for the invitation to include this volume in the NSBT series but also for the impact, through his writing and speaking over several decades, in shaping my biblical-theological instincts;[8] to my colleagues at the IBB, for 'holding the fort' during the period of study leave; to the team at Tyndale House, for the welcome in the autumn of 2017; to Hebrew 4 students at the IBB who have studied book 4 of the Psalter with me (several of these have become colleagues,

---

[7] Now the 'Academic and Pastoral Board'.

[8] I am even somewhat nervous of having taken on board an aspect of the thinking of Don Carson, Sylvain Romerowski, Henri Blocher or another great scholar and unwittingly having failed to acknowledge this along the way.

and one of them, Robbie Bellis, has sharpened me a lot along the way); to Steffen Jenkins, for facilitating my re-engagement with Psalms scholarship at various points and for interacting so helpfully with the early chapters; to Fabrice Dubus and other Governing Body members at the IBB, for their wisdom regarding the benefits of study leave; to Christophe Paya, current Doyen of the Faculté de Vaux-sur-Seine, and the publishing house Excelsis for which Christophe also works, for the permission to reuse material originally published in French; to Beth Dufour, for securing permissions clearances with other publishing houses; to Philip Duce, Tom Creedy and Rima Devereaux, at IVP, for guiding the material towards publication; to Mollie Barker, for the expert, painstaking copy-editing which led to the removal of errors of many shapes and sizes.

A particular challenge arose in late 2022, as the manuscript needed to be updated to take account of the literature that had been published since the Moore College Lectures in 2018. Here, I owe a huge debt of gratitude to Will Cunningham-Batt, a third-year student at the IBB with a gift for research. He not only identified the scholarly output needing my attention but also acted as a terrific conversation partner regarding several matters of debate. The quality of the finished product is considerably improved thanks to Will's comments on earlier drafts. Since this late-2022 updating was conducted without the benefit of study leave, it needs to be recorded that this was only possible thanks to the competence, efficiency and servant-heartedness of Anne Mindana, Academic Secretary at the IBB; she also produced the diagrams in this book.

There is no claim here to provide the last word on covenant relationships in the Psalter, let alone covenant relationships in the Scriptures as a whole. The Bible is a long book, and synthesizing the data in this vast area of biblical theology is no easy task: most of us need to be open to adjusting or refining, here and there, our understanding of the contours of redemptive history as we try to integrate and do justice to the totality of relevant texts. If the present work can contribute to lending greater precision and accuracy to readers' grasp of God's breathtaking salvation plan (cf. Luke 24:32), ability to handle Scripture aright (cf. 2 Tim. 2:15) and worship of the Master (cf. Luke 1:68–75; Rev. 1:5b–6), its goal will have been fulfilled. May those of us who, by grace, are in Christ marvel at the extraordinary privilege of being new-covenant partners and beneficiaries! *Soli Deo gloria* (cf. Ps. 115:1: 'Not to us, YHWH, not to us . . .').

Abbreviations

ABC	Anchor Bible Commentary
ALBO	Analecta lovaniensia biblica et orientalia
AOTC	Apollos Old Testament Commentary
BBR	*Bulletin for Biblical Research*
BCOT	Baker Commentary on the Old Testament
BDB	F. Brown, S. R. Driver, C. A. Briggs (1906), *The New Brown-Driver-Briggs-Gesenius Hebrew and English Lexicon*, Peabody: Hendrickson.
BETL	Bibliotheca ephemeridum theologicarum lovaniensium
BST	Bible Speaks Today
BZAW	Beihefte zur Zeitschrift für die alttestamentliche Wissenschaft
CBQMS	Catholic Biblical Quarterly Monograph Series
CEB	Commentaire Evangélique de la Bible
CRB	Cahiers de la *Revue biblique*
DBY	1890 Darby Bible
EBC	Expositor's Bible Commentary
EBTC	Evangelical Biblical Theology Commentary
ESV	The ESV Bible (The Holy Bible, English Standard Version), copyright © 2001 by Crossway, a publishing ministry of Good News Publishers. Used by permission. All rights reserved.
EvQ	*Evangelical Quarterly*
FOTL	Forms of the Old Testament Literature
FS	Festschrift
GKC	E. Kautzsch (1910), *Gesenius' Hebrew Grammar*, 2nd English edn (rev. in accordance with the 28th German edn) by A. E. Cowley, Oxford: Clarendon.
HCSB	Holman Christian Standard Bible® Copyright © 1999, 2000, 2002, 2003, 2009 by Holman Bible Publishers. Used with permission by Holman Bible Publishers, Nashville, Tennessee. All rights reserved.

HSM	Harvard Semitic Monographs
IBB	Institut Biblique de Bruxelles (formerly Institut Biblique Belge)
Inst.	*Institutes of the Christian Religion* (see bibliography under Calvin)
JBL	*Journal of Biblical Literature*
JETS	*Journal of the Evangelical Theological Society*
Joüon	P. Joüon (1965), *Grammaire de l'hébreu biblique*, 2nd edn, Rome: Editrice Pontificio Istituto Biblico.
JSOT	*Journal for the Study of the Old Testament*
JSOTSup	Journal for the Study of the Old Testament: Supplement Series
JTS	*Journal of Theological Studies*
KEL	Kregel Exegetical Library
KJV	The Authorized Version of the Bible (The King James Bible), the rights in which are vested in the Crown, reproduced by permission of the Crown's Patentee, Cambridge University Press.
LD	Lectio divina
LHBOTS	Library of Hebrew Bible/Old Testament Studies
LXX	Septuagint: A. Rahlfs (ed.) (1935/1979), *Septuaginta*, Stuttgart: Deutsche Bibelgesellschaft.
MSS	manuscripts
MT	Masoretic Text
NAC	New American Commentary
NASB	The NEW AMERICAN STANDARD BIBLE®, Copyright © 1960, 1962, 1963, 1968, 1971, 1972, 1973, 1975, 1977, 1995 by The Lockman Foundation. Used by permission.
NCBC	New Century Bible Commentary
NIBC	New International Bible Commentary
NICOT	New International Commentary on the Old Testament
NIV	The Holy Bible, New International Version (Anglicized edition). Copyright © 1979, 1984, 2011 by Biblica. Used by permission of Hodder & Stoughton Ltd, an Hachette UK company. All rights reserved. 'NIV' is a registered trademark of Biblica. UK trademark number 1448790.
NIVAC	New International Version Application Commentary

NRSV	The New Revised Standard Version of the Bible, Anglicized Edition, copyright © 1989, 1995 by the Division of Christian Education of the National Council of the Churches of Christ in the USA. Used by permission. All rights reserved.
NSBT	New Studies in Biblical Theology
NT	New Testament
OBT	Overtures to Biblical Theology
OT	Old Testament
OTE	Old Testament Essays
OTG	Old Testament Guides
OTL	Old Testament Library
RB	*Revue Biblique*
sc.	*scilicet* ('namely', 'may it be understood')
SBL	Society of Biblical Literature
SBT	Studies in Biblical Theology
SJOT	*Scandinavian Journal of the Old Testament*
TOTC	Tyndale Old Testament Commentary
TynBul	*Tyndale Bulletin*
VT	*Vetus Testamentum*
Waltke and O'Connor	B. K. Waltke and M. O'Connor (1990), *An Introduction to Biblical Hebrew Syntax*, Winona Lake: Eisenbrauns.
WBC	Word Biblical Commentary
WTJ	*Westminster Theological Journal*
WUNT	Wissenschaftliche Untersuchungen zum Neuen Testament

1
This study's viability and method

My aim in this study could readily be misunderstood. It is neither to offer a primer on relationships between biblical covenants,[1] nor to provide my reading of the shape of the book of Psalms.[2] Rather, I seek to examine a particular question that lies at the intersection of these two areas of study. The question may be formulated as follows: *what is new about the new covenant, according to the book of Psalms?*

It is understandable that this undertaking might seem strange and difficult to justify even at the level of method. I will be seeking to adjudicate, from a *single* book of the *Old Testament*, on a major and long-standing debate that concerns the *new covenant* and involves the *whole of Scripture*. In addition, I will be doing so by building on the potentially shaky foundation of a recent consensus in the area of Psalms scholarship. Some explanations are called for before we can begin.

Problem 1: a single book for a whole-of-Scripture debate?

While it might seem reductionist to mine a single book in order to offer a 'verdict' on a debate that necessarily involves all of Scripture, I consider this to be a strength and not a weakness. In principle, if this exercise were undertaken (successfully) for all the canonical books, the aggregate result would be to provide the accuracy of biblical-theological understanding that has eluded (and divided) believers who claim to have equal respect for the authority of Scripture. If the only outcome of this study were to be enhanced accuracy regarding the flow of redemptive history as it emerges from one book of the Scriptures, that would be worthwhile.

---

[1] Cf. P. R. Williamson 2007; Hely Hutchinson 2022.
[2] Hely Hutchinson 2013b.

There are, though, reasons to believe that this biblical book has particular explanatory power. The Psalter has often been viewed as something of a 'mini-Bible': Athanasius, Basil, Luther, Calvin, Hooker and Henry spoke along those lines.[3] If they were meaning that the book of Psalms is a microcosm of Scripture from a *systematic*-theological perspective, the same could also be argued from a *biblical*-theological perspective.

The legitimacy of our study does not depend on the veracity of the idea that the book of Psalms is a microcosm of Scripture, whether from a systematic-theological perspective or from a biblical-theological perspective. It is not my aim to defend either postulate. Yet there is a correlation between the potential reach of this study and the extent to which the Psalter may be viewed as a mini-Bible in a biblical-theological sense. If we are able accurately to present the stance on covenant relationships of this biblical book, that is already helpful as a contribution to anyone's quest to understand the message of Scripture. But what if this particular biblical book itself provides something of a synthesis of the entire scriptural stance on how covenants relate? The importance of this study would clearly be enhanced. Yet that question of whether the Psalter is a microcosm of Scripture can be examined by others, and the material in this book may help to that end.[4]

As we look to answer the question of new-covenant newness from the Psalter, I will be walking on a tightrope in one respect. On the one hand, I am convinced of the unity of Scripture and thus the need for the voice of the New Testament to be heard as it bears on the Psalms. On the other hand, I will be consciously avoiding the temptation to jump too quickly to the New Testament. Our main aim in this study will be to listen to the Psalter itself.

Problem 2: an Old Testament book for a new-covenant debate?

If it is deemed odd that an *Old* Testament book should be selected to address a *new*-covenant debate, considerations regarding the Psalter as a potential microcosm of Scripture are, again, relevant. But since, as I have just stated, this is not a critical factor for this study, I should mention my

---

[3] Mays 1994: 1; T. L. Johnson 2003: 262–263; Nichols 1996: iv.
[4] As also our brief study: Hely Hutchinson 2013b.

reasons for believing that the Psalter sets forth new-covenant theology.[5] A little historical sensitivity may be necessary here: we should beware of confusing 'Testament' as it has come to be used in Christian tradition with 'covenant' as it is used biblically. There is no biblical basis for considering all the canonical books preceding Matthew's Gospel as constituting the 'old covenant'; and these same canonical books – that have collectively come to be known as the 'Old Testament' – contain much information that pertains to the *new* covenant.

With regard to the Psalter, the following initial pointers can suffice at this stage.

1. In 2005, I argued that the formula 'Give thanks to YHWH, for he is good, for his *ḥesed* (covenant faithfulness) endures for ever' 'is closely associated with the idea of covenant, and bespeaks, in particular, the anticipation of *new*-covenant fulfilment'.[6] This formula is rooted in Jeremiah 33:11, part of the prophet's exposition of new-covenant realities in his so-called 'book of consolation' (Jer. 30 – 33). It plays an important part in the Psalter, especially in book 5. We will be presupposing that the demonstration contained in that 2005 article is robust.

2. The well-documented linguistic and thematic correlation between Isaiah 40 – 55 and parts of books 4 and 5[7] makes it unsurprising that new-covenant theology should be present in those two books of the Psalter.

3. One key aspect of the new covenant as set forth in the Latter Prophets (e.g. Isa. 40 – 55; Jer. 30 – 33; Ezek. 34 – 37) is that it provides a definitive solution to the problem of the Babylonian exile. A key concern of the Psalter turns on the psalmist's perplexity in the face of that exile and YHWH's apparent disregard for his promises to David (Ps. 89); the two books that follow this psalm (books 4–5) provide a response to this (hence the title of this volume). These are the two books that will be the particular focus of our study.

---

[5] Note the presence of the hyphen. We are not referring to the movement 'new covenant theology'.

[6] Hely Hutchinson 2005a: 100; emphasis original.

[7] Predating the rise of editorial criticism. See e.g. Feuillet 1975: 364–365.

4. Psalm 2, which serves an introductory and programmatic function for the Psalter, alludes to the Davidic covenant but exhibits a *new*-covenant outlook in its presentation of the messiah. I defend this assertion at the beginning of chapter 3.

Problem 3: a recent consensus in Psalms scholarship?

This study is predicated on the belief that the Psalter is a book with a message that is greater than the sum of its parts. But might I not be simply building on the shaky foundation of a recent fad among Psalms scholars? I do not deny the subjective judgments and speculation that have characterized some recent scholarly output in the area of Psalter shape, and I would not presume to suggest that I am immune from them myself. But interest in the arrangement of the book of Psalms has a rich and ancient heritage (which can be traced back to Hippolytus, Origen, Jerome, Basil, Gregory of Nyssa and Augustine).[8] If some generations have proven to be less interested in this aspect of Psalms study than our current one, this is not necessarily cause for alarm.

In a similar way, matters of biblical theology have come to be explored with greater vigour over the past forty years, and the new insights and emphases that this has yielded are (where they are correct!) cause for thanksgiving.[9] In relation to the institution to which I owe so much, Moore College, the influential figure of T. C. Hammond was not associated with biblical theology in the same way as Donald Robinson, Graeme Goldsworthy and William Dumbrell. That the insights of the latter three scholars are relatively new is not, though, a reason to call into question their validity and usefulness.

In any case, it is not so much a question of whether one wants to 'jump on this bandwagon' (that of the configuration of the Psalter) as of whether one wants to take the Word of God seriously in its final form. It would not be possible to be wedded to a high view of Scripture and dismiss the notion of Psalter context. A simple reading of Psalm 72:20 confirms this ('This concludes the prayers of David son of Jesse' [NIV]): this is, so to speak, an editorial footnote that we take seriously because it is breathed

---

[8] Mitchell 1997: 33–40; Auwers 2000: 12–14; Jenkins 2020; 2022: 28–30.
[9] Many of the volumes in the current series could be cited in this connection.

out by God himself (cf. 2 Tim. 3:16). There is, of course, room for discussion as to how far one goes in subscribing to the idea of an overarching message that is discernible from Psalter structure, but even the sceptics are persuaded of a certain degree of intentionality in the ordering of the Psalms.[10] It is, for example, difficult to have no regard for Psalter shape when faced with a group of five psalms in a row that all begin and end with an identical call to praise YHWH (Pss 146 – 150). In fact, anyone who concedes that there is a 'book' of Psalms and is open to examining its constituent parts in their given order is necessarily an 'editorial critic' (or 'canonical critic'). There are some parallels here with the Gospels, which contain clearly identifiable 'pericopes' (units of text) whose order nevertheless reflects the evangelists' design.

My duty is to ensure that appropriate caveats and safeguards are built into this work – that I avoid fanciful readings that have no clear, objective basis in the data of this part of God's Word. It should become apparent in what follows that I am essentially building on indicators of shape that are uncontroversial (I set out in appendix 1 a checklist of these main indicators). One of the assured results of editorial criticism is that Psalm 89 – the last in book 3 – plays a pivotal role in the unfolding of the Psalter with its anguished calling into question of YHWH's covenant faithfulness.[11] This is a fundamental assumption for what follows in this book as we look to understand the answer to the psalmist's perplexity. At least from the perspective of consensus convictions from the past few decades, there is nothing shaky about this foundation!

I should add a final point regarding method in relation to Psalter shape. At the turn of the twenty-first century, it was necessary to interact with the thesis of Gerald Wilson concerning book 5's putative pessimism with regard to a human king.[12] But this pessimism has not been embraced by the scholarly consensus.[13] Again, I have also decided to take

---

[10] Longman 2014: 35–36; regarding Goldingay, see chapter 3 of this book, n. 70, and p. 64.

[11] The scepticism of R. D. Anderson (1994: 239) on this point may be considered to be answered by Hely Hutchinson 2013b and chapter 4 of this book.

[12] As we did for our doctoral dissertation (2006).

[13] See e.g. Snearly 2016. Robertson (2015: 148 n. 3) explains: 'Wilson's effort to disregard the assurances of the Davidic promise as recorded in Psalm 132 . . . fails to reckon with the constant emphasis in the Psalms and elsewhere in Scripture on the merger of David's throne with God's throne. His disparaging treatment of the messianic promise in Psalm 110 . . . involves him in a laborious effort to avoid the focal thrust of the text.' Wilson is not, however, entirely bereft of contemporary advocates: see Goswell 2020.

the 'risk' of interacting only minimally with views on Psalter shape that I believe are speculative and unconvincing; this is a risk inasmuch as it could give the impression that I endorse all the scholarly output in this area, but the gain will be a more streamlined focus on the topic at hand.

The key line of attack

I stated at the outset of this chapter that my goal is not to produce 'a reading' of the Psalter (I have done this, briefly, already).[14] But inasmuch as one acts as a Psalter reader, one does find that close to the heart of the agenda of this scriptural book is the question of how covenants relate. In particular, the question of the permanence of the Davidic covenant in the face of the exile is explored. In line, then, with one of the Psalter's own concerns, my task will be to determine how the Davidic and new covenants fit together. Thus, my key line of attack in this study will be to ask what is new about the new covenant relative to the covenant with David. This will, though, require us to interact with the biblical covenants more generally and explore how they are interlinked.

The plan of this book

As we approach this question, we will have in mind six or seven points of view that have currency in contemporary evangelicalism. I will begin by setting out these models (chapter 2). The bulk of the book will then consist of an examination of the data of the Psalter that will allow us to assess the merits and demerits of those models (chapters 3–5). A significant consideration raised by a comparison of the models is the question of how the new-covenant believer relates to the Mosaic law, and so I will devote some space to this (chapter 6). In the conclusion, I will summarize the Psalter's perspective on covenant relationships and comment on how the models match up against our findings (chapter 7). At that concluding stage, I will also widen the scope to consider some New Testament data and draw attention to some theological and practical implications of our study.

---

[14] Hely Hutchinson 2013b.

Three presuppositions

Primacy of the Masoretic Text

As we examine the Old Testament, I give pride of place to the Hebrew Masoretic Text (MT), following the principle that Ernst Würthwein articulates as follows ('m' corresponds to the MT): 'As a general rule m is to be preferred over all other traditions whenever it cannot be faulted either linguistically or for its material content . . . [I]f a reading of m is rejected, every possible interpretation of it must first have been fully examined.'[15]

Post-exilic dating for the Psalter

I believe that the final form of the Psalter dates to the post-exilic period. As argued in appendix 3, it may be that the author of Chronicles[16] creates a composite psalm from three psalms within the Psalter (I rule out dependence in the other direction but not the explanation of no dependence in either direction). If this is correct, the implications for the dating of the Psalter are significant. Given that the final doxology of book 4 is cited by the Chronicler, it is probable that the latter had access to the Psalter in its final form (we will have occasion to note the rapprochement between the closing doxology of the fourth book and that of the fifth book:[17] it is likely to reflect the work of the same redactor). If 390 BC is an appropriate *terminus ad quem* (or latest date) for Chronicles,[18] the Psalter reached its current form by the late fifth century BC (or very early fourth century at the latest) – two centuries before the Septuagint (Greek translation of the Hebrew Bible). This view is markedly different from that of Gerald Wilson,[19] who considers that the final form of the Psalter owes its origins to a period later than the destruction of the temple in AD 70; in my opinion, Wilson sets too much store by evidence from Qumran.[20]

---

[15] Würthwein 1980: 114. I follow the approximate order of the value of witnesses that he advocates (1980: 112).

[16] It is possible that the author of the composite psalm is distinct from the Chronicler himself. In that case, we should recognize that the perspectives of the two authors are in harmony with each other: 'the editor of the hymn faithfully followed in the footsteps of the Chronicler' (Butler 1978: 149).

[17] See p. 63.

[18] Pratt 1998: 9–11.

[19] E.g. Wilson 2002a: 26–30.

[20] On this matter of the order of the Psalms as found in the Dead Sea Scrolls, I line up behind Beckwith (1995: 1: '[t]he eccentric Psalms MSS from Qumran are probably liturgical

Placement in the Writings

I attach some significance to the placement of the Psalter in the last part of the tripartite Hebrew canon (Law, Prophets, Writings). This structure for the Old Testament is apparently reflected in Jesus' teaching (Luke 24:44) and is attested as early as the second century BC (in the prologue of Ecclesiasticus).[21] It makes sense to follow this arrangement of the books.[22]

This means that the book of Psalms follows the Latter Prophets. It is probably the book that *immediately* follows them. It *may* be more appropriate to consider that Ruth precedes the Psalter, but that has little bearing on this study. What should, however, be noted (for the purposes of our study) is that I will be presupposing in particular that Isaiah and Jeremiah precede the book of Psalms both chronologically and canonically. Less crucially, I will also be assuming that Chronicles is placed at the end of the Hebrew canon.[23]

(note 20 *cont.*) adaptations') and McFall (2000: 225: '[w]hatever the Qumran sect did with its store of Psalms is probably confined to them').

[21] It is also 'frequently mentioned in the Talmud' (Beckwith 1985: 110).

[22] This approach is also favoured by, e.g., Van Pelt 2016.

[23] As reflected in Jesus' words in Matt. 23:35; Luke 11:51 (the martyrdom of Zechariah being not the last one chronologically but the last canonically, in 2 Chr. 24:20–21). For a full discussion of the order of the books within the Old Testament, see Beckwith 1985: 181–234. Jenkins (2022: 54) draws attention to the instability in the order of the Writings: 'Most mediaeval MSS have Psalms second, often after Chronicles, despite which the printed tradition settled on Psalms first.' For our purposes, the tripartite structure of the Hebrew canon is of far greater significance than the precise order of the books within the Writings.

2

The covenant-relationships spectrum

The Psalter invites us to consider a particular angle on the vexed question regarding what is new about the new covenant. It is that newness *relative to the Davidic covenant* that is notably on the agenda in the book of Psalms. Determining what is new about the new covenant relative to the Davidic covenant inevitably requires grappling with relationships between other biblical covenants, but the Davidic–new relationship will need to be our focus. In this chapter, I look to summarize the key characteristics of the approaches to covenant relationships that we find in the evangelical marketplace. I do so with a particular eye to how they articulate the newness of the new covenant relative to the Davidic covenant.

These approaches may be viewed as being on a spectrum (see Fig. 2.1). At the respective poles of this spectrum, exponents advocate a tight connection between the new covenant and what precedes it (Westminster covenantalism) and a loose connection (classical dispensationalism). As one moves from model 1 to model 7 – from left to right on the spectrum – one observes increasing discontinuity between the new covenant and biblical covenants set up prior to the new covenant.

1	2	3	4	5	6	7
Westminster covenantalism	Reformed Baptist covenant theology	1689 federalism	progressive covenantalism	new covenant theology	progressive dispensationalism	classical dispensationalism

Figure 2.1 **Evangelical models of covenant relationships viewed on a spectrum**

Some readers may prefer to skip to the summary at the end of this chapter and/or read this chapter just before the concluding chapter 7.

Model 1: Westminster covenantalism / classical Presbyterianism

Our first position, Westminster covenantalism or classical Presbyterianism, advocates a (single) 'covenant of grace' that

> was differently administered in the time of the law, and in the time of the gospel: under the law, it was administered by promises, prophecies, sacrifices, circumcision, the paschal lamb, and other types and ordinances delivered to the people of the Jews, all fore-signifying Christ to come; which were, for that time, sufficient and efficacious, through the operation of the Spirit, to instruct and build up the elect in faith in the promised Messiah, by whom they had full remission of sins, and eternal salvation; and is called the old testament.[1]

Under the gospel dispensation, 'Christ, the substance, was exhibited', but '[t]here are not . . . two covenants of grace, differing in substance, but one and the same, under various dispensations'.[2]

Westminster covenantalism stands in the lineage of Calvin, who could speak of the Abrahamic covenant as being the same as the Sinaitic covenant and the same as the new covenant,[3] allowing for infants to be 'participants in the covenant'.[4] But we choose as our contemporary representative of this school Palmer Robertson in view of the influence exerted by his 1980 work *The Christ of the Covenants*. Robertson stands in the Westminster lineage, although he prefers the phrase 'covenant of redemption' where Westminster employs 'covenant of grace',[5] and his precise stance is not always easy to determine. On the one hand, he declares that 'the new covenant, promised by Israel's prophets, does not

---

[1] The Westminster Confession of Faith (1647), ch. 7.

[2] Ibid.

[3] 'Since, therefore, Abraham is at this time the father of all the faithful, it follows that our safety is not to be thought otherwise than in that covenant which God established with Abraham; but afterwards the same covenant was ratified by the hand of Moses' (Calvin, Commentary on Ezekiel 16:61, <www.ccel.org/ccel/calvin/calcom23.v.lxii.html> accessed 22 August 2018). For the identity of this covenant and the new covenant, see *Inst.* II.X.2 ('the two are actually one and the same': Calvin 1960: 429).

[4] *Inst.* IV.XVI.5 (Calvin 1960: 1327–1328).

[5] 'Covenant of redemption' has come to be used subsequently by those in the Westminster tradition as designating an intra-trinitarian covenant. Cf. Fesko 2016.

appear as a distinctive covenantal unit unrelated to God's previous administrations'. Indeed:

> [the] organic relation of the new covenant to the covenants of Abraham, Moses, and David finds explicit development both in the Old Testament prophecies concerning the covenant and in the New Testament realizations of this consummating covenant. From either perspective, the new covenant may be understood in no other way than as a realization of the prophetic projections found in the Abrahamic, Mosaic, and Davidic covenants.[6]

Designating the latter three covenants together as 'the old covenant',[7] Robertson also maintains that

> a clear line of continuity must be seen in the relationship of the old covenant to the new. While the new covenant will be at radical variance with the old covenant with respect to its effectiveness in accomplishing its goal, the substance of the two covenants in terms of their redemptive intention is *identical*.[8]

His diagram (see Fig. 2.2) is designed to show that 'each successive covenant [sc. of what he terms 'the covenant of redemption'] expands on previous administrations',[9] with each of them finding fulfilment in Christ (i.e. in the new covenant).

On the other hand, Robertson identifies seven motifs that distinguish the new covenant from these three covenants that had previously been established:[10] 'The Return of Exiled Israel to the Land of Promise'; 'Full Restoration of God's Blessing on the Land of Promise'; 'Divine Fulfillment

---

6 Robertson 1980: 41.

7 Ibid. 281.

8 Ibid. 282; emphasis added.

9 Ibid. 63. It is worth noting that there is a strand of covenant-theological thought that rejects continuity between the Abrahamic and Sinaitic covenants. The latter covenant is viewed as a 'republication' of the covenant of works (cf. Parker and Lucas 2022: 10). Michael Horton considers that 'the Sinai theocracy was a parenthesis within the history of the covenant of grace' (2022: 56). This is clearly at odds with Robertson's diagram and, e.g., with this clear affirmation from Walter Kaiser: 'God *renewed* the ancient patriarchal promise, which continued to appear in the Sinaitic and Davidic promises . . . Jesus by His death renewed the covenant, but He did not institute an entirely "new" covenant' (1978: 268; emphasis original). For further consideration of the variety of stances on the Sinaitic covenant within Reformed thought, consult Ferry 2009.

10 Robertson 1980: 274–278.

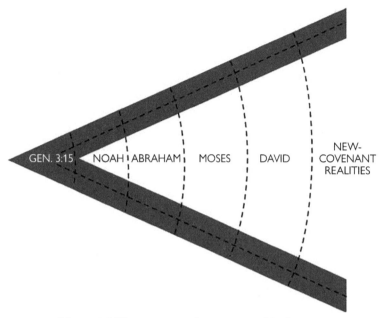

Figure 2.2 The covenantal structure of Scripture
Adapted from Robertson 1980: 62. Used with permission

of Previous Covenantal Commitments'; 'Internal Renewal by the Work of God's Holy Spirit' (he particularly emphasizes the uniqueness of this aspect of God's dealings with his people under the new covenant); 'The Full Forgiveness of Sins'; 'The Union of Israel and Judah'; 'The Everlasting Character of the New Covenant' – the fact that it will never be superseded.

We should note three other points in relation to Robertson's development of some of these motifs.

1 He indicates that the law that will be written on the heart is 'essentially the same' as that of the old covenant;[11] he also states that this law should be understood in a broad sense as referring to the teaching of Old Testament Scripture in general.[12]

---

[11] The Westminster Confession of Faith (ch. 19) embraces a tripartite division for the law of Moses, specifying the abrogation of the ceremonial and judicial laws and the binding nature of the moral law (the latter consisting of the Ten Commandments).

[12] Robertson 1980: 282, including n. 13. More precisely, Robertson speaks of 'old covenant Scriptures', but he seems to be referring to the Old *Testament*.

2 With regard to the forgiveness of sins, the new element consists of the end of the sacrificial system thanks to its antitype, the once-for-all sacrifice.[13]

3 The need for a mediatorial office (teacher, prophet or priest) to bridge the gap between YHWH and the people disappears.[14]

Given the intimate connection between the Abrahamic, Mosaic and Davidic covenants that he advocates, Robertson implies that the Davidic covenant is annulled owing to the people's disobedience.[15] That the covenant is 'eternal' needs to be understood in a typological sense, for the 'persistent disobedience of the vassal has the effect of making null and void the promises of blessing associated with the covenant relationship'.[16] That said, 'the substance of blessing which [the Davidic covenant] promises remains',[17] and the fact that 'the "root of Jesse" rules as the hope of the Gentiles, in accord with the covenant with David', testifies to the 'continuing significance of [this covenant] into the present'.[18]

Robertson seems to lean on Jeremiah 31:31 in defining the new-covenant people of God as 'Israel', understood in an antitypical sense: 'the new covenant people of God are the actualized realization of a typological form.'[19] This typological relationship is paralleled by other structures:

The old covenant 'serpent of brass' typologically anticipated the new covenant Christ cursed on the cross. The old covenant tabernacle typologically anticipated the new covenant dwelling of God in the midst of his people. The old covenant nation of Israel typologically anticipated the new covenant reality of the chosen people of God assembled as a nation consecrated to God.[20]

Although the beneficiaries of the new covenant are made up of believing Jews and non-Jews,[21] Robertson plays down the idea of a transition from

---

[13] Ibid. 282–284.
[14] Ibid. 293–297.
[15] Ibid. 284–286.
[16] Ibid. 285–286.
[17] Ibid. 285.
[18] Ibid. 183. It seems hard to reconcile the viewpoints summarized in this paragraph.
[19] Ibid. 289.
[20] Ibid.
[21] This point emerges more clearly from his more recent work, *The Israel of God* (Robertson 2000: 38–50).

the corporate relationship (under the old covenant) to the individual (under the new covenant).[22]

Model 2: Reformed Baptist covenant theology

The second model, Reformed Baptist covenant theology, is close to the first: it subscribes to a single covenant of grace. '[T]he one Covenant of Grace exponentially builds, increases, and heightens throughout redemptive history until it crescendos in heaven.'[23] This covenant is variously administered from stage to stage, just as the Constitution of the United States has undergone particular phases of administration; each biblical administration (or covenant) is preliminary to the one that follows and is 'subservient' to the initial promise of Genesis 3:15 (and 3:21).[24] Indeed, the gospel promises of Genesis 3:15, 'by which Adam was saved', become progressively clearer with each succeeding covenant but remain 'identically the same'.[25] The covenant with Abraham should not be considered to be '"the" Covenant of Grace' but only one of its administrations.[26]

The Sinaitic covenant contains a conditional dimension, but this does not undermine 'salvation by grace through faith', which applies to individual believers and not to the nation:

> [The Israelites] broke the covenant (as it related to them as a nation) and did not enjoy His blessing. Thus, God divorced them and destroyed them as a nation ... For the individual people of God (true believers) who lived under the Mosaic covenant, it was an administration of the covenant of grace. But for the nation as a whole, in terms of the *temporal* blessings promised, it was based on their covenant faithfulness.[27]

This Mosaic covenant may be viewed as 'the paradigm and representative covenant, which incorporated all of the former covenants', that is, all the

---

22 'Jeremiah does not set a personal faith-relationship in the new covenant in opposition to a corporate relationship. He maintains both of these features with equal emphasis. The prophet explicitly states that the new covenant shall be made corporately' (Robertson 1980: 287).

23 Blackburn 2013: 35; cf. Chantry 2013: 129.

24 Blackburn 36–38.

25 Chantry 2013: 129–130.

26 Blackburn 2013: 40.

27 Ibid. 47 n. 48; emphasis original; cf. 45.

covenants preceding the new covenant. The Davidic covenant is one of these 'Old Covenant administrations'.[28] These covenants are all defective in the following ways:

> (1) the knowledge and work of Christ was not clear and full; (2) the sacrifices had no power in themselves to save; (3) the Holy Spirit, though active and working, was not given in universal fullness; (4) the gift of salvation was confined almost entirely to the nation of Israel; and (5) people were saved in the Old Covenant, but not all in the Old Covenant were saved.[29]

The blessings promised in Jeremiah 31:31–34 'were possessed by *some* members of the OT administrations of the Covenant of Grace'.[30] By contrast, under the new covenant, they apply to all members; such new-covenant beneficiaries are those who are regenerate.[31] Unlike under old-covenant administrations, such new-covenant members cannot fall away, and the new covenant cannot be broken:[32] 'One could be a true member in good standing of any one of the administrations of the Old Covenant, but still *not* be a recipient of God's grace and salvation. That is not the case in the New Covenant.'[33]

The 'eternal, moral, perpetual, abiding law of God as codified in the Ten Commandments'[34] is written on the hearts of new-covenant believers. The latter are called to obey these commandments and thus 'establish the law'[35] (Rom. 3:31).

Model 3: 1689 federalism

In recent years, a movement has emerged which has come to be known as '1689 federalism'. Its aim is to rediscover and recover the outlook on covenant relationships embraced by seventeenth-century Particular Baptist theologians and notably that enshrined in the Second London

---

[28] Ibid. 49–50.
[29] Ibid. 49.
[30] Ibid. 51; emphasis original.
[31] Ibid. 50–51.
[32] Ibid. 53–54.
[33] Ibid. 60; emphasis original.
[34] Ibid. 55.
[35] Ibid. 52–55.

Baptist Confession of Faith (hence the date 1689). This movement is self-consciously defined over against other approaches on the spectrum that we are considering in this chapter.[36]

In common with our second model, 1689 federalism is close to Westminster covenantalism. 'If the Westminster federalism can be summarized in *one covenant under two administrations*, that of the 2LCF would be *one covenant revealed progressively and concluded formally under the New Covenant*.'[37] Yet:

> [p]roper weight must be given to the *newness* of the *New* Covenant by seeing it as something that has not yet come about from the perspective of the Old Testament. This is not merely a scale in which the New Covenant is 'more of the same.' It is not merely quantitatively different from the Old Covenant. It is something qualitatively different.[38]

By virtue of its being 'made and sealed in the blood of Christ and . . . revealed in Christ . . . the New Covenant is different in substance from all the Old Testament covenants'.[39]

This emphasis on the newness of the new covenant is reflected in terminology which differs from that of the first two models: it is the *new* covenant that is labelled the 'covenant of grace'.[40]

As in the case of our second model, the people of this new covenant are those who are 'in Christ' by the Spirit – circumcised of heart rather than merely circumcised of the flesh; they profess faith and should receive baptism upon such profession.[41] Yet the new covenant can be retroactively applied during the era of the old covenant: 'Although it is not accomplished in history until Christ comes, we see the gathering in of the elect who believe in Christ from the fall onwards.'[42]

What of the Davidic covenant? It forms part of the old covenant and exhibits continuity with the Abrahamic and Mosaic covenants: 'the

---

[36] See the diagrams at <www.1689federalism.com> (accessed 7 November 2017).

[37] Denault 2014: 86; emphasis original. '2LCF' designates the Second London Baptist Confession of Faith.

[38] Renihan 2014: 499; emphasis original.

[39] Ibid. 500.

[40] Denault 2017: 84.

[41] Renihan 2014: 504–505.

[42] Ibid. 477.

Mosaic Covenant cannot be divided or disconnected from the Abrahamic and Davidic covenants, and thus all three combine to form the Old Covenant';[43] 'the Abrahamic, Mosaic and Davidic Covenants were national, temporary, and typological covenants'.[44] The conditional dimension of all three covenants needs to be understood ('[t]he condition of the Abrahamic Covenant was clarified and codified in the Mosaic Covenant'[45]), and 'the Mosaic Covenant controls both the Abrahamic and the Davidic Covenants'.[46] Specifically, '[t]he Davidic Covenant brings all of the Abrahamic promises to consummation and focuses the Mosaic Covenant into one person'.[47] 'Every single part' of it typologically reveals the new covenant.[48]

The law of Moses has 'abiding moral validity under the New Covenant',[49] the Decalogue in particular, as 'the basic, fundamental law of the New Covenant'.[50] It is 'binding'[51] on the believer.

Model 4: progressive covenantalism

'Progressive covenantalism' is self-consciously defined over against 'covenant theology' (Westminster – our first model) and 'dispensationalism and its varieties' (our seventh and sixth models).[52] According to Peter Gentry and Stephen Wellum, it is not satisfactory, either on the one hand to speak of one 'covenant of grace', or, on the other hand, to 'partition history in terms of dispensations'.[53] God's plan of salvation 'unfolds step-by-step', primarily by means of the progression of the biblical covenants, and 'ultimately culminating in Christ'.[54]

The new covenant (in Christ) *'is the fulfillment, telos, and terminus of the biblical covenants'*.[55] Thus, the 'God-intended end' of what the prior covenants 'revealed, anticipated, and predicted through instruction and

---

[43] Ibid. 482.
[44] Ibid. 483.
[45] J. D. Johnson 2014: 249.
[46] Renihan 2014: 482.
[47] Ibid. 481.
[48] Ibid. 482.
[49] Barcellos 2001: 61. This volume predates the emergence of 1689 federalism as an identifiable school but anticipates it.
[50] Ibid. 59.
[51] Ibid. 86.
[52] Gentry and Wellum 2018: 51–52.
[53] Ibid. 655.
[54] Ibid. 656.
[55] Ibid. 660; emphasis original.

various patterns' is reached.[56] In relation to the Davidic covenant, the fulfilment comes about through Christ's proving to be 'David's greater son, who rules the nations and the entire creation as King of kings and Lord of lords'.[57] A growing tension across the redemptive-historical plot line is created by the combination of unconditionality and conditionality in the biblical covenants (including in the Davidic) until the tension is resolved in Christ.[58]

The Davidic covenant is 'the *epitome* of the Old Testament covenants'.[59] 'It brings the previous covenants to a climax in the king, who is the representative of Israel, the seed of Abraham, and an Adamic-like figure.'[60] The Davidic covenant is 'a subset of the old covenant (for the Davidic king was under Torah as a covenant), and . . . Israel's representative, sonship role is now narrowed in the king, as the corporate representative of the people'.[61] It is also 'organically related' to two other prior covenants. First, regarding the Abrahamic covenant, 'the Davidic covenant serves to identify the promised line of "seed" that will mediate blessings to all nations'.[62] Second, regarding the Adamic covenant,[63] 'the Davidic king also inherits the role of Adam and Israel as "son of God" to humanity as a whole', the Davidic covenant being 'the charter by which humanity will be directed', following Walter Kaiser's reading of 2 Samuel 7:19b:[64]

> [U]nder the Davidic king, the Abrahamic promise of the great nation and the great name come together. In fact, the ultimate fulfilment of the Abrahamic covenant coincides with the fulfilment of the Davidic covenant. The Abrahamic blessings, linked back to Adam and creation, will be fully realized only through the Davidic son. Indeed, the final fulfilment of the Abrahamic promise of blessing in a Promised Land will take place under the rulership of the Davidic king. The Davidic king, then, becomes the mediator of covenant blessing,

---

[56] Ibid.
[57] Ibid. 661.
[58] Ibid. 662–666.
[59] Ibid. 700.
[60] Ibid.
[61] Ibid. 701.
[62] Ibid.
[63] Gentry and Wellum prefer to speak of 'the creation covenant under Adam's representative headship' (ibid. 641).
[64] Ibid. 701, citing Kaiser 1974.

tied back to Abraham, and ultimately tied back to Adam as head of the human race.[65]

The new covenant is contrasted with the old covenant established with Israel (the Mosaic or Sinaitic).[66] It brings about (1) a change in mediation (spiritual and direct, in Christ – as opposed to 'natural-biological' and indirect, via certain leaders), (2) a change in the composition of the covenant community (made up solely of those born of the Spirit [circumcised of heart] and knowing God – as opposed to being a mixed group comprising believers and unbelievers), (3) 'complete forgiveness of sin', 'the reversal of what took place under Adam'.[67]

New-covenant believers are not 'under … previous covenants as covenants'.[68] The new covenant replaces the old.[69] The Mosaic law belongs to the Mosaic covenant: the new-covenant believer's ethical life is not governed by it. Yet it 'has continuing relevance as an *indirect* guide'.[70]

Model 5: new covenant theology

Gentry and Wellum explain that they had previously identified their progressive covenantalism 'as a species of "*new covenant*" theology'[71] – our fifth model – but distance themselves from some of the positions that are associated with that label.[72] New covenant theology is a broad category,[73] but it majors on its stance on the law of Moses[74] – and, accordingly, is known for this and particularly associated with it. 'New Covenant Theology is often accused of being antinomian due to its denial of the Decalogue as the eternal moral law of God.'[75] That Christians are 'no longer subject to the temporary Mosaic law-covenant'[76] is a significant

---

[65] Ibid. 701–702.

[66] Ibid. 694, 706; cf. 342.

[67] Ibid. 706–711; emphasis original.

[68] Ibid. 661; emphasis original.

[69] Ibid. 789–790.

[70] Meyer 2016: 93–94; emphasis original.

[71] Gentry and Wellum 2018: 35; emphasis original.

[72] Ibid. 35 n. 9: 'some deny a creation covenant, others deny Christ's active obedience, and others are unnuanced in their understanding of God's moral law in relation to the Decalogue.'

[73] White 2008: 142. Parker and Lucas (2022: 31) explain that, though 'very difficult to define since it lacks definitive scholarly representation', new covenant theology 'is clearly not monolithic'.

[74] White 2012; Wells and Zaspel 2002.

[75] White 2008: 56 n. 141.

[76] Ibid. 41.

theme in Blake White's presentation of the new covenant as 'fundamentally and radically *new*'.[77] Further, progressive covenantalism (model 4) rejects the stance of new covenant theology in holding 'little instructive place for the Mosaic law in the church's life'.[78]

So it seems necessary to keep our fourth and fifth models distinct. According to the most recent work I have seen that considers the relationship between progressive covenantalism and new covenant theology, the two models may be described as 'first cousins'.[79]

Model 6: progressive dispensationalism

According to Darrell Bock, a prominent exponent of our sixth model, there are 'three key covenants', namely 'the three covenants of promise (Abrahamic, Davidic, new)'.[80] Craig Blaising, another leading representative of progressive dispensationalism, directly tackles the question of the relationship between the new covenant and the Davidic covenant.[81] The new covenant replaces the Sinaitic covenant and is superior to it;[82] 'the new covenant is the form in which Abrahamic-covenant blessing will be fulfilled.'[83] The new covenant has 'a purpose similar to the Mosaic covenant – that is, to bring the blessing of the Abrahamic covenant back into the present experience of a generation or generations of Israel'.[84] This fulfilment is dependent on the king of the Davidic covenant: 'new covenant blessing will be mediated by the Davidic king.'[85] For the Abrahamic blessing 'comes upon the king',[86] who mediates it to 'the Israel of faith – that remnant of physical Israel which trusts in God – and to all those of the nations who trust in God through this king'.[87]

'The king . . . greatly surpasses in character, power, and length of reign both David and Solomon, the greatest of Israel's former kings.'[88] The king

---

[77] Ibid. 1; emphasis original; see 7–53.

[78] Wellum and Parker 2016: 3. See also n. 72 above.

[79] Frey 2022: 154.

[80] Bock 2022: 127.

[81] Blaising 1993, esp. 169–171.

[82] Ibid. 155, 169.

[83] Ibid. 170.

[84] Ibid. 151.

[85] Ibid. 170.

[86] Ibid.

[87] Ibid. 173.

[88] Ibid. 170.

fulfils a priestly function, that of the order of Melchizedek, in line with Psalm 110:4, and '[t]here should be no doubt that the Melchizedekian priesthood is part of the Davidic covenant'.[89]

The blessing envisaged by the new covenant is permanent and may be summarized as 'the renewal and sanctification of the human heart by the indwelling Holy Spirit, along with resurrection from the dead and everlasting life'.[90] The Davidic covenant, which consists of 'the promises concerning the establishment of David's house and the promises concerning the intimate relationship between God and David's descendant',[91] is unconditional, but 'a continuous, uninterrupted reign is . . . conditioned upon the faithfulness of the Davidic kings'.[92] In sum, the provisions of the new covenant and the Davidic covenant are clearly distinct from each other, but they converge in their fulfilment.

This fulfilment occurs in stages.[93] Already, 'the Davidic promised ruler . . . executes the benefits of salvation that include the granting of forgiveness and imparting of the Spirit'.[94] Non-Jews – in the church of today – are included among the beneficiaries.[95] But we await the 'consummated kingdom with the king physically and visibly present' and 'national, territorial Israel' enjoying 'an eternal shalom' alongside the nations,[96] beginning in the millennium.[97]

Going hand in hand with the replacement of the Mosaic covenant by the new covenant is the replacement of the Mosaic law by a new-covenant law.[98]

Model 7: classical dispensationalism

For our seventh and final model, classical dispensationalism, we turn to Dwight Pentecost, who considers that Scripture presents five major covenants, four of which are gracious and eternal.[99] These four major covenants are the Abrahamic and those that develop an aspect of this

---

[89] Ibid. 162.
[90] Ibid. 169.
[91] Ibid. 159–162.
[92] Ibid. 164.
[93] Ibid. 180, 192–194.
[94] Bock 2022: 132.
[95] Ibid. 132, 136.
[96] Ibid. 115, 132–133, 136.
[97] Ibid. 133.
[98] Blaising 1993: 194–199.
[99] Pentecost 1958/1964: 67–71.

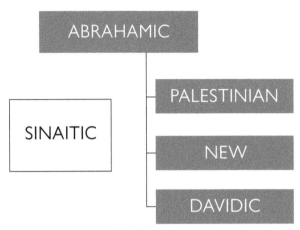

Figure 2.3 **The five major covenants
according to Dwight Pentecost**

fundamental covenant, namely the Palestinian, Davidic and new (see Fig. 2.3).[100] The Mosaic covenant, though major, is conditional, temporary and not 'determinative' for God's prophetic programme.[101]

Regarding the covenants that are our primary focus (the Davidic and the new), 'the [Abrahamic] seed promises are developed in the Davidic covenant, and the [Abrahamic] blessing promises are developed in the new covenant'.[102] These two covenants, the Davidic and the new, are unconditional,[103] the only element of conditionality in the Davidic covenant being the continuing presence of a Davidic king on the throne ('[d]isobedience might bring about chastening, but never abrogate the covenant').[104]

The two covenants must be understood in literal terms,[105] which implies that a physical temple will be built in Jerusalem at the time of the restoration of the Israelite kingdom. Indeed, since the partner in the new covenant is the Jewish people, its fulfilment will take place for the benefit of this people when the Davidic throne is established in the millennium.[106]

---

[100] Ibid. 71–72.

[101] Ibid. 66–67.

[102] Ibid. 71–72. He specifies that the promise of land is developed by the Palestinian covenant; in this connection, he quotes Deut. 30:3–5 and Ezek. 20:33–37, 42–44.

[103] Ibid. 103–104, 118–119.

[104] Ibid. 103.

[105] Ibid. 105–111, 118–119.

[106] Ibid. 114–115, 119–128.

Thus, these two covenants, though having little in common other than their anchorage in Genesis 12, converge in their fulfilment.

Pentecost summarizes the new-covenant provisions:

> This covenant . . . has to do with the regeneration, forgiveness, and justification of Israel, the outpouring of the Holy Spirit with His subsequent ministries, [and] Israel's regathering and restoration to the place of blessing, all founded on the blood of Jesus Christ.[107]

He leaves the door open to the possibility that non-Jews benefit from this covenant ahead of the millennium. Whether this reflects a secondary application to believers or the existence of two new covenants (one of which applies to 'the church in this age'),[108] 'the new covenant of Jeremiah 31:31–34 must and can be fulfilled only by the nation Israel and not by the church . . . [T]his was a literal covenant made with the physical seed of Abraham.'[109] This physical seed is the sole covenant partner;[110] 'promises to Israel may not be transferred to the Gentiles'.[111]

Summary of issues – and a glimpse of the stakes

What a comparison of these models throws up is a host of interrelated matters concerning:

1. continuity and discontinuity across redemptive history;
2. degrees of proximity of relationship between particular covenants;
3. covenant membership (ranging from non-elect being included at some level in model 1 through to the Jewish people being the new-covenant partner in model 7);
4. covenant beneficiary (might this be different from covenant member/partner?);

---

[107] Ibid. 118.
[108] Ibid. 121–124. There is a third, more extreme dispensationalist position, namely that '[t]he new covenant is actually not applied to the church in any manner in the NT' (Parker and Lucas 2022: 19). Snoeberger (2022: 176) exemplifies this: 'the church has *no* legal relationship to or participation in the new covenant'; emphasis original.
[109] Ibid. 124–125.
[110] Ibid. 119.
[111] Ibid. 73; cf. 84.

5 typology, tension, progressive revelation, fulfilment;
6 the Mosaic law in relation to the new-covenant believer (in force, serving as a guide or having no validity).

We should be careful to avoid overstating what is at stake.[112] This is a debate that is conducted among those who have a high view of Scripture. At all points on the spectrum there is a desire to understand and submit to biblical revelation in its entirety. There is no position to the left of model 1 on the spectrum (that would be Judaism or jettisoning the New Testament). There is no position to the right of model 7 (that would be Marcionism or jettisoning the Old Testament). In our concluding chapter, we will be able to observe how key gospel truths are embraced all along the spectrum.

Nor, however, should we underestimate what is at stake. Speaking practically, our stance on the questions raised in this chapter can have a bearing on the following issues:[113] whether and to what extent our Christian ethic should be that of the Mosaic law; the relationship between church and state; evangelism (centripetal or centrifugal – a dynamic that is inward-looking or outward-looking?); prosperity theology; how much money we want to spend on the reconstruction of the temple in Jerusalem; whether we think President Trump was right to move the US embassy from Tel Aviv to Jerusalem in 2018; how Christ-centred and cross-centred we are in our theology; how thrilled we are by the gospel; baptism; the question of whether one can be a 'Christian' yet not saved (covenant objectivism: can one be a new-covenant partner without being a new-covenant beneficiary?). Not all of these issues are of critical importance, but one's stance on biblical theology can play a major part in the stance that one adopts in these areas.

So where does one want to position oneself on the spectrum? We turn to the Psalter in order to find out.

We will return to the seven models at the end of our enquiry.

---

[112] Cf. Frey (2022: 55): 'Whether reformed, dispensationalist or new-covenantalist, we have more in common than what divides us.'
[113] Which I explore in Hely Hutchinson 2022: 161–181.

3

Scene-setting for the psalmist's perplexity (Psalms 1 – 89)

Introduction

In Psalm 89, in the face of what seems to be the collapse of the Davidic covenant, the psalmist is perplexed. Against the background of the Babylonian exile[1] and the absence of a Davidic king on the throne, we hear the psalmist's anguished cries and pleas: 'You have renounced the covenant with your servant'; 'How long, O LORD?'; 'Lord, where is your steadfast love of old, which by your faithfulness you swore to David?' (Ps. 89:39, 46, 49 ESV [MT 89:40, 47, 50]). The stakes are high. In verse after verse in the closing part of the psalm (vv. 38–51 [MT vv. 39–52]), it is as if the psalmist is on the brink of despair. Is he really accusing YHWH of covenant unfaithfulness?[2]

Our study focuses on the two books of the Psalter that follow this psalm and constitute an answer to the perplexity. This will enable us to see how the Psalter understands the newness of the new covenant, notably relative to the Davidic covenant.

But this is not where the book of Psalms begins. So, first, in this chapter, we must turn our attention to the Psalter's introduction and first three books. There are some significant data on covenant relationships that feature in Psalms 1 – 89. Indeed, from the outset, we must reckon with the relationship between the Davidic and new covenants.

---

[1] For the compatibility of this historical context, which we will note (see p. 47), with the person mentioned in the psalm's title, see the comments on Asaph in Kidner 1973: 35.

[2] In 2004 or 2005, Henri Blocher kindly helped me with this question. There are enough data in the context to allow us to speak of an accusation in form but not in essence. The psalmist prays and does not exclude a change of circumstances (Ps. 89:46–51 [MT 89:47–52]), indicating that he does not necessarily believe that God has reneged on his promises.

A new-covenant agenda for the Psalter set by Psalm 2

It is widely held that the first two psalms form the gateway into the Psalter.[3] I have elsewhere sketched why and how I believe Psalms 1 and 2 fulfil this function:[4] the '*tôrâ*' meditation referred to in Psalm 1 has as its object the content of Psalm 2 which, in turn, is programmatic for the entire Psalter. It is not critical for our present purposes that readers follow my precise understanding of how the first two psalms fit together – only that they recognize the importance of the introductory role played by the first two psalms. Given this key introductory function, if Psalm 2 addresses questions of covenant relationships, such questions cannot be considered peripheral to the design of the book of Psalms.[5] More specifically, if the reading of Psalm 2 that we develop in this chapter is correct, it will need to be acknowledged that pinpointing the newness of the new covenant is an undertaking that this part of Scripture invites us to pursue.

Psalm 2:7 contains a clear allusion to a promise made to David (see Table 3.1).[6] Although the term *běrît* ('covenant') itself is absent in both 2 Samuel 7[7] and Psalm 2 (where *ḥōq* serves as an approximate substitute),[8]

Table 3.1 God's promise to David evoked in Psalm 2

2 Sam. 7:14a	I will be a father to him and he will be a son to Me (NASB)
Ps. 2:7	I will declare the LORD's decree: He said to Me, 'You are My Son; today I have become Your Father.' (HCSB)

---

[3] Erich Zenger could speak of this consensus as having been established as early as 1999 (Zenger 1999: 116; see the bibliography at his n. 4). More recently, David Willgren (2016: 136) states that 'recent scholarship has regarded them [sc. Pss 1 – 2] as having the function of a preface to the "Book" of Psalms (although some include only Ps 1)'. Cf., more recently still, Ellison 2021: 535–537. Jenkins (private correspondence, 1 March 2023), however, cautions that 'scholarship is much less united on this than is often claimed'.

[4] Hely Hutchinson 2013b: 25–28; 2015a: 111–113.

[5] Cf. Hensley (2018: 153): 'Given Pss 1–2's introductory function, the Davidic covenant . . . is clearly a central concern of the Psalter.'

[6] Among the numerous authors who mention this link, several use language that highlights how they believe it to be obvious: '[o]f course' (House 1998: 409); '[u]ndoubtedly' (Haney 2002: 108); 'clearly' (Wilson 2002a: 111); 'clearly' (Lucas 2003: 36).

[7] 'While the word "covenant" does not appear in the chapter, there is sufficient ancillary covenant terminology throughout to endorse its use in the key texts which comment on this oracle, viz., 2 Samuel 23:5, Psalm 89:3, 28, 34, and Psalm 132:12' (Gordon 1984: 71).

[8] In Ps. 105:10 *ḥōq* and *běrît* are parallel and apparently quasi-synonymous. Cf. also Jones (1965: 337–338), who cites similar texts outside the Psalter; the sense that Delitzsch (1894: 124) attributes to *ḥōq* in Ps. 2:7; von Rad 1957: 49 n. 7.

YHWH's 'dynastic promise' in 2 Samuel 7:11b–16 is in the background to the psalm. This means that, as we read the psalm, we need to have in mind the promise that David's seed (*zera'*) would become a son for YHWH and that this son's throne would be established for ever. There is a clear consensus on this point.

Does this mean that the second psalm presents the perspective of the Davidic covenant? The question of how we should understand the precise connection between 2 Samuel 7 and its evocation in Psalm 2 is not a major concern of the commentators,[9] but a Davidic-covenant outlook does often seem to be assumed, implied or even stated. Thus, Peter Craigie maintains that the psalm sets forth a 'renewal' of the Davidic covenant;[10] Gerard Van Groningen sees in the psalm a perpetuation of 'Yahweh's covenanting act with David';[11] Daniel Block surmises that the psalm was 'composed for some formal public celebration of what had transpired in 2 Samuel 7'.[12]

Yet several considerations point in a different direction. We will look at each in turn.

1 Referent in historical context difficult to determine

The interpreter of this psalm is faced with the considerable problem of determining the original historical context. Who is the son of verse 7? Is it David himself (Calvin),[13] Solomon (Kirkpatrick),[14] Josiah (Briggs)[15] or every Davidic king (A. A. Anderson,[16] Motyer,[17] Ross[18])? Should we avoid seeking a referent from among the kings of Judah, perhaps by virtue of a

---

[9] But see Goldingay (2006: 95, 102), who discerns a connection between the Abrahamic and Davidic covenants in this psalm.

[10] Craigie 1983: 67. To be sure, Craigie recognizes the messianic character of the psalm 'from the perspective of early Christianity', yet, in his opinion, '[t]he concept of an "anointed one" or messiah . . . originally attached only to an earthly king (2:2)' whose coronation is evoked by the psalm (ibid. 68).

[11] Van Groningen 1997: vol. 1, 336. Cf. the similar remarks in the last paragraph on ibid. 337. While Van Groningen also speaks of an elaboration of the 2 Sam. 7 promises in Ps. 2:8–9, he appears not to consider this to be a theological development relative to the dynastic oracle: 'This *continuity* is elaborated in verses 8 and 9 in which the king *repeats* the promises of a universal kingdom' (ibid.; emphasis added).

[12] Block 2021: 132.

[13] Calvin 1859: 5ff.

[14] Kirkpatrick 1891: 5–6.

[15] Briggs and Briggs 1907: 13.

[16] A. A. Anderson 1972a: 64.

[17] Motyer 1994: 489 (with hesitation: 'possibly').

[18] Ross 2011: 200.

particular *Sitz im Leben* (or sociological setting; Terrien),[19] an exilic setting (Bullock)[20] or a post-exilic setting (Zenger),[21] or maybe in line with the psalm's prophetic character and/or in the light of the New Testament (cf. Williams[22])? Even if the presupposition of an enthronement ceremony continues to be favoured by commentators,[23] the psalm 'alludes to no precise historical circumstance'.[24]

It is true that the question of authorship is settled by Acts 4:25–26: David wrote Psalm 2. But the enigma remains regarding the time and circumstances to which David was referring. The question needs to be addressed: is identifying a royal referent in Israel's history a necessary hermeneutical quest in the case of Psalm 2?

2 Davidic-covenant promises surpassed

In this psalm, the promises which immediately follow verse 7 outstrip those of the Davidic covenant. Nowhere else in the various narratives or mentions of the promises to David do we learn that his son will inherit the nations or that he will shatter them like earthenware (vv. 8–9):[25] possession and destruction of the nations are promises of a more grandiose order than the former. Louis Jacquet speaks of an 'exploitation' of the dynastic oracle of 2 Samuel 7 such that it has 'universal scope'.[26] As Stephen Dempster puts it, '[t]he second psalm stresses the importance of the Davidic king's meditating on Nathan's oracle to David, which *now* has universal scope'.[27]

3 YHWH's role shared and rank equalled[28]

The Psalm 2 king enjoys a status which, again, is of a different order relative to what is envisaged in the passages in Samuel, Kings and

---

[19] Terrien (2003: 87): 'The poet of Psalm 2 probably lived in the time of the monarchy. He knew the liturgy of royal coronation. For him, however, Yahweh was enthroned in heaven as the only king of the earth (Isa 6:3, 5). During the dark reign of Manasseh, vassal of Assyria (687–642 B. C. E.), the psalmist may have found courage in Isaiah's daring oracle (8:9–10).'

[20] Bullock 2001: 60.

[21] Zenger in Hossfeld and Zenger 1993: 50.

[22] Williams 1986: 32.

[23] Schaefer 2001: 8; Weber 2001: 53; Wilcock 2001a: 23; Grogan 2008: 42 ('probably'); Ross 2011: 199–200; Longman 2014: 59–60.

[24] Beaucamp 1976: 45.

[25] Although Ps. 89:27 (MT 89:28) and 2 Sam. 23:3 go some way in this direction.

[26] Jacquet 1975: 222.

[27] Dempster 2003: 194–195; emphasis added.

[28] Hely Hutchinson 2015a: 109–110.

Chronicles relating to the Davidic covenant. To be sure, the dynastic oracle promises a throne that is perpetually established (2 Sam. 7:13, 16), and David's reputation is to be likened to the 'great(est) of the earth' (2 Sam. 7:9). But in Psalm 2, YHWH, who is in *heaven* (v. 4), confers on his son a role and rank that correspond to his own. YHWH's response to the rebellious nations is to assert the kingship of his son (vv. 5–6). Conspiring against YHWH and conspiring against his anointed one are not separable concepts (v. 2b). Indeed, the nations express their desire to rid themselves of '*their* bonds' and '*their* cords' (v. 3 ESV; emphasis added) – those of YHWH *and his messiah.*

4 Ambiguity between YHWH and his son in evidence

We can go further by noting the ambiguity between YHWH and his son. Consider Psalm 2:12:

> Pay homage to the Son or He will be angry
> and you will perish in your rebellion,
>   for His anger may ignite at any moment.
> All those who take refuge in Him are happy.
> (HCSB)

Remarkably few commentators discuss this, but the referent of the pronouns 'He', 'His' and 'Him' could be 'the Son' (as the first clause of the verse favours[29] – so Calvin[30]) or YHWH (as the rest of the psalm and the Psalter favour[31] – so Kirkpatrick[32]). We may wish to argue, alongside Craigie,[33] that submission to YHWH is evinced by means of ('through') submission to the king and therefore that there is ultimately no particular interpretative problem. But our point is not that the ultimate interpretation is difficult but that the ambiguity is in evidence. Why is this significant? We find ourselves recognizing the proximity between Psalm 2

---

[29] The doubts that Kidner (1973: 53) expresses concerning the translation 'Kiss the son' (the absence of a definite article and the presence of the Aramaic term for 'son', *bar*) are not, in my view, sufficient to call into question the MT. See Terrien's discussion (2003: 86; to his bibliography should be added Vang 1995).

[30] Calvin 1859: 14.

[31] Hely Hutchinson 2015a: 110.

[32] Kirkpatrick 1891: 12–13.

[33] Craigie 1983: 68. Cf. Kirkpatrick 1891: 13.

and a series of passages in the Latter Prophets. These passages exhibit the same ambiguity of referent and speak of an eschatological David in connection with a new covenant: Hosea 3:5; Micah 2:13–14 (cf. Ezek. 34:7–31); Zechariah 11:10; 12:10.

One example should suffice,[34] namely the enigma of Micah 2:13–14. These verses constitute the book's first prophecy of hope applying to a remnant. Who is the shepherd-king of these verses? Allen,[35] Schibler,[36] Smith[37] and Waltke[38] favour the option that identifies the king with YHWH. McComiskey,[39] Sweeney,[40] Van Groningen[41] and the *Bible d'étude Semeur*[42] consider this to be a figure who is distinct from YHWH. Exegetical caution is necessary.[43] On the one hand, it becomes clear that a shepherd-saviour-king will come forth from Bethlehem (Mic. 5:2ff. [MT 5:1ff.]). On the other hand, it is *YHWH* who is the shepherd-'gatherer': he (according to 4:6–7) will reign over a remnant and (according to 7:14) shepherd his flock (although a reference to the messiah in this latter text cannot be ruled out). Again, the transition from first person (in 2:12) to third person (in 2:13) suggests that the one who says 'I will gather' and 'He who opens the breach' (ESV) are to be distinguished; on the other hand, YHWH himself is spoken of in the third person at the end of the oracle, the 'and' (*wāw*) in 'And the LORD at their head' (2:13 NASB) possibly being epexegetical ('the LORD' indicating the identity of the king).

5 Holiness of the king underscored

A contrast with the first expression of the Davidic covenant is suggested by the second half of Psalm 2:6: 'on Zion, my holy mountain'. For 2 Samuel 7 evokes the scenario of David's son committing iniquity

---

[34] A second example of ambiguity between YHWH and his new-covenant king is given in appendix 2.

[35] Allen 1976: 300–303 (he understands this to be an oracle of salvation relating to the events of 701 BC).

[36] Schibler 1989: 74: '*Their king*, that is Yahvé, goes ahead of them'; emphasis original.

[37] Smith 2001: 481–483.

[38] His reading (Waltke 1993: 652–654) presupposes an allusion to the events of 701 BC, but he notes that the majority of commentators consider that this passage speaks of a new exodus following Babylonian captivity.

[39] McComiskey 1985b: 414–416.

[40] Sweeney 2000: 365–367; Dumbrell (2002: 208) follows this reading.

[41] Van Groningen 1997: vol. 2, 507.

[42] *Bible d'étude Semeur 2000* 2001: 1327–1328 (note on 2:13).

[43] McConville 2002b: 198.

(v. 14b),[44] and even calls attention to Saul's rebellion in this connection (cf. v. 15), whereas YHWH's anointed in Psalm 2 is established in a holy rule that is inseparable from the temple (so Calvin[45]). Hear Samuel Driver: 'In the original promise . . . the possibility of the ruler spoken of *sinning* is expressly contemplated (v. 14b). In Psalm ii., however, the poet takes the promise of v. 14a absolutely, and leaves this possibility out of the question.'[46]

6 New covenant implied by the democratization of blessing and the Isaiah 55 background

The final line of Psalm 2, considered in context, requires that the beneficiaries of the decree of verse 7 be plural. This, again, stands in contrast to the Davidic covenant. The opening word of verse 10, *wě'attâ*, serves as a conjunction that draws a conclusion[47] from the preceding content of the psalm (concerning the son's kingship). One of these conclusions, featuring right at the end of the psalm, is that 'all' those who find refuge in YHWH / the son are 'happy' (*'ašrê*) – fortunate, privileged, blessed (v. 12). While it would be mistaken to downplay the solidarity between the king and his subjects in the Davidic covenant, the dynastic oracle of 2 Samuel 7 highlights the king *alone* as being the object of divine *ḥesed*. By contrast, here in Psalm 2, 'all' who find refuge are blessed.

This democratization of blessing relative to the Davidic covenant has a ready and illuminating new-covenant parallel in Isaiah 55 which, chronologically and canonically, stands in the background to the book of Psalms. In Isaiah 55:3, God promises to make an 'everlasting covenant'. Continuity with the Davidic covenant is specified in the same verse ('my steadfast, sure love for David'[48] [ESV]), but the covenant partner on view is not the (singular) David (cf. 2 Sam. 23:5) but the plural 'you'. In context,

---

[44] The construction (*bêt* with infinitive construct) in 2 Sam. 7:14b does not imply that sins will necessarily be committed: it can be understood as a conditional clause. Cf. GKC §159k, 494; contra Eslinger 1994: 58.

[45] Calvin 1859: 8.

[46] Driver 1915: 57; emphasis original.

[47] Gibson (1994: §72, rem. 4, p. 91): *wě'attâ* 'introduces a corollary of what has happened and leads to a fresh statement of intent, command, etc.' (he quotes Ps. 2:10 among his examples). Cf. Waltke and O'Connor §38.1e, 634; Delitzsch 1894: 126.

[48] I discuss in Hely Hutchinson 2022: 195–196 the possibility that we should understand the phrase *ḥasdê dāwid* (lit. 'faithfulnesses of David') in Isa. 55:3 to speak of the faithfulness exhibited by a future David (a subjective genitive, defended by Gentry and Wellum [2018: 464–479] and Block [2021: 342]). The debate is finely balanced. Either way, the text points to the establishment of the throne of the Davidic king.

the referent of 'you' must comprise 'all who are thirsty' (Isa. 55:1) – the 'servants of YHWH' (Isa. 54:17) or faithful Israelites. These same people are also the beneficiaries of the covenant – those who enjoy complete, free satisfaction (Isa. 55:1–2) and abundant pardon (v. 7). This is not the Davidic covenant but the new covenant.[49]

7 New covenant implied by the blessing for the nations

I have touched on the globalization on view in the psalm relative to the Davidic covenant in our second consideration (above). It is possible that 2 Samuel 7 itself testifies to an international scope for the Davidic covenant: Walter Kaiser's[50] influential[51] interpretation of verse 19b could be invoked ('the law of man' being understood as 'the charter for humanity') – or Ralph Davis's reading of 2 Samuel 23:3 ('ruler over mankind').[52] These texts are, though, obscure.[53] It is less controversial to note that the nations are not left behind when Solomon appeals to the Davidic covenant in his prayer at the inauguration of the temple (1 Kgs 8:41–43; cf. vv. 22–26). Yet it seems significant that *blessing for the nations* is never set forth as a *constitutive element* of the promises made to David. It is true that aspects of the Abrahamic covenant come to be incorporated in the Davidic covenant,[54] and also that blessing for the nations is a key component of the Abrahamic promises (cf. Gen. 12:3).[55] But these two covenants need to be distinguished, and inasmuch as they come together in this psalm, this is not a function of the Davidic covenant but of the new covenant. The 'all' of Psalm 2:12 certainly encompasses the nations: the referents of the vocatives in verse 10 correspond to the subjects of verses 1–2. The call to the nations to find refuge in YHWH / the son (Ps. 2:10–12) is a new-covenant trait – as, again, Isaiah 55 envisages ('so you will summon a nation you do not know, and nations who do not know you will run to you' [v. 5 HCSB]).

---

[49] I discuss further the connection between Ps. 2 and Isa. 55 in the interim conclusion below (see p. 35).

[50] Kaiser 1974.

[51] Among those who have been so influenced are Dumbrell 1984: 151–152; A. A. Anderson 1989: 126–127; Davis 1999: 83; Block 2003: 40 (cf. Block 2021: 319); Gentry and Wellum 2018: 456–458; Harmon 2020: 89; Emadi 2022: 85.

[52] Davis 1999: 246.

[53] So Gordon regarding 2 Sam. 7:19b (1986: 241; cf. 1984: 77): the parallel in 1 Chr. 17 is far removed from Kaiser's suggestion ('according to the rank of a man of high degree' [v. 17 DBY]).

[54] As we will see on p. 43.

[55] Cf. note regarding Goldingay's observation on Ps. 2 (see p. 27).

8 New David of Micah 5 suggested

If, as is possible – though not, in my view, probable – the Septuagint carries the original reading of the verb at the start of verse 9,[56] the image is one of shepherding, not shattering. In this case, one would be particularly led to note an eighth consideration, namely the rapprochement with Micah 5:2–5 [MT 5:1–4]. This passage features a new David in the context of the new covenant. With or without the image of shepherding, one is struck by the number of correspondences between Psalm 2 and Micah 5:4 [MT 5:3]:

> He will stand and shepherd them
> in the strength of Yahweh,
> in the majestic name of Yahweh His God.
> They will live securely,
> for then His greatness will extend
> to the ends of the earth.
> (HCSB)

To be noted are the tight connection between YHWH and the messiah, the messiah's universal greatness and the security[57] of the people. Psalm 2 and Micah 5 both reflect a new-covenant outlook.

9 Davidic king contrasted with David of Psalm 3

We should consider that the grandiose character of the Psalm 2 king is reinforced by the juxtaposition with Psalm 3. It is not necessary to have a developed view of Psalter arrangement to be struck by the contrast between the Davidic figure of Psalm 2, 'installed . . . on Zion, [YHWH's] holy mountain', and the David of Psalm 3, who is running away from his

---

[56] The reading of the Septuagint (the verb 'to shepherd', *poimainō*) presupposes the root *r-ʿ-h* rather than *r-ʿ-ʿ*. Only the vocalization differs. Context favours the MT: the action of breaking has as parallel, in the second half of the verse, the action of shattering. Yet, in the Septuagintal reading, the two parts of the verse do not necessarily clash (*pace* Terrien 2003: 85), for acting as shepherd does not need to entail protecting the entire flock (cf. Ezek. 34:17–22). Further, the MT is not without difficulty: it also requires a considerable transposition of images between the two halves of the verse inasmuch as a rod is not the tool of a potter. I owe this latter point to Émile Nicole.

[57] The security is implied in the context of Mic. 5:4 (MT 5:3), although it is not explicit in the original.

son Absalom (Ps. 3 heading [MT 3:1]). To be sure, the 'holy mountain'[58] also features in Psalm 3 (in v. 4 [MT v. 5]), though in such a way as to highlight the *absence* of David and the presence of YHWH. Here in this third psalm, we are a long way from the scenario of others finding refuge in David,[59] who is lonely and beleaguered, threatened by many[60] enemies.[61] While these observations do not amount to proof of a new-covenant outlook in Psalm 2, they do help the Psalter reader correctly to evaluate the figure who is on view in that introductory psalm. The greatness of the messiah-king-son of Psalm 2 is not to be underestimated.[62]

Interim conclusion: Davidic covenant encompassed and transcended by the new covenant

In sum, Psalm 2 conveys a new-covenant perspective. But the allusion to the Davidic covenant in verse 7 invites the question as to how the Davidic and new covenants relate. We can expect this question to be elucidated as the remainder of the Psalter explores the concerns of this programmatic second psalm. What we have seen thus far is that the Davidic 'seed' of 2 Samuel 7 turns out to occupy the same rank as YHWH himself: he is a new, holy David who is heir and judge of the nations and the locus of blessing for all (including among non-Jews) who take refuge in him/YHWH. It seems that, under the new covenant, the original promises of the dynastic oracle are, on the one hand, confirmed and encompassed and, on the other, extended and even transcended.

While it is clear that the theology of Psalm 2 incorporates the Davidic covenant without being a mere reprise of it, the overall picture that we gain from the above data precludes our asserting that the new covenant

---

[58] Since the phrase is relatively rare, this observation is not anodyne. The occurrences in the Psalter of *har* ('mountain') followed by the noun *qôdeš* ('holiness') with a pronominal suffix (that renders the second term functionally adjectival) are Pss 2:6; 3:4 (MT 3:5); 15:1; 43:3; 48:1 (MT 48:2); 99:9.

[59] Even if YHWH, rather than the king, is the place of refuge (Ps. 2:12; cf. the discussion in our fourth point, above), we have noted (in our third and fourth points) the close proximity between these two figures in Ps. 2. When we come to consider Ps. 72:17b (see pp. 42–45), we will have occasion to be confident that the referent of Ps. 2:12 is the king.

[60] Note the four occurrences in this short psalm of words belonging to the family *r-b-b* (vv. 1, 2, 6 [MT vv. 2, 3, 7]).

[61] Indeed, we notice elsewhere that David takes refuge in YHWH (e.g. Ps. 7:1 [MT 7:2]; 18:2 [MT 18:3]).

[62] As Mays (1994: 44) comments, Ps. 2 is 'the only text in the Old Testament that speaks of God's king, messiah, and son in one place'.

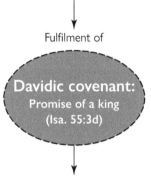

Covenant with 'all who thirst' (Isa. 55:1)

Fulfilment of

Davidic covenant:
Promise of a king
(Isa. 55:3d)

Complete, free satisfaction and abundant pardon (Isa. 55:1–2, 7)

Figure 3.1 **The covenant of Isaiah 55 encompassing
and transcending the covenant with David**

represents a *modification* of the Davidic covenant. The aggregate of
the differences between the two covenants in the psalm is simply too
great. Commentators of the parallel passage in Isaiah 55 advocate
speaking of a change of partner or a change of beneficiary for the Davidic
covenant,[63] but our treatment of both passages requires no such hypoth-
eses. Rather, we should presume that the Davidic covenant both remains
intact and comes to be integrated into the larger schema of the new
covenant (see Fig. 3.1). The evidence points in the same direction for
Psalm 2: the new covenant *encompasses* and *transcends* the Davidic
covenant.

If the programmatic Psalm 2 has begun to answer our question
regarding new-covenant newness relative to the Davidic covenant, it is
primarily books 4 and 5 that develop this. But there are important data
for our enquiry that feature in several psalms in the first three books of
the Psalter, and our immediate concern in the remainder of this chapter
is to throw the spotlight on these key texts.

---

[63] Cf. the discussion in H. G. M. Williamson 1998: 117–119. He summarizes the two options
as follows: 'the covenant with David is here potentially transferred to the people as a whole';
'by reaffirming the covenant with David as an individual the people will be brought into the
enjoyment of the blessings' (ibid. 117). Williamson himself follows the first line of interpretation; cf. also, e.g., Martin-Achard 1989: 161. Given these two options advocated by exegetes,
Isa. 55 is often not considered to be a new-covenant passage as such (cf. ibid.).

New-covenant typology incorporated in the Davidic covenant (Psalms 18; 20 – 21)

There is much that could be said about typology from the book of Psalms. I have elsewhere sketched some thoughts as to how David serves as both type and reverse type (contrastive type) of the Psalm 2 king.[64] For our current purposes, we will need to restrict our enquiry in this area to what is clearly germane to our quest for precision as to the newness of the new covenant. Psalms 18 and 21 are intriguing in this regard and may lead us to re-evaluate our understanding of how the Davidic covenant functions.

The covenantal perspective set forth by Psalm 18 is enigmatic. There are many data that recall Psalm 2 and thus suggest a new-covenant outlook.

1 Here is a messiah (v. 50 [MT v. 51]) whose deliverance in the face of enemies is total (heading [MT v. 1]).
2 His supremacy is absolute (vv. 40–44, 47–48 [MT vv. 41–45, 48–49]).
3 He is righteous (vv. 20–24 [MT vv. 21–25]) in such a way as to parallel YHWH: he has kept YHWH's 'ways' (v. 21 [MT v. 22]) and has been 'perfect' (v. 23 [MT v. 24]); 'as for God, his way is perfect' (v. 30 [MT v. 31]).
4 The transcendent YHWH is angry (vv. 7–15 [MT vv. 8–16]; cf. Ps. 2:4–5).
5 YHWH dwells simultaneously in the heavens and in an earthly structure (the tabernacle [v. 6 (MT v. 7)]; cf. Ps. 2:5–6; 1 Kgs 8).
6 As becomes much clearer in the light of Paul's quoting[65] of verse 49 (MT v. 50), non-Jews are beneficiaries of God's mercy (cf. Ps. 2:10–12).

On the other hand, a Psalm 2 perspective is belied by the following considerations.

1 In contrast to Psalm 2:12, there is no ambiguity in Psalm 18 as to whether YHWH or the messiah is the place of refuge: only YHWH fulfils this function.[66]
2 Whereas in Psalm 2:7 David's *son* (cf. 2 Sam. 7:14) speaks to YHWH, here in Psalm 18 David himself is the speaker (heading [MT v. 1]).

---

[64] Hely Hutchinson 2015a: 114–117; 118.
[65] In Rom. 15:9.
[66] Compare the formula of Ps. 18:30 (MT 18:31) with that of Ps. 2:12.

3 Whereas Psalm 2 is strongly reminiscent of the new-covenant theology of Isaiah 55, the climactic, final verse of Psalm 18 provides a summarizing commentary on the whole and anchors the psalm firmly in the Davidic covenant of 2 Samuel 7 (compare Ps. 18:50 [MT 18:51] with 2 Sam. 7:12–16; see Table 3.2).

Similar remarks are called for in relation to Psalm 21. On the one hand, the king on view recalls the supreme son of Psalm 2:

1 He makes 'all his enemies' (v. 8 [MT v. 9]) 'like a fiery furnace' (v. 9 [MT v. 10]).
2 He acts in tandem with YHWH (v. 2 [MT v. 3]).
3 He acts in a context in which YHWH is angry (v. 9 [MT v. 10]).
4 The life he receives consists of 'length of days for ever and ever' (v. 4 [MT v. 5]) – a striking compounding of terms!
5 YHWH has made the king 'a blessing for ever' (v. 6 [MT v. 7])[67] – a source of blessing to others, the people as a whole being saved (v. 13 [MT v. 14]; cf. Ps. 20:9 [MT 20:10]).[68] There is a possible allusion in v. 6 (MT v. 7) to the promises made to Abram in Genesis 12:2c ('you will be a blessing').

On the other hand, the king in question is David. Although the connection between the 'David' of Psalm 21's heading (MT v. 1) and the king whom the psalm showcases is not made explicit, this interpretation – if it does not already suggest itself by default – is strongly favoured by Psalter context. Here, editorial criticism plays a legitimate and useful part. One of the most widely accepted results of scholarly enquiry into Psalter shape, one that can be traced back to Pierre Auffret's 1982 study,[69] is that Psalms 15 – 24 form a concentric structure within which Psalm 18 has as counterpart the twin Psalms 20 – 21.[70] In Psalm 20, intercession for the salvation

---

[67] The form is a poetic plural of intensity (cf. GKC §124e, 397–398). Contra several translations, we should not understand that YHWH grants the king blessings but that YHWH renders the king a blessing to others. See Goldingay 2006: 310.

[68] Via first-person plural, Ps. 21:13 (MT 21:14) echoing 20:9 (MT 20:10) (first-person plural occurring from 20:5 [20:6 MT]).

[69] Auffret 1982; for some idea of the influence of Auffret's analysis of these psalms, see Sumpter 2013: 186.

[70] The significance of the juxtaposition of these two psalms is widely recognized, even by Goldingay (2006: 313) and Longman (2014: 124), who are generally sceptical of editorial criticism. For a discussion of these links, see Delitzsch 1894: 358–359; Wilson 2002a: 397.

Table 3.2 Similar perspectives on the Davidic and new covenants in 2 Samuel 7 and Psalms 18 and 21

2 Sam. 7:12–16	I will raise up your **seed** (*zar'ăkā*) after you . . . and I will establish his kingdom . . . I will establish the throne of his kingdom for ever . . . my **covenant faithfulness** (*ḥasdî*) will not depart from him . . . Your house and your kingdom will be before you **for ever** (*'ad-'ôlām*); your throne will be established **for ever** (*'ad-'ôlām*).
Ps. 18:50 (MT 18:51)	Granting great deliverances to his king, showing **covenant faithfulness** (*ḥesed*) to his messiah, to David and his **seed for ever** (*zar'ô 'ad-'ôlām*).
Ps. 21:4, 6–7 (MT 21:5, 7–8)	[Y]ou gave him length of days **for ever and ever** (*'ôlām wā'ed*) . . . For you have made him a blessing **for ever** (*lā'ad*) . . . For the king is trusting in YHWH, and in the **covenant faithfulness** (*ḥesed*) of the Most High he is not moved.

(the root *y-š-'* occurring four times in ten verses) of the 'messiah' (v. 6 [MT v. 7]) / 'king' (v. 9 [MT v. 10]) recalls the key final verse of Psalm 18: 'Great salvation he brings to his king, and shows steadfast love to his anointed [= 'messiah'], to David and his offspring for ever' (Ps. 18:50 ESV [MT 18:51]). Further, as already noted in relation to Psalm 18, YHWH dwells simultaneously in the Zion sanctuary (Ps. 20:2 [MT 20:3]) and in heaven (Ps. 20:6 [MT 20:7]). In Psalm 21, the answer to prayer for the 'salvation' (root *y-š-'* in vv. 1 and 5 [MT vv. 2, 6]) of the 'king' (in vv. 1 and 7 [MT vv. 2, 8]) is cause for rejoicing. In short, there would need to be some weighty arguments to counter the idea that the identity of the king of Psalm 18 – David (heading [MT 18:1] and 18:50 [MT 18:51]) – is different in Psalms 20 – 21.

We have seen that the *historical David* enjoys some considerable measure of the fulfilment of promises that apply to his *son* and that ultimately go hand in hand with the realization of the *new* covenant. This may require that we make some adjustment to our understanding of how the Davidic and new covenants relate, but the perspective of Psalms 18 and 21 chimes in with that of 2 Samuel 7 (see Table 3.2). The syntax of Psalm 18:50 (MT 18:51) highlights the intimate connection between 'David and his seed' as beneficiaries of YHWH's covenant faithfulness. This idea may feel foreign to us. In the light of 2 Samuel 7, we are not wrong to understand that the promise concerns David's seed and son. But there is a sense in which it concerns David himself too; and verse 16 of the original promise in 2 Samuel 7 does speak of *David's* 'house', 'kingdom' and 'throne' being established 'before [*him*]'[71] – during his lifetime. And so those glimpses of what seemed like *new*-covenant fulfilment in *David* were not mistaken!

Appeal to Psalter context allows us to articulate this in terms of typology. Psalm 19, the central psalm of the concentric structure that juxtaposes the psalms that we have been considering, presents David as a model patterned after the righteous man of Psalm 1. Other parts of book 1 (and book 2) show him to be a reverse type (contrastive type).[72] But this part of book 1 elucidates an aspect of the Davidic covenant that we can now summarize as follows: David is not the Psalm 2, new-covenant king, but it is a feature of the Davidic covenant that he should serve as a *type* of this king.[73]

If Psalms 18 and 20 – 21 serve as partial echoes of Psalm 2, there are two important psalms in book 2 that echo that programmatic psalm more fulsomely and that provide further information regarding new-covenant newness. So we move on to consider these two key 'Psalm-2-lookalikes' (Pss 45 and 72).

Fulfilment of the Davidic covenant entailed by fulfilment of the new covenant (Psalms 45 and 72)

Book 2 opens with a crisis[74] whose solution frames the remainder of the book. This solution, set forth in Psalms 45 and 72, takes a new-covenant form.

---

[71] Emphasis added. I am aware of the textual variant 'before me' (referring to YHWH), but the harder reading represented by the MT needs to be reckoned with. The phrase 'for ever' need not mean 'for all eternity'; that it can be restricted to the lifetime of an individual is clear from 1 Sam. 1:22 (also Exod. 21:6).

[72] Cf. brief remarks on p. 138 n. 89 (and Hely Hutchinson 2015a: 115–117, 118).

[73] There are some parallels here with the portraits of David and Solomon that we find in Chronicles. That there is no mention of the Uriah–Bathsheba incident (in David's case), nor the 700 wives and 300 concubines (in Solomon's case), seems to serve a purpose in painting a typological picture of the Messiah to come.

[74] Which I summarize in Hely Hutchinson 2013b: 30–31 as 'enemy oppression and spiritual depression tied to God's absence – twin problems confronting an individual (Pss 42 – 43) and the nation of Israel as a whole (Ps. 44)'.

1. The psalmist envisages (or desires)[75] a king whose enemies are defeated (Ps. 45:5 [MT 45:6]) and who rules 'from sea to sea and from the Euphrates to the ends of the earth' (Ps. 72:8 HCSB: these words are identical in the new-covenant text Zech. 9:10; cf. also Ps. 2:8). It is also envisaged (or desired) that this king's enemies 'lick the dust' (Ps. 72:9),[76] that all kings bow down to him and that all nations serve him (Ps. 72:11). Unmistakably, this picture of absolute, universal supremacy recalls that of the Psalm 2 king.

2. The king's justice is centre stage, occupying three verses of Psalm 45 (vv. 4, 6–7 [MT vv. 5, 7–8]) and eight verses of Psalm 72 (vv. 1–4, 7, 12–14), the former recalling[77] the portrait of Isaiah 9:6–7 (MT 9:5–6) and the latter recalling Isaiah 11:3–5. There is no doubt that this king is worthy of being installed on YHWH's holy mountain (Ps. 2:6)!

3. The prospect of peace (Ps. 72:3, 7) and prosperity (Ps. 72:16), when considered against the background of parallels in the Latter Prophets, points to a future – beyond the exile – associated with the coming of the messiah and the fulfilment of the new covenant (Isa. 9:2–7 [MT 9:1–6] [cf. Isa. 11:1–9]; Ezek. 34:25–31; 36:24–38; Hos. 2:14 – 3:5 [MT 2:16 – 3:5]; Joel 2:18–27; 4:17–21; Amos 9:11–15; Mic. 4:1–4; Zech. 8:7–12).

4. The king is to enjoy the same status as YHWH himself, fitting – again – the Psalm 2 bill: as 'God' (Ps. 45:6 [MT 45:7]), here is one who acts in full harmony with 'his God' (Ps. 45:7 [MT 45:8]). He is endowed with the 'judgments' and 'justice' of YHWH himself (Ps. 72:1), the object of fear in perpetuity (Ps. 72:5), possessing renown for ever (Ps. 72:17).

5. The honour and fame conferred on the king are likened to the duration of the sun and moon (Ps. 72:5, 17). This alludes to passages in Jeremiah that fall within the lengthy exposition of the new covenant of chapters 30 – 33[78] (and to which we will return).[79]

---

[75] Depending on whether one takes the morphologically ambiguous verb forms as imperfective or jussive.

[76] The other two occurrences of the expression 'to lick the dust' feature in the Latter Prophets (Isa. 49:23; Mic. 7:17) in relation to the eschatological (post-exile) prospect of the nations' submission (see following note). Cf. Van Winkle 1985: 451–452.

[77] The final form of the Psalter is post-exilic, and the Writings follow the Latter Prophets.

[78] Jer. 31:35–37; 33:20–26.

[79] See, notably, p. 52.

Table 3.3 Echoes of 2 Samuel 7 in Psalm 45

Ps. 45:2 (MT 45:3)	You are the most handsome of men; grace flows from your lips. Therefore God has blessed you **forever** (*lĕʿôlām*). (HCSB)
Ps. 45:6 (MT 45:7)	**Your throne** (*kisʾăkā*), God, is **forever and ever** (*ʿôlām wāʿed*); the **scepter* of Your kingdom** (*šēbeṭ malkûtekā*) is a **scepter** (*šēbeṭ*) of justice. (HCSB)
Ps. 45:17 (MT 45:18)	I will cause your name to be remembered for all generations; therefore the peoples will praise you **forever and ever** (*ʿôlām wāʿed*). (HCSB)
2 Samuel 7:12–16	I will establish **his kingdom** (*mamlaktô*) . . . I will establish **the throne** of **his kingdom for ever** (*kissēʾ mamlaktô ʿad-ʿôlām*) . . . my covenant faithfulness will not depart from him . . . Your house and **your kingdom** (*mamlaktĕkā*) will be before you **for ever** (*ʿad-ʿôlām*); **your throne** (*kisʾăkā*) will be established **for ever** (*ʿad-ʿôlām*).

* Term used with a different sense in 2 Sam. 7.

Yet, in these two *new*-covenant psalms, a *Davidic*-covenant outlook is also entailed. This may already be suggested by the fact, which I have defended elsewhere,[80] that both psalms present the king as Solomonic. But we can go further. For Psalm 45, consider how verses 2, 6 and 17 (MT vv. 3, 7, 18) echo the dynastic oracle of 2 Samuel 7 (see Table 3.3). Regarding Psalm 72, allusions to the Davidic covenant are not as clear, but it is the '*son* of the king' who is on view (v. 1; cf. 2 Sam. 7:14); and, as already noted, he is to be feared *perpetually* and to enjoy *perpetual* renown[81] (vv. 5, 17; 2 Sam. 7:12–16).

What these observations point to is an indissoluble link between the new covenant and the Davidic covenant. Stated simply, fulfilment of the new covenant could not be envisaged were it not for God's faithfulness to his promises to David. This is similar to what we have already seen in Psalm 2.

---

[80] Esp. Hely Hutchinson 2015a: 119–120 (also, more briefly, 2013b: 31).
[81] Cf. also the preamble to the dynastic promise in which David's reputation is to be likened to the 'great(est)' of the earth' (2 Sam. 7:9).

But we need to go further: the new covenant also encompasses the Abrahamic covenant. This is already suggested by the allusion to Jeremiah 33 (in Ps. 72) that we have touched on. In Jeremiah 33:21–22, the innumerable host of heaven and grains of sand of the sea – images drawn from the promises to *Abraham* (Gen. 15:5; 22:17) – will be the fruit of the line of *David*, for whom there will unerringly be 'a son reigning on [the] throne' (Jer. 33:21). Again, according to this same passage, the 'seed of Abraham, Isaac and Jacob' will have as rulers (here is a striking phrase!) 'the seed of *Jacob and David*' (Jer. 33:25–26).[82] We should recall that, in context, the prophet is setting forth the character of the *new* covenant.

An even more direct allusion in Psalm 72 to the Abrahamic covenant features in verse 17b, to which we now turn.[83]

Fulfilment of the Abrahamic covenant entailed by fulfilment of the new covenant (Psalm 72:17b)

We do well to remind ourselves that this verse constitutes the climactic conclusion to Psalm 72, for the verses that follow do not belong to the psalm itself: verses 18–19 form the doxology concluding book 2, and verse 20 is (so to speak) an editorial 'footnote'. Here, then, are the closing words of Psalm 72: 'They will be blessed in him, and all nations will call him blessed.' The allusion to Genesis 12:3 and related texts (18:18; 22:18; 26:4; 28:14) is clear and uncontroversial.[84] The pronouns 'him' refer to the king – who corresponds to the new-covenant king of Psalm 2. This king is the locus of the fulfilment of the promises made to Abraham: 'They will be blessed in him.' In other words, if blessing for the nations is to be

---

[82] Emphasis added.

[83] It is possible, following Wilson's (2002a: 992 n. 25) tentative suggestion, that the first half of the verse already contains an allusion to the Abrahamic promise of a 'name' (cf. Gen. 12:2). Yet the language of a 'great name' also features in the preamble to the dynastic oracle and thus could more directly reflect the Davidic covenant (2 Sam. 7:9; cf. Gen. 12:2).

[84] This allusion is recognized not only by contemporary commentators but also by early Church Fathers (cf. Jean-Nesmy 1973: 379). Regarding the hithpael conjugation employed with the verb 'bless', we should beware of exaggerating the semantic distinction relative to the niphal. This distinction is not even visible in the New Testament where Genesis texts carrying both conjugations are quoted by the passive 'will be blessed' (Acts 3:25 [cf. Gen. 22:18; 26:4]; Gal. 3:8 [cf. Gen. 12:3; 18:18; 28:14]). For a discussion of this debate, see Gentry and Wellum 2018: 274–277.

attained, the new covenant must be fulfilled by means of the messiah of the Davidic covenant. We are reminded of the programmatic Psalm 2: 'happy (*'ašrê*)[85] are all who take refuge in him' (v. 12; we can now be more dogmatic about the latter text referring to the son rather than to YHWH).[86]

We have already noted in relation to Psalm 2 that the new covenant entails a democratization and globalization relative to the Davidic covenant – democratization because the covenant partner is plural and globalization because the covenant beneficiary is drawn from all nations. The conclusion of Psalm 72 enables us to understand more clearly than hitherto why these aspects of newness come about. The explanation lies with the fact that the new covenant encompasses not only the Davidic covenant but also the Abrahamic covenant. It is true that we anticipated this point in our discussion of Psalm 2.[87] It is also true that Psalm 21 has already drawn our attention to the idea of the king as a source of blessing to others,[88] and we touched on the idea of the salvation of the nations courtesy of the king in Psalm 18.[89] Further, although it is not our direct concern, the theme of blessing for the nations is majored on in book 2.[90] But it is here, at the conclusion of the final psalm of book 2, that these notions are integrated with peculiar clarity: the future Davidic–Solomonic

---

[85] This term is cognate with the rare verb *'-š-rê* which we find in parallel with *b-r-k* in Ps. 72:17.

[86] Cf. the debate in our discussion of Ps. 2 (pp. 29–30).

[87] See p. 32.

[88] See p. 37.

[89] See p. 36. Within book 1, this idea is clearer in Ps. 22 (from v. 27 [MT v. 28]).

[90] The international scope of divine blessing that is on view in Ps. 72:17 constitutes one of the key ideas of the book. That this emphasis distinguishes book 2 from book 1 is highlighted by a comparison of the closing doxologies of the respective books: despite significant overlap between the two doxologies, the wish that 'the whole earth be filled with his glory' (Ps. 72:19 NIV) is peculiar to that of book 2 (cf. Ps. 41:13 [MT 41:14]). In other words, in book 2 context, Ps. 72:17 is not an isolated text: there is a certain emphasis on the fact that the Abrahamic covenant must be fulfilled! Ps. 47:9a (MT 47:10a) is particularly striking in this regard (notwithstanding the LXX variant). '[T]he people of the God of Abraham' are in apposition to '[t]he princes of the peoples' (ESV; cf. Feuillet's discussion [1975: 375–376]; here we find the only occurrence of the phrase 'God of Abraham' in the Psalter, and the name 'Abraham' will recur only in Ps. 105). See also, in the immediate context, Ps. 47:4, 7–9 (MT 47:5, 8–10); cf. Ps. 48:1, 9 (MT 48:2, 10) (the 'faithfulness' or *ḥesed* of this latter text reflects the promises made to Abraham). Further, Zion, God's 'holy mountain' (cf. Ps. 2:6), is 'the joy of all the earth' (Ps. 48:2 [MT 48:3])! The idea that the nations submit to God emerges particularly from Pss 65 – 68, towards the end of the book (Pss 65:5, 8–13 [MT 65:6, 9–14]; 66; 67; 68:28–34 [MT 68:29–35]; cf. Pss 57:9–11 [MT 57:10–12]; 59:13 [MT 59:14]; 64:9 [MT 64:10]). The logic of the desire expressed in Ps. 67 is particularly noteworthy: the Israelites seek blessing from God *in order to* (purpose clause at the start of v. 2 [MT v. 3]) be a blessing to the nations (cf. Gen. 12:1–3).

king will be the 'conduit of divine blessings'[91] for a worldwide people. His military exploits and justice are to be deployed in the service of peace and prosperity for the sake of people drawn from all nations.

We should notice how the closing words also differ from the formulations of the original Abrahamic promises. For the final clause of the psalm informs us that 'all nations will *call him blessed*' (emphasis added). The beneficiaries of the new covenant are blessed by the king and will, in turn, call the king blessed! It seems that the new-covenant people will be centred on their king.

The close connection between the Abrahamic and Davidic covenants here in Psalm 72, though striking by virtue of its clarity, should not surprise us in the light of earlier scriptural revelation. In addition to Jeremiah 33 and Psalm 21, already considered, 2 Samuel 7 itself evokes the Abrahamic promise in its preamble. The 'great name' of 2 Samuel 7:9 recalls Genesis 12:2, and the 'place' of 2 Samuel 7:10 recalls the land promised to Abraham.[92] More striking still, the language employed regarding the seed – 'who will come from your entrails' – is a phrase that is common only to expressions of these two covenants (Gen. 15:3ff.; 2 Sam. 7:12).[93] Further, the covenant with Abraham envisaged that kings would come from his line, the texts in question suggesting that these kings would be inseparable from the covenant's fulfilment (Gen. 17:6, 16; 35:11–12; cf. Gen. 49:10).[94]

We have seen that the new covenant encompasses the Abrahamic covenant and the Davidic covenant: the three converge in their fulfilment. It is worth mentioning that this does not mean that the Abrahamic and/ or Davidic covenants are *reconfigured*. Somewhat tentatively, Gerald

---

[91] E. Jacob, *Théologie de l'Ancien Testament*, 2nd edn, Neuchâtel: Delachaux & Niestlé, 1968, 191, quoted in Renaud 1989: 321.

[92] The 'place' (*māqôm* [2 Sam. 7:10]) recalls the designation, in Deuteronomy, not only of a central location (Deut. 12:5, *passim*) but also of the land promised to the patriarchs considered as a totality (compare Deut. 11:24 with Gen. 15:18 [cf. Dumbrell 2002: 87]; cf. Deut. 26:9).

[93] Firth 2005: 92.

[94] In a similar and parallel manner, regarding the land promise, the Abrahamic covenant already contains, in embryonic form, the more grandiose (new-covenant) promise that we find in Ps. 72:8–11: 'your seed shall possess the gate of their enemies' (Gen. 22:17b NASB); 'The LORD appeared to [Isaac] and said, "Do not go down to Egypt. Live in the land that I tell you about; stay in this land as a foreigner, and I will be with you and bless you. For I will give *all these lands* to you and your offspring, and I will confirm the oath that I swore to your father Abraham. I will make your offspring as numerous as the stars of the sky, I will give your offspring *all these lands*, and all the nations of the earth will be blessed by your offspring' (Gen. 26:2–4 HCSB; emphasis added). Thus, although Gen. 15:18, which refers to the promised land as being 'from the river of Egypt to the great river, the river Euphrates' (ESV), is in the background to Ps. 72:8, the idea of a worldwide territory in this psalm must be recognized as lying in the trajectory of the Abrahamic promise. Cf. P. R. Williamson 2000b: 19–22.

Fulfilment of the new covenant:

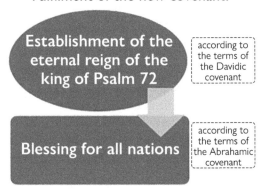

Figure 3.2 **How the new covenant is fulfilled by the king of Psalm 72**

Wilson opines that 'the whole psalm [sc. 72] functions as David's attempt to transfer the blessings of his covenant with YHWH to his descendants'.[95] But this would seem to downplay the fact that the dynastic promise already concerns David's seed and son (2 Sam. 7:11b–16). What our exegesis points to is a more straightforward understanding: the Abrahamic and Davidic covenants both retain their integrity and come to be fulfilled within the framework of a new covenant that encompasses them and transcends them. The fulfilment of the new covenant will depend on the realization of the Davidic covenant (namely, a messianic throne established for ever) and will manifest itself in the realization of the Abrahamic covenant (namely, the blessing of all nations) (see Fig. 3.2).

Should it be asked where the Sinaitic covenant fits into this schema, another book 2 psalm – to which we now turn – provides some pointers.

Need for repentance and mercy highlighted by the conditionality of the Sinaitic covenant (Psalms 50 – 51)

Psalm 50 is suffused with the language of the covenant set up at Mount Sinai,[96] the fire and storm of verse 3 evoking that occasion (Exod. 19;

---

[95] Wilson 1986: 89; cf. Wilson 1985: 211.
[96] Cf. e.g. Eveson 2014: 316–322; Harman 1998: 197–200.

Deut. 5). The covenant in question is bilateral in the sense that the people agree to its terms in the context of a sacrifice-based ceremony (Ps. 50:5; cf. Exod. 24:3–8). They 'take [his] covenant on [their] lips' (v. 16 HCSB). He is 'God, [their] God' (v. 7; cf. Exod. 20:2; Lev. 26:12; Deut. 5:6),[97] and they must not 'forget' him (v. 22; cf. e.g. Deut. 4:23; 6:12; 8:11): they are required to put into practice his stipulations, chief among which are the Ten Words,[98] although sacrifices are also part of what is required (v. 8a).[99]

Allen Ross summarizes YHWH's indictments of the people in the psalm as 'formalism' (vv. 7–15) and 'hypocrisy' (vv. 16–23) and discerns a link between the two, suggesting that flouting of the first part of the Decalogue (regarding worship of God) gives rise to flouting of the second part (regarding relationships with others).[100] Three of the Ten Commandments are alluded to as having been disdained (vv. 18–20). Heaven and earth were witnesses at the time of the setting-up of the Sinaitic covenant (Deut. 4:26)[101] and are witnesses again as the charges are brought against the people (v. 4). There is a call to repent lest 'there be none to deliver' (v. 22 ESV) but also the prospect of deliverance for the 'one who orders his way rightly' (vv. 14–15, 23 ESV). The two 'closing verses . . . are suggestive of the covenant curses and blessings with which God's covenant with Israel was concluded (see Leviticus 26:3–39; Deuteronomy 28)'.[102]

If, within the framework of the Sinaitic covenant, obedience is all-important and even necessary for blessing, the following psalm (Ps. 51) presents a case – King David's – in which capital offences have been committed. What hope of blessing can there be following sins of 'a high hand' (cf. Num. 15:30) – murder and adultery? The Sinaitic covenant does not cater for such extremes in its sacrificial system (Ps. 51:16 [MT 51:18]).[103]

But David, evincing repentance, appeals to YHWH's *ḥesed* (v. 1 [MT v. 3]; cf. Ps. 65:3 [MT 65:4]). This is an important term in the Psalter. It will require our attention as we now turn to the end of book 3.

---

[97] This formula is not, however, exclusive to the Sinaitic covenant, its first occurrence featuring in the context of the Abrahamic promises (Gen. 17:7–8).

[98] It is possible that the term 'words' in v. 17 denotes the Decalogue. Cf. Harman 1998: 200; Eveson 2014: 320.

[99] In our (penultimate) chapter on the law, we return to this question of the subcategories within the law of Moses.

[100] Ross 2013: 167–168.

[101] Cf. Goldingay 2007: 112 (for this reference).

[102] Eveson 2014: 321.

[103] Cf. Nicole 2004: 42.

An unconditional covenant broken by God himself (Psalm 89)?

One of the most clear-cut results of editorial criticism is the recognition that Psalm 89 leaves the unfolding story of the Psalter on a 'cliffhanger' as book 3 draws to a close.[104] It is important to note that the doxology of verse 52 (MT v. 53) serves as the conclusion to book 3 as a whole rather than the end of its closing psalm.[105] The end of Psalm 89 itself is striking for the intensity of its expression of gloom and perplexity. It is fitting that it is juxtaposed with Psalm 88,[106] the gloomiest psalm in the Psalter. Indeed, Psalms 88 and 89 share some striking lexical links: the vocabulary of Psalm 88:11–12 (MT 88:12–13) fetches up at the beginning of Psalm 89 (see Table 3.4).[107]

Patently, the cause of the perplexity is YHWH's apparent failure to honour his commitments to his messiah (vv. 38–51 [MT vv. 39–52]) – what *seems* to be his lack of ḥesed and 'ĕmûnâ[108] ('steadfast love' and 'faithfulness' [ESV]) in the shape of his *apparent* breaking of a covenant that had been unconditionally and perpetually established (vv. 1–37 [MT vv. 2–38]). That covenant is the Davidic – what YHWH 'swore to David' (v. 49 [MT v. 50]). The historical circumstances giving rise to the crisis are those of the Babylonian exile (v. 39 [MT v. 40], 45 [MT v. 46; cf. 2 Kgs 24:8ff.]).[109]

---

[104] Wilson is the key figure here (see e.g. 1986: 89–91). This does not, however, mean that we are required to consider the first three books to be 'the first major segment' of the Psalter (Wilson 1986: 91): a cesura is already signalled by Ps. 72:20, and the specific character of book 3 should not be downplayed (cf. Hely Hutchinson 2013b: 32–34; 2015b: 121–123).

[105] As a comparison of its counterparts demonstrates: Ps. 89:52 (MT 89:53); cf. Ps. 41:13 (MT 41:14); Ps. 72:18–19. The formula has been stripped to its barest bones, in keeping with the gloomy character of book 3 in general.

[106] See our comments in Hely Hutchinson 2013b: 32–33 regarding the structure of the beginning and end of this third book.

[107] Goulder 1982: 211; Tate 1990: 418. The terms in bold in the table are, in Hebrew, ḥesed ('steadfast love'), 'ĕmûnâ ('faithfulness') and pele' ('wonder').

[108] Cf. vv. 1, 2, 5, 8, 14, 16, 19, 24, 28, 33, 37, 49 (MT vv. 2, 3, 6, 9, 15, 17, 20, 25, 29, 34, 38, 50).

[109] A fair number of scholars argue for a pre-exilic date. Girard (1994a: 496 n. 25) is inclined to rule out an exilic date on the grounds of the 'openness and hope' of the opening section of the psalm, but it is precisely the contrast between these verses and those of the last part of the psalm that serves to point up the seriousness of the crisis. Kraus (2003: 783–784) considers that v. 43 (MT v. 44) is not compatible with the note of catastrophe that the exile would evoke, but links with the book of Lamentations should be noted in this section of the psalm (Kidner 1975: 324; it is striking that the four occurrences of the phrase *kol 'ōbĕrê derek/dārek* ['all who pass along the way' (Ps. 80:12 ESV)] should feature in book 3 [Pss 80:12 (MT 80:13); 89:41 (MT 89:42)] and in Lamentations [1:12; 2:15]). Weiser (1962: 591) declares that the psalm contains no pointer to 'the capture of the king', but the data of v. 45 (MT v. 46) square readily with the young king Jehoiachin who was taken captive by Nebuchadnezzar (2 Kgs 24:8ff.). There can be no doubting

Table 3.4 Lexical links between Psalms 88 and 89

Psalm 88:11–12 (MT 88:12–13)	Psalm 89:1–2, 5 (MT 89:2–3, 6)
Is your **steadfast love** declared in the grave, or your **faithfulness** in Abaddon? Are your **wonders** known in the darkness, or your righteousness in the land of forgetfulness? (ESV)	I will sing of the **steadfast love** of the LORD, for ever; with my mouth I will make known your **faithfulness** to all generations. For I said, '**Steadfast love** will be built up for ever; in the heavens you will establish your **faithfulness**.' Let the heavens praise your **wonders**, O LORD, your **faithfulness** in the assembly of the holy ones! (ESV)

The psalmist stresses the unconditionality of the Davidic covenant in such a way as to render his perplexity all the more acute and poignant. The length of the psalm – the third or fourth longest in the Psalter – is, in part, a reflection of its serving as a vehicle for conveying this emphasis. Right from the start, the psalmist insists on the unbreakable character of the Davidic covenant: YHWH's everlasting faithfulness is associated not only with creation (v. 2 [MT v. 3]) but also with the promise of an everlasting seed and throne for David (vv. 3–4 [MT vv. 4–5]). The covenant comes in 'the most solemn form that a word can take':[110] an oath (v. 3 [MT v. 4]). Later, this swearing[111] of an oath is reinforced by YHWH's

---

(note 109 *cont.*) the degree of catastrophe in this psalm. Floyd's comments are apt (1992: 456): 'Though the description of the catastrophe in *vv.* 39–46 may in itself be vague with respect to historical reference, in the context of the psalm as a whole this part of the text can be seen to describe the kind of defeat that violates the terms of the oracle, and thus calls the terms of the oracle into question. This is the kind of defeat that threatens both Judah and the Davidic dynasty with extinction . . . [T]here is only one defeat that would have signified what Ps. lxxxix is making complaint about, namely the fall of Judah to the Babylonians in 587 BCE (2 Kgs xxiv–xxv).' For other noteworthy references to the Babylonian exile in book 3, see Pss 74:3–7; 79:1–4.

[110] Amsler 1992: 195.

[111] In all cases, the verb is *š-b-ʿ* (conjugated in the niphal, with YHWH as subject). It is associated with unconditional promises made by YHWH at the setting-up (and/or confirming) of the Noahic covenant (Isa. 54:7) and Abrahamic covenant (e.g. Gen. 22:16; Exod. 32:13; Num. 14:16; Mic. 7:20) as well as the Davidic covenant (Ps. 89); it is also found in contexts of conditionality, the oath then being valid under circumstances that are specified in the context (Jer. 11:4–5; Ps. 132:11–12).

holiness[112] (v. 35 [MT v. 36]) and constancy (v. 49 [MT v. 50]): it would be hard to imagine how God's character could be more clearly 'on the line' in what he promises to David. It is unthinkable that YHWH would prove to be a liar (v. 35b [MT v. 36b])! The oath is, further, sworn 'once and for all'[113] (v. 35a [MT v. 36a]): it cannot be revoked.

This insistence on the unconditional character of the Davidic covenant in Psalm 89 is even more striking when one takes into account the background of the texts in 1 Kings that bespeak its conditionality (see Table 3.5). Unlike their counterparts in 1 Kings, the conditional clauses in Psalm 89 are expressed negatively ('if your sons . . . do not . . .'), and, accordingly, the two verbs that are connoted negatively ('forsake', 'profane') do not feature in the Kings texts. But the other two verbs ('walk' [*hālak*], 'keep' [*šāmar*]) feature at least once each in each of the four Kings passages. Regarding the four nouns that designate the law,[114] three are attested at

Table 3.5 The contrast between Psalm 89 and 1 Kings regarding the conditionality of the Davidic covenant

Ps. 89:30–31 (MT 31–32)	If his **sons** forsake my law and do not **walk** in **my judgments**, if they profane **my statutes** and do not **keep my commandments**
1 Kgs 2:4	If your **sons keep** their way, to **walk** before me in truth, with all their heart and all their soul
1 Kgs 6:12	if you **walk** in **my statutes** and perform **my judgments** and **keep** all **my commandments** to **walk** in them
1 Kgs 8:25	if only your **sons keep** their way to **walk** before me as you **walked** before me
1 Kgs 9:4	if you **walk** before me as David, your father, **walked** . . . to perform according to all that I **commanded** you, if you **keep my statutes** and **my judgments**

---

[112] Such reinforcement of the verb *š-b-ʿ* by this phrase features only here and in Amos 4:2 (a context not related to the setting-up of a covenant), but we should also note this formula tied to the Abrahamic covenant: 'By myself I have sworn, declares the LORD . . .' (Gen. 22:16 ESV; same verb again).

[113] For the adverbial role played by the first word in this verse (an attributive adjective), see Waltke and O'Connor §15.2, 275.

[114] *tôrâ* ('law'), *mišpāṭ* ('judgment'), *ḥuqqâ/ḥōq* ('statute'), *miṣwâ* ('commandment').

least once in the four Kings passages taken as a whole (including all three together in 6:12).

But the key observation is that, in context, the conditionality is left to stand in the Kings passages, whereas it is ruled out in Psalm 89. Thus, for example, in 1 Kings 6:12, the declaration 'I will fulfill My promise to you, which I made to your father David' (HCSB) is valid only in the event of Solomon's proving to be obedient. Indeed, a binary structure of blessing and cursing will be operating. Israel's fortunes rest on the ability of Solomon and his sons to obey, as YHWH's words following the temple dedication spell out:

> As for you, if you walk before Me as your father David walked, with a heart of integrity and in what is right, doing everything I have commanded you, and if you keep My statutes and ordinances, I will establish your royal throne over Israel forever, as I promised your father David: You will never fail to have a man on the throne of Israel.
>
> If you or your sons turn away from following Me and do not keep My commands – My statutes that I have set before you – and if you go and serve other gods and worship them, I will cut off Israel from the land I gave them, and I will reject the temple I have sanctified for My name. Israel will become an object of scorn and ridicule among all the peoples.
>
> (1 Kgs 9:4–7 HCSB)

In other words, the Davidic promises may well 'fail'. By contrast, according to the perspective of Psalm 89, nothing can stand in the way of the covenant's inviolable character. Should David's sons prove disobedient, says YHWH:

> then I will punish their transgression with the rod
>   and their iniquity with stripes,
> *but I will not remove from him my steadfast love*
>   *or be false to my faithfulness.*
> (Ps. 89:32–33 ESV [MT 89:33–34]; emphasis added)

The unconditional character of the promise that we find here in Psalm 89 is aligned with the original formulation of 2 Samuel 7:14b–15.

At first sight, the perspectives of 1 Kings and Psalm 89 would seem contradictory. Before the conclusion of our study, we will have occasion to appreciate how and why 'contradiction' is not the right category. The conditional and unconditional dimensions of the Davidic covenant prove to be readily reconcilable. At this stage, however, of the unfolding flow of the Psalter, we do well to let the tension stand. I fear that, in some proposals for harmonizing the conditionality with the unconditionality of this covenant, this difficulty may be resolved artificially or prematurely, such that tension is alleviated at too early a stage in redemptive history. Ralph Davis, commenting on the relationship between the 1 Kings 2 passage and 2 Samuel 7, suggests that 'the unfaithfulness or disobedience of Solomon (or of any Davidic king) would not negate the promise to David; but . . . there will be no *enjoyment* of the blessedness of that promise unless a king remains faithful'.[115] Similar proposals abound.[116] Yet it seems that what is at issue when the conditionality comes into play is the presence or absence of a Davidic king on the throne *according to the terms of the promise made to David*. In other words, the stakes are high! Such high stakes are reflected in Psalm 89. 'What bothers the psalmist in Psalm 89 is that the promises made to David seem to be withdrawn'.[117]

An additional dynamic is at work in Psalm 89 that, again, highlights the unbreakable nature of the Davidic covenant. We consider this now.

The Messiah of the new covenant set forth within the framework of the Davidic covenant (Psalm 89)

The close connection between the Davidic covenant and the new covenant, which we explored in relation to Psalms 18 and 20 – 21,[118] is clearly

---

[115] Davis 2002: 27; emphasis original.

[116] 'Although the line of David may be chastened, the terms of this covenant, the *ḥesed* (חֶסֶד) of God, will never be withdrawn' (Grisanti 1999: 242); '[i]n general terms, the line would not fail. Yet in particular terms its benefits might be withdrawn from individuals' (Dumbrell 1980: 45); '[the] condition turns only on sanctions that do not form part and parcel of the covenant itself' (Buis 1976: 57); cf. Pentecost 1958/1964: 103–104; Kaiser 1972: 18; McComiskey 1985a: 164; Gileadi 1988: 161–162; Waltke 1988: 132; Kim 1989: 379; Blaising 1993: 168; Walton 1994: 115; Freedman 2003: 16; Block 2021: 384–385. Gentry and Wellum (2018: 459–464) speak of 'later interpretations of 2 Samuel 7' that emphasize either the human obligation (conditionality) or the divine obligation (unconditionality) in the covenant.

[117] Schreiner 2017: 77.

[118] See pp. 36–39.

on view. By way of reminder, we saw (in relation to those book 1 psalms) that the *historical David* enjoys some considerable measure of the fulfilment of promises that apply to his *son* and that ultimately go hand in hand with the realization of the *new* covenant. This is also the case here in Psalm 89.

Consider, first, the comparison between the permanence of creation and that of the Davidic covenant: the latter is established for ever, 'like the days of the heavens' (v. 29 [MT v. 30]), 'like the sun' (v. 36 [MT v. 37]), 'like the moon' (v. 37 [MT v. 38]). Here is the *new*-covenant language, already touched on,[119] of Jeremiah 31:35–37; 33:20–26 and Psalm 72:5, 17.

In the second place, we must observe how the king, David, is presented. As in Psalm 2, which portrays the Messiah of the *new* covenant, here, in Psalm 89, 'the regal power is the exact reflection of the divine power: the king is therefore not YHWH's vassal but the one who acts in YHWH's very stead – his stand-in'.[120] Yet, as in the case of Psalm 18, the framework of this 'new-covenant outlook' is explicitly that of the Davidic covenant (Pss 18:50 [MT 18:51]; 89:2–3, 28, 35, 49 [MT 89:3–4, 29, 36, 50]). Specifically, just as in Psalm 18 David stands 'at the head of the nations' (Ps. 18:43 [MT 18:44]) within the framework of the *Davidic* covenant, so here, according to the promise of Psalm 89, he will be ranked 'more highly than the kings of the earth' (v. 27 [MT v. 28]). Terms that would normally be reserved for YHWH himself are applied to the earthly king David: 'Most High'[121] (*'elyôn* [v. 27 (MT v. 28)]), 'Shield [of Israel]' (v. 18 [MT v. 19], by implication of parallelism).[122]

It is telling that the distinguished systematician Henri Blocher can wonder whether verse 27 (MT v. 28) does not attribute the terms 'First-born' and 'Most High' to the *new* David.[123] His exegetical reason for leaning in this direction is that verse 26a (MT v. 27a) harks back to 2 Samuel 7:14 which speaks of David's son. But one needs to allow the 'shock' to be felt: such exalted titles are conferred upon the earthly monarch, the referent not changing between verse 20 (MT v. 21) (David) and verse 26 (MT v. 27).

---

[119] See p. 40.

[120] Dumortier 1972: 193.

[121] This word is also used to refer to Israel's potential status at the head of the nations (Deut. 26:19; 28:1 [cf. BDB]).

[122] Cf. Renaud (1997: 223) who rightly acknowledges that Ps. 84:9 [MT 84:10] constitutes another exception, 'shield' being employed with reference to the 'anointed one'.

[123] Blocher 2002: 35.

Indeed, the focus in this psalm is very much on David himself. Whereas in 2 Samuel 7:13–15 there is an *individual* offspring – designated by the use of singular personal pronouns – who benefits from YHWH's *ḥesed*, the closest equivalent individual in Psalm 89 is David himself. To be sure, a reference to David's seed does emerge in verse 29 (MT v. 30), but it is developed as a collective by means of the plural nouns ('his sons') and pronouns that feature in the ensuing verses 30–32 (MT vv. 31–33). Once these plurals revert, in verse 33 (MT v. 34), to the singular in speaking of the unshakeable *ḥesed*, it appears that it is David who is, again, on view.[124] 'I will not violate my *ḥesed* towards him' (Ps. 89:33 [MT 89:34]) does, of course, echo the dynastic promise of 2 Samuel 7:15 ('[M]y *ḥesed* will not leave him'), but the 'him' in question is not the same. Whereas the original oracle's referent is the seed/son of David, the referent in Psalm 89 is probably David, in keeping with the fact that the *ḥesed* of this covenant invariably refers to David (as opposed to his offspring) elsewhere in this psalm (vv. 1–4, 24, 28, 49 [MT vv. 2–5, 25, 29, 50]).

In short, according to the perspective of Psalm 89, the partner of the *Davidic* covenant – that is, David, son of Jesse – bears close resemblance to the *new*-covenant figure who is his seed and son. Rhetorically, this heightens the sense of crisis at the close of book 3 as the psalmist laments the apparent collapse of the Davidic covenant. With the advent of the exile, it appears that the remedy – the coming of the new-covenant king – is in doubt. Theologically, the resemblance (1) reinforces our observations from book 1 regarding the typological dimension of the Davidic covenant (its function of setting forth David as a type of the new-covenant king) and (2) enables us to appreciate the tightness of the connection between the Davidic and new covenants.

If conditionality is excluded from the Davidic-covenant perspective of Psalm 89, it does feature elsewhere in book 3. So we move on to consider Psalms 78 and 81.

Sinaitic conditionality flagged elsewhere in book 3 (Psalms 78 and 81)

The Sinaitic dynamic of disobedience to the Mosaic law giving rise to covenant curses is clearly on view in Psalm 78, and the sheer length of the

---

124 Contra VanGemeren 2008: 676.

psalm – the second longest in the Psalter – means that it receives peculiar emphasis. Its introduction serves to warn the people of the dangers of failing to keep the commandments of the *tôrâ* (vv. 1–8). The lesson to be heeded concerns the '[sons of Ephraim] ... [who] did not keep God's covenant and refused to live by His law' (Ps. 78:9–10 HCSB). As a result, God 'rejected the tent of Joseph and did not choose the tribe of Ephraim' (Ps. 78:67 HCSB). But there are other important strands in the psalm: God's patience and grace are highlighted,[125] as is his choice of 'the tribe of Judah – Mount Zion which he loved' and of 'David, his servant' (Ps. 78:68, 70). From the perspective of Psalm 89, this choice of David, which constitutes the climax of the psalm, no doubt renders the Babylonian exile all the more calamitous. Yet Psalm 78 does provide the theological ammunition that accounts for that exile, namely the seriousness of covenant unfaithfulness on the human side (cf. Ps. 78:37) and, in particular, the Israelites' failure to comply with the conditions of the Sinaitic (Mosaic) covenant (cf. Lev. 26; Deut. 28).

Psalm 81 clearly indicts the people for precisely such failure. God had appeared at Mount Sinai, in the 'secret place of thunder'[126] (v. 7 ESV [MT v. 8], recalling Exod. 19 – 20), and had established a covenant with the people that can be summarized by verses 9–10 (MT vv. 10–11):

There must not be a strange god among you;
you must not bow down to a foreign god.
I am Yahweh your God,
who brought you up from the land of Egypt.
Open your mouth wide, and I will fill it.
(HCSB)

But, immediately afterwards, we learn that this is how the Israelites signally failed to live (vv. 11–13 [MT vv. 12–14]): neglecting to 'heed' God's voice (the verb *šāmaʿ* features twice), they proved to be unsubmissive and

---

[125] I would argue that the structure of the psalm throws into sharp relief the theme of God's patience in the face of the Israelites' unfaithfulness. Following the introduction, the psalm unfolds in two cycles which highlight the sinfulness of the people but which culminate in God's grace (there is some overlap in the structure I propose with Harman 1998: 268): the people's sin (forgetfulness) (vv. 9–11 and 40–43), divine miracles (vv. 12–16 and 44–55), the people's rebellion (vv. 17–20 and 56–58), divine wrath (vv. 21–31 and 59–64), divine grace (vv. 32–39 and vv. 65–72).

[126] For the meaning of this phrase, cf. Kidner 1975: 294 n. 3.

stubborn, and they followed their own devices and paths (the verb 'walk [in]', *hālak*, features twice). According to the terms of this covenant, blessing is contingent upon obedience (vv. 13–16 [MT vv. 14–17]).

New-covenant fulfilment as framework for fulfilment of the Abrahamic covenant (Psalms 84 – 87)

We have seen that book 3's gloomy outlook is explained by its emphasis on the conditionality of the Sinaitic covenant: the curses of that covenant are an entailment of the people's disobedience. This makes the exile inevitable. We do not yet understand how the Sinaitic curses can square with the unconditional promise to David regarding the perpetual establishment of the Davidic throne. But, as I have indicated elsewhere,[127] I contend that book 3 provides a glimpse of the solution, notably in the four psalms that follow the Asaph group and precede the outer frame (Pss 84 – 87).[128]

These psalms paint positive pictures of the temple (Ps. 84), the land (Ps. 85), a 'servant' of YHWH who expresses confidence in God's *ḥesed* (Ps. 86) and the city of Zion (Ps. 87). It appears that these psalms foreshadow the fulfilment of the Abrahamic covenant within the framework of the new covenant. Most clearly, in Psalm 87, people from a diverse range of nations[129] enjoy the *knowledge* of YHWH (v. 4), which is a new-covenant privilege (Jer. 31:34; Hos. 2:20 [MT 2:22]). Here is the blessing of all nations promised to Abraham. It is cast in a striking mould: non-Israelites are citizens of Zion![130] Again, the previous psalm envisages that

---

[127] Hely Hutchinson 2013b: 33–34; 2015b: 122.

[128] Also in the allusion to the Abrahamic covenant in Ps. 74:20. Cf. the data that Hensley (2018: 86) adduces in favour of 'the covenant mediated by Moses after the Exodus', although the covenant in question is the Abrahamic, not the Mosaic – as indicated by, e.g., Exod. 32:11–14 and expounded extensively in our next chapter.

[129] Relative to Israel, nations that are proximate, distant, superpowers and persecutors (v. 4) – 'a representative sample of the Gentile world' (Kidner 1975: 315).

[130] Emerton (2000) describes as 'legal fiction' the idea that 'people (whether Jews or gentiles) would be said to have been born in Zion, when in fact they had been born elsewhere'; Mitchell (1997: 257) appeals to a midrash according to which '*[t]his man and that man* refer to the Messiahs of the Lord, to Messiah ben David and Messiah ben Ephraim'; emphasis original. But we need to face the clear biblical information head on and benefit from the shock that should be felt here (this powerful metaphor of Zion citizenship for non-Jews comes to be explored in Heb. 11 – 13).

'all nations . . . will come and bow down before' God and 'honour [his] name' (Ps. 86:9).

We should note that a prominent feature of Psalm 86 is its recalling, in verses 5 and 15, of Exodus 34:6–7 ('Yahweh – Yahweh is a compassionate and gracious God, slow to anger and rich in faithful love and truth, maintaining faithful love to a thousand generations, forgiving wrongdoing, rebellion, and sin' [HCSB]):

> For You, Lord, are kind and ready to forgive,
> rich in faithful love to all who call on You.
> (Ps. 86:5 HCSB)

> But You, Lord, are a compassionate and gracious God,
> slow to anger and rich in faithful love and truth.
> (Ps. 86:15 HCSB)

This is significant because this passage in Exodus 34 reflects the Abrahamic covenant. In context, the grace that YHWH manifests at the time of the golden calf incident is explicitly rooted in the promises to Abraham (Exod. 32:11–14). It is true that the continuation of Exodus 34:7 – which speaks of punishment – recalls the Sinaitic covenant (cf. Exod. 20:5), but this part is not cited by the psalmist. Further, if blessing, in that Sinai context, is set forth as being conditional upon loving YHWH and keeping his commandments (Exod. 20:6), such is not the case in Exodus 34; and the psalmist specifies that it is those who 'call on' YHWH who benefit from his *ḥesed* (v. 5). One additional datum points in a new-covenant direction: the affirmation that YHWH is 'kind' or 'good' (*ṭôb* [v. 5]) departs from Exodus 34 language[131] but is a key term in the new-covenant formula which plays an important role in book 5 ('Give thanks to YHWH, for he is good . . .').[132]

The other two psalms (84 and 85) do not portray as clearly as Psalms 86 and 87 the prospect of Abrahamic-covenant fulfilment within the framework of new-covenant fulfilment, but their theology does seem to be cut from the same cloth. Here, we learn that those who are 'happy' (*'ašrê*) draw their strength from YHWH (Ps. 84:5 [MT 84:6]) and trust in him (Ps. 84:12 [MT 84:13]). We read too that '[a]ssuredly, his salvation is

---

[131] Although see Exod. 33:18–19 (as pointed out by Dan Wu in conversation, 13 August 2018).
[132] Hely Hutchinson 2005a.

near to those who fear him' (Ps. 85:9 [MT 85:10]). In other words, blessing is bestowed not on the basis of ethnicity but on the basis of faith in YHWH.

Summary

We have covered a lot of ground in this chapter. Reductionism can be the enemy of good biblical theology, and so we need to reckon with a lot of biblical data![133] But where does the wealth of data we have seen leave us, with respect to our overall quest for clarity regarding covenant relationships?

We have already made good headway. The headings I have provided along the way provide the key 'take-home' points. Here, I propose to rearrange their order for the sake of grouping ideas thematically.

We noted, with regard to the Davidic-covenant-new-covenant relationship, that:

1 the Davidic covenant is encompassed and transcended by the new covenant (Ps. 2);
2 new-covenant typology is incorporated in the Davidic covenant (Pss 18; 20 – 21): the Messiah of the new covenant is set forth within the framework of the Davidic covenant (Ps. 89);
3 fulfilment of the Davidic covenant is entailed by fulfilment of the new covenant (Pss 45 and 72).

Turning to the Abrahamic–new relationship:

4 fulfilment of the Abrahamic covenant is entailed by fulfilment of the new covenant (Ps. 72:17b);
5 new-covenant fulfilment is the framework for fulfilment of the Abrahamic covenant (Pss 84 – 87).

With regard to the Sinaitic covenant, we saw that:

6 the need for repentance and mercy is highlighted by the conditionality of the Sinaitic covenant (Pss 50 – 51);
Sinaitic conditionality is also flagged in book 3 (Pss 78 and 81).

---

[133] At the end of the book of Acts, we see Paul doing biblical theology 'from morning until evening' (NASB; see Acts 28:23). Biblical theology takes time and requires that one cover a considerable amount of biblical ground!

Finally, we still have questions regarding what seems like:

7 the unconditional Davidic covenant broken by God himself (Ps. 89); how can this be?

I should put some flesh on these bones by way of summarizing the chapter.

The introductory and programmatic Psalm 2 enables us to appreciate that the question of how the new covenant relates to the Davidic covenant is on the agenda of this long book. It seems that the Davidic covenant, which promises a perpetually established throne for David's son and seed, is encompassed and transcended by the larger schema of the (eschatological) new covenant. Yet, already, Psalms 18, 20 – 21 and 89 showcase the *historical David* enjoying some considerable measure of the fulfilment of promises that apply to his *son* and that ultimately go hand in hand with the realization of the *new* covenant. This strong link between the Davidic covenant and the new covenant is established by means of typology and is signalled in the original dynastic oracle of 2 Samuel 7 which speaks of *David's* 'house', 'kingdom' and 'throne' being established 'before [*him*]'.

Once the new covenant comes to be fulfilled, this must involve not only fulfilment of the Davidic covenant (Pss 45 and 72) but also that of the Abrahamic covenant. Indeed, it is precisely in the new-covenant king, promised according to the terms of the Davidic covenant, that the Abrahamic promise of blessing for all nations will come to be realized (Ps. 72:17b).

According to Psalm 89, nothing can stand in the way of the Davidic covenant's being fulfilled: it was established unconditionally and thus is characterized by inviolability. God would never lie! And so the psalmist is perplexed when, in the face of the Babylonian exile, the Davidic throne becomes vacant. What has happened to YHWH's covenant loyalty (*ḥesed* and *'ĕmûnâ*)? Yet we also saw that there was a need for obedience, on the part of king and people, to Sinaitic-covenant stipulations (Pss 50 – 51; 78; 81).

We were keen to let the tension stand. It is true that we caught a glimpse of the eschatological Abrahamic–Davidic solution towards the end of book 3 (Pss 84 – 87), but we still have questions. How is it that the curses of the Sinaitic covenant can square with the unconditional promise to David regarding the perpetual establishment of the Davidic throne? What is it that can make the post-exilic new-covenant solution possible? Under what conditions can it come about?

When we arrive at book 4 (which we move on to next), the perplexity expressed by the psalmist at the end of book 3 starts to receive a developed response, and we are taken more directly to the heart of the matter of how the covenants relate.

4

The building blocks
of the answer in book 4

Introduction

Our overall quest is to determine the Psalter's perspective on a question which it invites us to grapple with: what is new about the new covenant relative to the Davidic covenant? The first three books of the Psalter have enabled us to come some way in our answer. Only, however, after the expression of perplexity in Psalm 89 do we find that a sustained treatment of the question is on the agenda in the book of Psalms. The Babylonian exile gives rise to the question: what has happened to YHWH's covenant loyalty? Following Psalm 89, we discover the answer to the psalmist's perplexity (Pss 90 – 150). As we tackle book 4 (Pss 90 – 106) in this chapter, we will be led to see that the theological firepower for answering the psalmist's perplexity lies in the *first five books of the Scriptures*.

Exile alluded to in Psalm 106

In order to understand how the fourth book of the Psalter connects with the perplexity expressed at the end of the third book, we need to turn to the end of the book – the end of Psalm 106.

Book 4 closes with a prayer:[1]

Save us, Yahweh our God,
and gather us from the nations,
so that we may give thanks to Your holy name
and rejoice in Your praise.
(Ps. 106:47 HCSB)

---

[1] Followed by the book's concluding doxology.

It is important for our thesis that we establish that this prayer is found on the lips of those in exile in Babylonia. From the perspective of the unfolding flow of the book of Psalms, it may seem uncontroversial to assert that those who need to be gathered are the exiles of the sixth century BC. But we need to confront a difficulty: 1 Chronicles 16:35–36 corresponds to the prayer and doxology of Psalm 106, apparently found on the lips of Levites appointed by David to celebrate the arrival, in Jerusalem, of the ark of the covenant (1 Chr. 16:4–7). This could suggest that the last two verses of Psalm 106 predate the exile and even the setting-up of the Davidic covenant (which is recorded in the following chapter of 1 Chronicles, chronologically following the arrival of the ark in Jerusalem). Under this scenario, the prayer request – 'Save us . . . and gather us from the nations' – would need to be interpreted in the light of the third wave of Philistine oppression against the Israelites in 1010 BC.[2] This would mean that the historical survey in Psalm 106 ends more than four centuries before the deportation to Babylonia!

Indeed, the 1 Chronicles passage does lead some commentators to distance themselves from an allusion to the exile in Psalm 106. Alec Motyer is among them:

> *Gather us from the nations* may indicate that this psalm was written during the Babylonian captivity but the inclusion of these verses in the celebrations when David brought the Ark to Jerusalem (1 Ch. 15, 16) speaks against this. In the psalm the *nations* are a place of scattering, a snare and a dominating force. There was no time, from the first entry into Canaan, when this was not the case to a greater or less (*sic*) degree.[3]

The stance of Motyer and others[4] is all the more reasonable in view of the last part of book 4's closing doxology: 'And let all the people say "Amen"! Praise Yah!' (Ps. 106:48b). These words are 'irregular' in the sense that they do not have counterparts in the doxologies that close the first three books (Pss 41:13 [MT 41:14]; 72:18–19; 89:52 [MT 89:53]). Yet they have a clear parallel in the narrative of 1 Chronicles 16: 'And all the people said,

---

[2] Cf. Payne 1988: 392; see also 369.
[3] Motyer 1994: 557; emphasis original.
[4] Briggs and Briggs 1907: lxxxiii; Gese 1974: 166; Wilson 1985: 184–185; cf. Weiser's hesitation (1962: 680–683). See also the list of authors cited by Auwers (2000: 81 n. 249).

"Amen", and praised YHWH' (v. 36). Is there not an obvious explanation for this irregularity, namely that the psalmist or redactor–compiler of the Psalter quotes the Chronicles passage? Is the Chronicler's historical framework not incorporated in this quotation? Thus do we not have here, at the end of book 4, an allusion to David's era?

Despite the force of this argument, I submit that the allusion to the exile is secure. The immediately preceding context in Psalm 106 holds the key: 'He caused them to be pitied by all those who held them captive' (v. 46 ESV). As Derek Kidner notes, 'examples of this clemency (for which Solomon prayed in his Temple prayer, 1 Ki. 8:50) are recorded for us only from a later age (*e.g.* 2 Ki. 25:27–30; Ezr. 1:2–4)'.[5] Similarly, Allan Harman argues that

> the use of language relating to 'pity' draws attention to the promises made in similar terms of what would happen when the people repented of their sins (see 1 Kgs. 8:50; 2 Chr. 30:9; Jer. 42:12). Therefore this reference to captivity means specifically the Babylonian exile, because *of no other captivity is this language used.*[6]

Indeed, the vocabulary of 'pity' and 'captivity' (more precisely, 'those holding them captive') in Psalm 106:46 does not feature in 1 Chronicles 16. And it is, in any case, an unproven assumption that there must be dependence in one direction or the other between these two passages: the Chronicler may have drawn on (Davidic) sources that are independent of those that fetch up in the book of Psalms (cf. 1 Chr. 16:4–7). The Chronicles passage overlaps only with the equivalent of the first verse and the last two verses of Psalm 106, and the 'irregularity' in the last part of book 4's doxology looks decidedly less irregular when compared with the closing line of the Psalter: 'And let all the people say "Amen"!' (Ps. 106:48b) is (more or less) the 'same closing thought' as 'Let everything that has breath praise Yah!' (Ps. 150:6).[7]

We are not required to choose between this explanation – independent sources – and that of dependence by the Chronicler on the Psalter, whose case is made in appendix 3. The essential point (for our purposes) is that the natural reading of Psalm 106 in Psalter context does not need to be

---

5 Kidner 1975: 382.
6 Harman 1998: 351; emphasis added.
7 Delitzsch 1889: 133.

modified in order to accommodate the data of 1 Chronicles 16. It is the voice of the Babylonian exiles that is heard at the end of Psalm 106.

Mosaic covenant not invoked in 'Mosaic' response to the crisis of the exile

With that prayer on the lips of the exiles at the end of book 4, the reader of the Psalter is probably slightly further on in history than at the end of book 3. On the one hand, in Psalm 89 it would seem that the psalmist is voicing a fairly immediate reaction to the events of 586 BC, namely the Babylonian destruction of Jerusalem and the start of the exile (Ps. 89:40b–46 [MT 41b–47]). On the other hand, in Psalm 106:47 the exiles pray for restoration to their land. But if we set aside this verse and the one that precedes it (Ps. 106:46–47), book 4 amounts to a flashback: the historical progression through the era of David (in books 1 and 2), Solomon (book 2) and the exile of the two kingdoms (book 3) is interrupted and gives way to what John Walton calls, by way of a heading, 'Introspection about Destruction of Temple and Exile'.[8] The calamity of the exile engenders theological reflection, and a whole book is given over to it. I believe that Gerald Wilson is justified in calling these seventeen psalms the 'editorial "center" of the final form of the Hebrew Psalter'.[9] That this editorial concern is to respond to the crisis of Psalm 89[10] is uncontroversial among those who engage in editorial criticism of the Psalter.[11]

It is also a consensus observation that book 4 is Mosaic.[12] Even John Goldingay, who is unenthusiastic about the study of Psalter shape,[13] gives some assent to Marvin Tate's label 'Moses-book'.[14] But the 'Mosaic' character of the book needs to be unpacked lest it prove misleading. In book 4, we are exposed to all the occurrences, bar one,[15] of the *name* Moses in the

---

[8] Walton 1991: 24.

[9] Wilson 1985: 215.

[10] Ibid.

[11] E.g., recently, Vesco 2008b: 1017 ('The fourth book of the psalter responds to the questioning of Ps 89 regarding the failure of the Davidic covenant'); McKelvey 2010: 15; deClaissé-Walford et al. 2014: 685; Tucker and Grant 2018: 333.

[12] See e.g. Goulder 1975; Tate 1990: xxvi–xxvii; Zenger 1994: 154–157; Weber 2003: 121; McKelvey 2010: 16; Ngoda 2014: 155. Hamilton (2021b: 64) proposes as title for book 4 'Moses Intercedes for the Davidic Covenant'.

[13] Goldingay 2008: 11.

[14] Ibid. 23.

[15] Ps. 77:20 [MT 77:21].

Psalter (Pss 90:1; 99:6; 103:7; 105:26; 106:16, 23, 32), the *figure* of Moses, his *era*, his five *books*, his *psalm* (90) and his *role as intercessor*. Yet at no point does book 4 appeal to the Mosaic *covenant* (the Sinaitic covenant) by way of solution to the problem of the exile.

This absence is striking and, it seems, significant given (1) the importance, in book 4, of the Pentateuch as the source of the answer to the exile, and (2) the prominence, in this same fourth book, of the theme of covenant. Indeed, one way of formulating the book's very aim could be this: to highlight the unbreakable character of the *Abrahamic* covenant with a view to demonstrating that the *Davidic* covenant has not been annulled and that the *new* covenant will be realized. My task in this chapter is to defend this thesis.

Abrahamic covenant as the basis for the exiles' prayer (Psalm 106:45–47)

Our starting point is to consider further what we have already begun to explore at the end of Psalm 106. In context, the prayer for restoration (v. 47) is tied to the fact of the captors' compassion (v. 46). This compassion is something that is *given* by YHWH (the verb *nātan* [v. 46]). The basis on which YHWH bestows this gift on the exiles is his covenant – 'and he remembered his covenant with them and relented according to the greatness of his *ḥesed*' (v. 45) – in line with his loving covenant commitment.

Which covenant is on view here in verse 45? The question is important, since this is a key verse – 'the psalm's capstone', writes Rolf Jacobson.[16] It is this verse that explains why optimism regarding a return from exile (cf. v. 47) is in fact realism despite the Israelites' unfaithfulness – and why praise is the fitting mood for the psalm (cf. v. 1). Yet there is something of a tradition of not identifying the covenant in question,[17] and this has even been considered a virtue.[18] In rare cases, it has been suggested that the covenant is that of Sinai. It seems, however, that this stems from unfortunate conflations – of the person of Moses and the Mosaic covenant (in the case of Erich Zenger)[19] or of 'the Sinai experience' and that covenant

---

[16] deClaissé-Walford et al. 2014: 805.
[17] Hoftijzer 1956: 73 n. 14. This tradition is followed even by Jacobson himself, who refers to 'the covenant' (deClaissé-Walford et al. 2014: 796, 807).
[18] Kraus 2003: 905.
[19] Zenger 1994: 174–175.

(in the case of Neil Richardson).[20] Hensley[21] argues that 'the psalm presupposes a seamless continuity between the Abrahamic and Mosaic "covenants" and regards them as essentially one and the same', 'one covenant of YHWH established with Abraham and graciously sustained and renewed at Horeb'. But he confuses 'Mosaic covenantal *context*' (his phrase, my emphasis) with 'Mosaic covenantal *content*' (my phrase).[22]

To the extent, however, that one can speak of a consensus regarding this question of which covenant is on view, it lies with the Abrahamic.[23] There are many reasons for asserting confidently that this is indeed the referent of 'his covenant' in Psalm 106:45, and we present them in the following sections.

1 Abrahamic covenant evoked by virtue of Pentateuchal allusions in the psalm

The data of the psalm itself, considered independently of Psalter context, point clearly in the direction of evoking the Abrahamic covenant. We summarize Psalm 106's key allusions to the Pentateuch in Table 4.1, to which we refer in relation to the discussion below.

In verse 23, we read:

So He said He would have destroyed them –
if Moses His chosen one
had not stood before Him in the breach
to turn His wrath away from destroying them.
(HCSB)

In context (v. 19ff.), this refers to Moses' role as intercessor in the golden calf incident, first reported in Exodus 32. The latter passage is explicit regarding the key factor that gives rise to the turning-away of YHWH's wrath: it is on the basis of the promises to Abraham that Moses' prayer is answered. Here is how Moses argues:

---

[20] Richardson 1987: 201.

[21] Hensley 2018: 105.

[22] Remarkably, Vesco (2008a: 815) asserts that '[i]n the psalter, the Davidic covenant is mentioned only in this psalm [sc. Ps. 89]. The other occurrences of the term in the psalter concern the covenant in general, namely that of Sinai – even in Ps 132,12.'

[23] The following authors espouse this point of view directly or acknowledge the parallel between this text and Lev. 26:42 (on which see discussion below): Kirkpatrick (1901: 633); Briggs and Briggs (1907: 354); Williams (1987: 271–272); Harman (1998: 350); Allen (2002: 73); VanGemeren (2008: 790); Goldingay (2008: 237–238); Dempsey (2015: 331); Estes (2019: 306).

Table 4.1 Key allusions to the Pentateuch in Psalm 106

Episode of rebellion in the desert	Section of Psalm 106	Passage in Pentateuch
Kibroth-hattaavah	vv. 14–15	Num. 11:4–34
Korah	vv. 16–18	Num. 16
Golden calf	vv. 19–23	Exod. 32 – 34; Deut. 9
Kadesh-barnea	vv. 24–27	Num. 13 – 14
Baal-Peor	vv. 28–31	Num. 25:1–13
Meribah	vv. 32–33	Num. 20:1–13

But Moses implored the LORD his God and said, 'O LORD, why does your wrath burn hot against your people, whom you have brought out of the land of Egypt with great power and with a mighty hand? Why should the Egyptians say, "With evil intent did he bring them out, to kill them in the mountains and to consume them from the face of the earth"? Turn from your burning anger and relent from this disaster against your people. Remember Abraham, Isaac, and Israel, your servants, to whom you swore by your own self, and said to them, "I will multiply your offspring as the stars of heaven, and all this land that I have promised I will give to your offspring, and they shall inherit it for ever."' And the LORD relented from the disaster that he had spoken of bringing on his people.
(Exod. 32:11–14 ESV)

But there is a second Pentateuchal text that reports the same incident and that is also in the background to Psalm 106:23, namely Deuteronomy 9:25–29. While, at first blush, these verses may appear not to add much to the Exodus 32 passage, brief consideration of their context will enable us to appreciate this: we need to view the Abrahamic covenant as being fundamental not only to the golden calf incident but *also to most of the other episodes* that feature in Psalm 106. We are driven to this conclusion because the golden calf episode serves as the grid through which to interpret other major incidents in which the Israelites sin.

The way in which this is signalled in Deuteronomy 9 is via an interruption in the narrative. Verses 8–21 provide an account of the golden calf event in which Moses' role as intercessor is on view. As for the content of Moses' praying, it is revealed only after a parenthetical section has been intercalated (vv. 22–24). When verse 25 resumes the account, it immediately does so in a way that clearly ties the narrative back to the golden calf episode, for it employs the same language of 'forty days and forty nights'[24] which has already featured three times (vv. 9, 11, 18), as well as the formula 'And I fell prostrate before YHWH' (recalling v. 18 directly). The usefulness of these observations turns on the way in which this narrative shapes our understanding of the material that is sandwiched in between its two parts: the intercalated material (vv. 22–24) is all of a piece with the golden calf incident. Thus, as we read 'And at Taberah, and at Massah, and at Kibroth-hattaavah' (Deut. 9:22 DBY), these other incidents need to be viewed as being under the same umbrella as the golden calf event – likewise the Kadesh-barnea episode (v. 23). All involve Israelite rebellion (v. 24), and all need to be understood as requiring the same response, namely intercession by Moses that is grounded in the Abrahamic promises.

Of the four episodes to which verses 23–24 refer, two occupy an important place in Psalm 106: Kibroth-hattaavah (Num. 11:4–34) and Kadesh-barnea (Num. 13 – 14). A third, Massah (Exod. 17:1–7), is tied, by virtue of its place name ('Massah and[25] Meribah' [Exod. 17:7]) and similar features, to another episode (in another location) that is referred to in the psalm as taking place 'by the waters of Meribah' (Num. 20:1–13).

The Kadesh-barnea episode, which we have already touched on in relation to Deuteronomy 9, contains its own attestation of Mosaic intercession that is similar to that of the golden calf incident (Num. 14:13–19; cf. Exod. 32:11–14): although, in this instance, he does not mention the patriarchs by name, Moses appeals to the Abrahamic promise concerning the land. Further, as he does so, he reminds YHWH (in Num. 14:18) of the words he (YHWH) addressed to him in Exodus 34:6–7. The latter text forms part of the golden calf narrative and underscores the Abrahamic connotations that we must associate with the key term *hesed* in these

---

[24] With only the slight variant that definite articles appear in v. 25.
[25] The way in which one construes the *wāw* is not critical for our purposes. Stuart (2006: 391 n. 187) argues in favour of two names for the one place.

contexts (Exod. 34:6, 7; Num. 14:18, 19).[26] It is significant that, aside from the oft-repeated formula of verse 1,[27] the (two) occurrences of this key term in Psalm 106 are preceded by the noun *rôb* ('greatness' [vv. 7, 45]): YHWH acts out of the 'greatness' of his covenant loyalty, reminiscent of those original Pentateuchal texts which speak of YHWH as being 'great of covenant loyalty' (*rab-ḥesed*).[28]

Two incidents of rebellion recorded in Psalm 106 remain unaccounted for. It may appear that no clear 'Abrahamic-covenant background' may be claimed for them, but this would be mistaken. First, we should note that intercession, or at least intervention, plays an important part in both. In the case of Korah's rebellion (Num. 16), Moses and Aaron intercede on behalf of 'all the community' (Num. 16:22), their prayer apparently answered by the fact that only Korah's people are put to death (Num. 16:16–21, 31–35). In the second case, the Baal-Peor episode (Num. 25:1–13), the intervention is that of Phinehas, grandson of Aaron,[29] which gives rise to '[YHWH's] covenant of peace . . . a covenant of an everlasting priesthood' (Num. 25:12–13; we return to this covenant later in this chapter).

Second, although it cannot be said that Phinehas' intervention is explicitly grounded in the promises to Abraham, we come across another throwback to the patriarch in the Baal-Peor episode as recalled in the psalm. Phinehas' act 'was counted to him as righteousness' (v. 31 ESV) – language that clearly alludes to Abraham's believing YHWH's promise regarding the number of his offspring (Gen. 15:6).[30]

Third, these two incidents are bound together with that of the golden calf by virtue of the 'panelling' that the Pentateuch exhibits, several themes of the Sinai sojourn recurring both at Kadesh and in the plains of Moab (see Table 4.2). In this case, it is the propitiation[31] of Exodus

---

[26] We have already had occasion to consider this important text in connection with Ps. 86:5, 15 (cf. p. 56).

[27] On which see Hely Hutchinson 2005a.

[28] In the psalm, the term *ḥesed* is plural. Although this may imply a less direct allusion to Exod. 34, the first and last occurrences of the term in Ps. 89 are also plural, and, in Psalter context, it is the crisis of that latter psalm that Ps. 106 is addressing. This formula (*rôb* followed by a plural form of *ḥesed*) is attested elsewhere in the Hebrew Bible only in Isa. 63:7 and Lam. 3:32 (a form of *rb* followed by a form of *ḥesed* has a further eleven attestations).

[29] Chronologically, the incident belongs to the period of the new generation: thirty-eight years elapse between Num. 19 and Num. 20.

[30] The key terms are identical, and the construction is very similar (though not identical).

[31] Act of rendering YHWH propitious, or favourably disposed towards the Israelites, following the latter's sinning.

Table 4.2 Themes of the Sinai sojourn recurring in Kadesh and Moab

	Sinai	*Kadesh*	*Moab*
Divine promises	Exod. 19:5–6	Num. 13:2	Num. 22:1 – 24:25
Rebellion	Exod. 32:1–8	Num. 14:1–12	Num. 25:1–3
Judgment/plague	Exod. 32:34–35	Num. 14:20–37	Num. 25:4–9
Propitiation	Exod. 32:26–29	Num. 16:36–50	Num. 25:7–13
Laws of sacrifice	Lev. 1:1 – 7:38	Num. 15:1–31	Num. 28:1 – 29:39
Priestly prerogatives	Lev. 6:1 – 7:38	Num. 17:1 – 18:32	Num. 31:28–30; 35:1–8
Impurity rules	Lev. 11 – 15	Num. 19:1–22	Num. 31:1–54; 35:9–34

Adapted from Wenham 1981: 16–17. © G. J. Wenham 1981; *Numbers: An Introduction and Commentary*, TOTC, Leicester: Inter-Varsity Press; Downers Grove: InterVarsity Press. Reproduced with permission of the Licensor through PLSclear.

32:26–29 (at Mount Sinai) that has counterparts in Numbers 16:36–50 (Kadesh) and Numbers 25:7–13 (Moab).

So, although the Baal-Peor incident includes some characteristics that might make it look exceptional, it should be held together with other episodes where the 'Abrahamic-covenant background' is unquestionably on view.

2 Abrahamic covenant presupposed by virtue of the links with Psalm 105

Although our first argument in favour of an allusion to the Abrahamic covenant in Psalm 106:45 is sufficient, it is worth being aware of others that buttress it. A second argument derives from the close ties between Psalms 105 and 106 which are well established: similarity of length, overlapping of praise formulae ('Give thanks to yhwh', 'Halleluyah'), sharing of key terms (such as 'to remember' [*z-k-r*], 'to forget' [*š-k-ḥ*], 'chosen one' [*bāḥîr*], 'inheritance' [*naḥălâ*], 'wonders' [*niplā'ôt*]), proper nouns ('Canaan', 'Ham')[32] and complementarity of theme.

That Psalm 105 showcases yhwh's faithfulness to his promises to Abraham is not, of course, adequate proof that those promises are still on

---

[32] In the Psalter, these two proper nouns occur only once each outside these two psalms. For further details on links between these two psalms, consult Weber 2003: 200; Zenger 1994: 174 n. 55.

view in Psalm 106:45. But the 'twinning'[33] of the two psalms requires that the reader reflect on *how* they are coordinated; and if the first celebrates YHWH's unshakeable commitment to the Abrahamic covenant, the second celebrates the fact that this (same) commitment remains inviolable even in the face of serious, repeated sin.[34] So Bernard Gosse is not exaggerating when he speaks of a '*reminder* of the theme of Covenant' in Psalm 106:45 and of the 'total and voluntary absence of reference to that of Sinai' in these psalms.[35] Further, he usefully draws attention to the link between the (Abrahamic) covenant and the gift of the land that features at the end of both psalms: if the prayer for restoration to the land in Psalm 106:47 is answered, this will be in line with Psalm 105:42–45.[36]

3 Abrahamic covenant alluded to in the parallel context of Psalm 90

A third reason why we may be confident that 'his covenant' in Psalm 106:45 refers to that of Abraham lies with the links between Psalms 90 and 106: these two psalms, which frame book 4, grapple with the inveterate sin of the people, the divine wrath that this provokes and the question of whether divine *ḥesed* is exhausted. I contend that the intertextual dialogue between the two psalms is instructive.

Psalm 90 is a 'prayer of Moses', and we also see Moses at prayer in Psalm 106. More specifically, the most explicit case of Mosaic intercession in Psalm 106 – that of the golden calf episode (v. 23) – is the one that fits the data of Psalm 90. While it is true that commentators do not generally draw on the Exodus 32 incident to explain the circumstances underlying Psalm 90,[37] this is partly owing to a refusal to see Moses as the author of the prayer.[38] That said, it is widely recognized – and highly significant –

---

[33] This term, as used to describe the relationship between the two psalms, can be traced at least as far back as Zimmerli's 1972 article.

[34] Cf. Zimmerli 1972: 111.

[35] Gosse 1998: 126; emphasis added.

[36] Ibid. 126–127.

[37] But see Hamilton 2021c: 154; also Freedman 1985 (cf. Tate 1990: 438; Creach 1996: 94; deClaissé-Walford 1997: 85), although, in the opinion of Freedman, 'the composer of the psalm based it on the episode in Exodus 32 and imagined in poetic form how Moses may have spoken in the circumstances of Exodus 32' (1985: 59); Tanner (in deClaissé-Walford et al. 2014: 690–691) espouses a similar view, leaning on R. J. Clifford, 'Psalm 90: Wisdom Meditation or Communal Lament?', in P. W. Flint, P. D. Miller, *The Book of Psalms: Composition and Reception*, Supplements to *VT*, Leiden: Brill, 190–205.

[38] E.g. Tate 1990: 437–438; Gerstenberger 2001: 158–159; Tanner in deClaissé-Walford et al. 2014: 690–691. In favour of the Mosaic authorship to which I hold, see Delitzsch 1889: 2–4; Maclaren 1903: 4–5.

that as the intercession begins, the language recalls Exodus 32:12b–13a: 'Return, O LORD! How long? Have pity on your servants!' (Ps. 90:13 ESV).[39] 'Return' (*šūb[â]*), 'have pity' / 'relent' (*wěhinnāḥēm*) and 'your servants' (*'ăbādêkā*) all feature in that Exodus 32 text in which Moses calls out to YHWH to 'remember Abraham, Isaac and Jacob' and reminds him of his oaths. When, therefore, in the psalm, Moses immediately continues by asking to be satisfied with YHWH's *ḥesed* (Ps. 90:14), we readers are required to vest this term with Abrahamic connotations (cf. also Exod. 34:6–7 and our discussion of this passage).[40] Given the collocation of *ḥesed* and *běrît* in Psalm 106:45, the dialogue with Psalm 90 drives us to recognize once again that it is the Abrahamic covenant that is alluded to at the end of book 4.

4 Abrahamic covenant on view in Pentateuchal texts that cohere with the theology of Psalm 106

I am not maintaining that Exodus 32 – 34 is the only Pentateuchal passage in the background to Psalm 90. Even in Psalm 90:13, which we have just considered, 'Have pity on your servants' also harks back to Deuteronomy 32:36[41] where we learn that YHWH 'will have pity on his servants' (same terms again). Does this Deuteronomy 32 text also suggest that the Abrahamic covenant is the basis for the intercession of Psalm 90 (and Ps. 106)? Indeed so, and it will lead us to spell out a fourth reason to be confident that Psalm 106:45 bespeaks the promises to Abraham; but we should not bypass a difficulty here.

Deuteronomy 32 forms part of a section of that fifth book of Moses in which another covenant is established in the plains of Moab (Deut. 29:1 – 32:52 [MT 28:69 – 32:52]).[42] It is both distinct from and complementary to,

---

[39] See Hengstenberg 1854: 134; Delitzsch 1889: 15; Kirkpatrick 1901: 552; A. A. Anderson 1972b: 654; Jacquet 1977: 132; Williams 1987: 164; Tate 1990: 443; Deissler 1993: 357; McCann 1993: 160; Creach 1998: 65; Kraus 2003: 800; Weber 2003: 121; Goldingay 2008: 32; Grogan 2008: 159; VanGemeren 2008: 695; Vesco 2008b: 852; McKelvey 2010: 33; Tanner in deClaissé-Walford et al. 2014: 695; Gundersen 2015: 110–115; Bullock 2017: 137; Estes 2019: 179–180; Hamilton 2021c: 154, 158.

[40] See p. 56.

[41] Cf. Kirkpatrick 1901: 552; Kidner 1975: 331; Kraus 2003: 800.

[42] I am assuming that each of the sections of Deuteronomy begins with a cataphoric (forward-pointing) demonstrative pronoun, the one relating to this section featuring at 29:1 (MT 28:69). In other words (and contra Craigie 1976: 353 and McConville 2002a: 401), I do not consider that this verse concludes the preceding chapters (cf. Olson 1994: 14–15; Nelson 2002: 338–339). Although I recognize that the debate is far from settled, the validity of my remarks

the Sinaitic covenant ('*in addition to* the covenant He had made with them at Horeb' [Deut. 29:1 HCSB (MT 28:69)]).[43] As this covenant is being set up, the Abrahamic promises are stressed:

> You stand today, all of you, before the LORD your God . . . that you may enter into the covenant with the LORD your God, and into His oath which the LORD your God is making with you today, in order that He may establish you today as His people and that He may be your God, just as He spoke to you and as He swore to your fathers, to Abraham, Isaac, and Jacob.
> (Deut. 29:10, 12–13 NASB [MT 29:9, 11–12])

But this Transjordanian covenant does not stray from the theology of the book of Deuteronomy as a whole which is simultaneously 'Abrahamic' and 'Sinaitic': both this last book of the Pentateuch in general and this supplementary covenant in particular confirm (1) the gracious promises that YHWH had made with Abraham and (2) the absolute necessity of keeping the Sinaitic commandments as a condition of blessing (Deut. 30:15–20; cf. Deut. 5 – 7). What is new in this additional covenant of Deuteronomy 29 – 32 (and esp. in Deut. 30:1–10) is the *clarity* with which the *compatibility* between these two strands is set forth. This is most instructive for our quest to understand covenant relationships.

Here is the scenario with which the reader is presented in this section of Deuteronomy. The Israelites will prove guilty of breaking the covenant established at Mount Sinai (Deut. 31:19–20; 32:5).[44] The curses of that Sinaitic covenant – including, notably, the exile (Deut. 30:1; 31:21) – will fall on the people. But this does not mean that there is no ultimate hope to which the people may cling (Deut. 32:36, 39, 43). The Abrahamic promises will come to be fulfilled eschatologically – beyond the people's being scattered among the nations – as they repent, are brought back to the land and enjoy blessing (Deut. 30:1–5). Significantly, YHWH will carry out an operation on the heart (Deut. 30:6; cf. Deut. 29:4 [MT 29:3]). Pierre Buis explains:

---

concerning the Transjordanian covenant does not depend on this question: there *is* a (supplementary) covenant set up in the plains of Moab (29:1 [MT 28:69]; 29:10–15 [MT 29:9–14; note the emphasis in the latter passage on 'today']) and it does contain significant new information relative to that of Sinai. For a more fulsome discussion of the Transjordanian covenant than is warranted for present purposes, see Hely Hutchinson 2022: 132–135.

[43] Emphasis added. 'Horeb' is the usual designation in Deuteronomy for Sinai.

[44] In this regard, it is noteworthy that the curses receive considerably more prominence than the blessings in the chapter that precedes this section, Deut. 28 (this is also true of Lev. 26).

For the people of God, the death resulting from unfaithfulness is not an end; from there, it is possible to start again on the journey towards faithfulness and life ... [B]eyond the exile, the contract will no longer be resumed under the same conditions: YHWH will have circumcised the hearts of his people who will be able to live out the great demand of Deuteronomy: 'love YHWH your God with all your heart so that you may live'[45]

The book can even conclude[46] with the prospect of Israel 'in safety ... in a land of grain and wine' (Deut. 33:28 ESV): such is the future of this people who are 'happy' (*'ašrê*) and 'saved by YHWH' (Deut. 33:29). It appears that the reader can be confident of the ultimate realization of the Abrahamic promises.

YHWH's intervention to circumcise hearts is certainly a new and radical element in the progress of biblical revelation up to this point. As the Pentateuch draws to a close, the mystery implied by the apparently competing Abrahamic and Sinaitic strands comes to be unravelled to a considerable extent: the Abrahamic promises will not be under threat when the Sinaitic curses fall, and, ultimately, heart circumcision will even obviate the need for further cursing.

But we should not exaggerate the explanatory power of the Transjordanian covenant. Moses has already insisted on the continuing validity of the Abrahamic covenant in the face of the exile, both in his first speech in Deuteronomy (4:25–31) and back in Leviticus 26. If, in the event of exile, the people repent

then I will remember my covenant with Jacob, and I will remember my covenant with Isaac and my covenant with Abraham, and I will remember the land. But the land shall be abandoned by them and enjoy its Sabbaths while it lies desolate without them, and they shall make amends for their iniquity, because they spurned my rules and their soul abhorred my statutes. Yet for all that, when they are in the land of their enemies, I will not spurn them, neither will I abhor them so as to destroy them utterly and break my covenant with them, for I am the LORD their God. But I will for their sake remember the

---

[45] Buis 1976: 100.
[46] That is, before the 'epilogue' that belongs to the Pentateuch as a whole (ch. 34). Sailhamer employs this term (1992: 36).

covenant with their forefathers, whom I brought out of the land of Egypt in the sight of the nations, that I might be their God: I am the Lord.

(Lev. 26:42–45 esv)

It is by virtue of '[his] covenant with Jacob . . . [his] covenant with Isaac and [his] covenant with Abraham' that yhwh 'will remember the land' (v. 42); it is because this covenant constitutes a commitment to the *descendants* of these patriarchs (yhwh's covenant 'with them', i.e. with the exiles, being unbreakable [v. 44])[47] that the total destruction of the people will not take place;[48] it is thanks to 'the covenant with their forefathers'[49] that the survivors will benefit ('for their sake' [v. 45]) from divine intervention such as had previously given rise to the exodus from Egypt. This is precisely the scenario that is in prospect at the end of Psalm 106: the exiles' supplication of verse 47 regarding a return to the land is based on the solid foundation of the promises to Abraham.

Davidic-covenant solution intimately connected to Abrahamic-covenant solution

The question arises as to why the *Abrahamic*-covenant solution to the exiles' problem, presented in the psalms that frame book 4, is an appropriate response to the preoccupation of Psalm 89. For the psalmist's perplexity turns on the apparent failure of the *Davidic* covenant. The reader of the Psalter is already clear on the answer provided by the end of

---

[47] It seems that succeeding generations of Israelites, including those who end up in exile, form part of the partner of the Abrahamic covenant (v. 44).

[48] Contrary to what vv. 36–39 might appear to suggest at first blush, there will be a remnant.

[49] It can be argued that this covenant is that of Sinai – the generation that yhwh 'brought out of the land of Egypt' (cf. Milgrom 2001: 2338–2339). In this case, the point would be that the realization of the Abrahamic promises in the post-exilic period will not short-circuit the need for subsequent obedience, and this would tie in with what we will see in Deut. 30 (see pp. 128–129). But (1) the context favours a further allusion to the Abrahamic covenant. In particular, the parallelism between 'I am yhwh, their God' (v. 44) and 'their God; I am yhwh' (v. 45) should be noted; (2) v. 44 has already indicated how several generations of Israelites can be viewed as being collectively the covenant partner (such solidarity between generations can also be observed in the parallelism between 'their iniquity and the iniquity of their fathers' [v. 40] and 'their iniquity [v. 43]); (3) the exodus, which is on view in v. 45, presupposes the promises to Abraham (Gen. 15:13–16).

book 2:[50] we noted, from Psalm 72:17b in particular, that fulfilment of the Abrahamic covenant comes via the Solomonic king who is the fruit of the Davidic covenant. We saw that this occurs within the framework of new-covenant realization. This means that, at the point of fulfilment, the Abrahamic covenant must entail the Davidic covenant. The perspective of book 4 is no different; but, here in book 4, we benefit from greater clarity – in keeping with the progressive nature of the revelation that the Psalter evinces – and greater detail.

Abrahamic solution to be applied to the exile (Psalms 89 – 90)

From the outset, on discovering Psalm 90, the Psalter reader is given an immediate clue as to the apposite character of book 4's answer to the crisis of book 3. This comes in the form of the striking intertextuality between the end of Psalm 89 and Psalm 90. While it would be an error to downplay the cesura that divides the two books, we should not allow this division to blind us to the significant links between these two 'seam' psalms (see Fig. 4.1).[51]

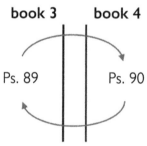

Figure 4.1 **The intertextuality between the two psalms at the 'seam' of books 3 and 4 of the Psalter**

First, the author of Psalm 89 voices the same concerns as Moses in Psalm 90 regarding the brevity of life. Towards the end of the psalm, he cries out to YHWH as follows:

---

51 We may smile at Evode Beaucamp's suggestion that 'with the name of Moses, behind that of Ethan, Heman, Asaph and the Sons of Korah, the psalm concludes the series of Levitical psalms' (1979: 96), and we may criticize his refusal to countenance the idea that a lament psalm might open a subgroup (ibid.), but we should recognize that he was ahead of his time in tackling such matters relating to the arrangement of psalms.

Remember how short my time is!
　For what vanity you have created all the children of man!
What man can live and never see death?
　Who can deliver his soul from the power of Sheol? *Selah*
(Ps. 89:47–48 ESV [MT 89:48–49])

It is, of course, true that Psalm 90 expresses these concerns in a more developed way. But second, and conversely, if the last part of Psalm 89 is characterized by anguished pleading, we should observe that, although this is not the dominant note sounded by Psalm 90, our key verses from that psalm – already discussed[52] – would nevertheless be perfectly 'at home' in that Psalm 89 context:[53]

Who considers the power of your anger,
　and your wrath according to the fear of you? . . .
Return, O LORD! How long?
　Have pity on your servants!
Satisfy us in the morning with your steadfast love
(Ps. 90:11–14a ESV)

How long, O LORD? Will you hide yourself forever?
　How long will your wrath burn like fire? . . .
Lord, where is your steadfast love of old . . .?
Remember, O Lord, how your servants are mocked
(Ps. 89:46, 49a, 50a ESV [MT 89:47, 50a, 51a])

Adamic problem exposed (Psalm 90:3–11)

The symbiosis between the two psalms at these levels requires us to consider the connections between the respective problems that they set forth. If Psalm 89 laments the apparent collapse of the Davidic covenant that comes into play with the Babylonian exile, Psalm 90 laments the problems of sin and its consequences – and does so in a way that clearly recalls Genesis 3. Indeed, whether or not one wants to speak of a 'covenant' between YHWH and Adam in the garden of Eden,[54] Adamic

---

[52] See pp. 71–72. Here we also quote v. 11.
[53] For (other) suggestions of links between Ps. 89 and Ps. 90, see Gundersen 2015: 74–90, and, for points of contact between book 4 (in general) and the last two psalms of book 3, consult Hossfeld 2002: 177–178.
[54] I believe we should, and I defend this position in Hely Hutchinson 2022: 47–56.

Table 4.3 Allusions to Genesis 3:19 in Psalm 90:3

Genesis 3:19	*Psalm 90:3*
You will eat bread by the sweat of your brow until you **return** to the ground, since you were taken from it. For you are dust, and you will **return** to dust.' (HCSB)	You **return** mankind to the dust, saying, '**Return**, descendants of Adam.' (HCSB)

disobedience to the commandment of Genesis 2:17 (the prohibition regarding eating from the tree of the knowledge of good and evil) lies in the background of the psalm, the consequences of transgressing being extensively on view. After speaking of the act of creating the world with an allusion to Genesis 2:4 (v. 2),[55] verse 3 recalls even more clearly Genesis 3:19 (see Table 4.3).[56]

Despite an allusion to the first man, Adam, the emphasis in Psalm 90:3 is on humanity as a whole.[57] More generally, the fall narrative underlies Psalm 90:7–11: the exposing of Adam's sin (v. 8; cf. Gen. 3:9–10, 17), death as a consequence of sin (vv. 8–9; cf. Gen. 3:19, 22, 24–25), the 'trouble and sorrow' of life (v. 10b NIV; cf. Gen. 3:16–19). Given these echoes,[58] it is reasonable to presuppose that the wrath of YHWH, which is mentioned five times in this part of the psalm (vv. 7, 9, 11) but not as such in the Genesis narrative, lies at the root of the curses of Genesis 3:14–24. In addition, it may well be that the 'thousand years' of Psalm 90:4 reflect Genesis 5:[59] following the sentence of Genesis 3, and prior to that of Genesis 6:3, such is the approximate human life span. It is also possible that the use of *zāram*[60] in the next verse (Ps. 90:5) recalls the following chapters of the Genesis narrative – the account of the flood (chs. 6–9).

---

[55] Cf. Kirkpatrick 1901: 549; Jacquet 1977: 726.

[56] As is widely recognized by the commentators. The term 'dust' is not, however, the same in the two texts. The verb 'return' is the same as that already noted in relation to Ps. 90:13 and Exod. 32:12b (*šûb*).

[57] As also in Ps. 8:5 (which exhibits the same parallelism as Ps. 90:3 between *'ĕnôš* ['humanity'] and *ben-ādām/bĕnê-ādām* ['son(s) of Adam']) and Ps. 89:47 (MT 89:48).

[58] Which bear resemblances to another wisdom text that reflects on Gen. 3, viz., Ecclesiastes; cf. Clemens 1994.

[59] Cf. Deissler 1993: 356; Motyer 1994: 545; Harman 1998: 309; Wilcock 2001b: 75; VanGemeren 2008: 691; Eveson 2015: 137 (mention of Methuselah); Hamilton 2021c: 155. Clifford (2000), neglecting the background in Genesis, seems to drive a wedge between knowledge of the brevity of human existence and knowledge of divine wrath.

[60] BDB 281: 'thou floodest them with rain, sweepest them (men) away'.

Conditional dimension of the Davidic covenant implicitly reaffirmed (Psalm 90)

We have seen that Psalm 90 simultaneously attaches itself to Psalm 89 and reaffirms the theology of Genesis 3. The bottom line is that we Psalter readers are driven to associate the problem of the exile (Ps. 89) with the problem of sin (Ps. 90). The nature of this association is not far to seek and has already emerged from book 3:[61] sin is the very problem that led to the exile! The problem of divine wrath is a recurring motif in book 3,[62] and Psalm 90 affords clarity regarding its close connection with sin.

The insistence on the unconditional and unshakeable character of the promises of the Davidic covenant – so marked in Psalm 89 – does not need to be called into question. But more needs to be said on this score if the psalmist's perplexity is to be alleviated: sinful human behaviour and the wrath that this provokes need to be taken into consideration within the framework of the Davidic covenant. Indeed, at least from one camera angle, that covenant with David is conditional (cf. 1 Kgs 2:4; 6:12; 8:25–26; 9:4–5).[63] The dynamic of the Sinaitic covenant – blessing conditional on obedience, cursing resulting from disobedience (Lev. 26; Deut. 28) – forms at least part of the formulation that one needs to give to the Davidic covenant if it is to be full-orbed. We continue to await further revelation from the Psalter in order to be in a position to reconcile the apparently irreconcilable perspectives of unconditionality and conditionality.

Remedy for the exile a consequence of the remedy for Adamic sin (Psalm 90:12–17)

We have seen that Psalm 90:3–11 enables the Psalter reader to grasp that the fundamental problem needing to be remedied is that of Genesis 3. This seems to be confirmed at the other end of the book. Psalms 104 – 106 trace salvation history as it unfolds through the remainder of Genesis and of the Pentateuch. What emerges from these psalms, as we will see, are the building blocks for the solution to the problem of the fall – the same solution that is the subject of Moses' intercession in the last part of

---

[61] See pp. 53–55.

[62] Pss 74:1; 76:7 (MT 76:8); 77:9 (MT 77:10); 79:5; 80:4 (MT 80:5); 85:5 (MT 85:6); 89:46 (MT 89:47).

[63] As we saw in the previous chapter (see pp. 49–50 and 53–55).

Psalm 90. The logic, then, of the way in which books 3 and 4 of the Psalter relate to each other is this: if Moses' pleading in Psalm 90:12–17 is answered, the human-sin-leading-to-divine-wrath problem will be resolved and, *as a result*, the problem of the exile will also be resolved. Expressed another way, finding a solution to the problem of the exile is not the absolute, primordial, radical imperative, but *finding a solution to the problem of sin* is that key imperative. Book 4 thus recalibrates the perplexing crisis of book 3. To be sure, resolving the exile problem is necessary, but this will come about as an entailment of a more fundamental solution.

This reading of the articulation between books 3 and 4 is further reinforced by what we have already discussed concerning the presenting problems in Psalms 90 and 106 which can be summarized as 'the golden-calf sin problem'. We have already demonstrated that the character of the solution to the Israelites' sin is 'Abrahamic'. This chimes in with the flow of the first book of Scripture: the solution to the problem of Genesis 3 – 11 finds its first sustained expression in the promises made to Abraham in Genesis 12. Our task at this juncture is to see how book 4 presents this 'Abrahamic' solution in the three long psalms that close this short book and make up almost 40% of its content (Pss 104 – 106).[64]

Noahic covenant as an indispensable part of the solution (Psalm 104)

With the advent of the flood of Genesis 6 – 9 (cf. Ps. 90:5), the survival of humanity and the world is at stake. Removing the threat of 'de-creation' is part of what is required to pave the way for the solution to the problem of Adamic sin. I suggest that, in the context of book 4, one of the functions fulfilled by Psalm 104 is to point up the stability of the created order as guaranteed by the covenant with Noah (Gen. 8 – 9).

---

[64] There are clear formal links, connecting one psalm to the next, from Ps. 103 through to Ps. 107. We recognize that Ps. 104 serves a 'Janus' function (pointing both ways) and that a strong case can be made for considering it to form a duo with Ps. 103: the formula 'Bless YHWH, my soul' features twice at the beginning of Ps. 103 and once each at the beginning of Ps. 104 and at the end of both psalms, and there is complementarity in the subject matter, respectively redemption and creation/providence (for more arguments in favour of viewing these as a 'psalm pair', see McKelvey 2010: 203–205). On balance, however, the formula 'Hallelujah' that concludes Ps. 104 also binds it together with the following two psalms which finish in the same way, and the progression through the Pentateuch is a stronger linking force across Pss 104 – 106 than is the content of Pss 103 – 104, especially given that one would expect creation/providence to precede redemption.

Psalm 104 celebrates[65] God's commitment to his creation. Several authors underline the parallels between this psalm and Genesis 1,[66] but it is important to observe that there is greater emphasis in Psalm 104 on YHWH's *continuing acts of providence* than on his initial act of creating the world.[67] The section that concerns us most directly is that of verses 5–9 which speak of YHWH's stabilizing of the creation ('it shall not be moved for ever and ever' [v. 5]) and his control of the waters. Should this be understood from a pre-flood (initial creation) or a post-flood (Noahic covenant) perspective?

The exegetical case for a pre-flood reading is probably stronger (v. 5 speaks of the time when YHWH 'established the earth on its foundations' [HCSB]), and the majority of commentators discern in these verses only the poetic equivalent of Genesis 1:9–10. But the possibility of *allusions* to the flood narrative should not be dismissed too quickly.[68] Consider verse 6 (see Table 4.4):[69]

Table 4.4 Possible allusions to the flood narrative in Psalm 104:6

Psalm 104:6	*Genesis 7:19–20*
You **covered** it [sc. the **earth**]* with the deep as if it were a garment; the **waters** stood above the **mountains**. (HCSB)	Then the **waters** surged even higher on the **earth**, and all the high **mountains** under the whole sky were **covered**. The **mountains** were **covered** as the **waters** surged above them more than 20 feet. (HCSB)

* This referent featuring in v. 5. With regard to the irregularity of the masculine pronominal suffix attached to the verb 'covered' (for *'eres*, 'earth', is feminine), Delitzsch (1889: 99) appeals to 'attraction . . . or . . . a reversion to the masculine ground-form in the further progress of the discourse'.

In addition, consider verse 9: 'You set a boundary they cannot cross; they will never cover the earth again' (HCSB). It is difficult to read this verse

---

[65] See vv. 1, 24, 31–35.

[66] See the summary of the literature provided by Allen 2002: 41–42; cf. also the position of Kidner (1975: 368), of Motyer (1994: 553) and of Goldingay (2008: 182).

[67] Goldingay's list of sections referring to YHWH's 'ongoing activity' is as follows: vv. 10–12, 13–18, 20–23, 24c–30; he notes that '[v]erses 16b and 26b also refer to past acts' (ibid.).

[68] Cf. D. G. Barker 1986.

[69] The terms indicated in bold are the same between the two passages. Weiser (1962: 667) also considers that this verse recalls 'the primeval flood which once covered the mountains'.

and think only of Genesis 1, for the waters *did* cover the earth at the time of the flood! So, even if one is persuaded that the allusion to the original creation is stronger (or even exclusive), it is hard to ignore the flood as the 'elephant in the room'.[70] Accordingly, Philip Eveson can assert that '[t]here is nothing in the context to suggest that these particular verses are describing the account of the Flood', but he feels compelled to discuss the latter event at some length, in order, notably, to explain what (on this understanding) is an exception: 'Only on that one occasion did God allow the great deluge to happen'.[71]

It may well be that we should understand Psalm 104:9 to be recalling the covenant with Noah,[72] for the following reasons:

1 the major significance of this flood event in the Genesis account as an overturning of creation;[73]
2 the close parallels between initial creation and post-flood recreation;[74]
3 the emphasis in the psalm on God's sustaining of creation;
4 the fact that Psalm 104 presupposes not only the realities of Genesis 1 – 2 but also those of Genesis 3, since it speaks of sin and death (vv. 29, 35);
5 the way in which the succeeding psalms[75] pick up the Pentateuchal narrative at Genesis 12 and, again, assume *at least* one chapter further on from Genesis 1 – 2.

Even if we are wrong to discern an allusion to the Noahic covenant, there remains a sense in which verse 9 still needs to be construed as, so to speak, a 'proto-Noahic covenant' or an expression of YHWH's commitment to creation with regard to the danger of a (whole-earth) flood. Again, however directly or indirectly it should be understood, the Genesis 8 – 9

---

[70] This laconic commentary by Rogerson and McKay (1977: 29) illustrates the point (the biblical references quoted should be noted): 'At God's command (Gen. 1:9) the waters went to their appointed places, never to *return to cover the earth* (cp. Gen. 9:11)', emphasis original. Grogan (2008: 174) considers it 'possible' that v. 9 echoes both Gen. 1 and Gen. 8 – 9. Hensley (2018: 237–238) considers that Ps. 104 'reflects concerns central to the Noahic covenant'.

[71] Eveson 2015: 222.

[72] Boice (1996: 841), *Bible d'étude Semeur* (2001: 841) and VanGemeren (2008: 765) mention Gen. 9 in relation to Ps. 104:9.

[73] Clines 1997: 80.

[74] Ibid. 81.

[75] To which Ps. 104 is tied (cf. n. 65 on p. 80).

background provides a strikingly good fit for Psalm 104. There is an accent on regularity in both passages:

As long as the earth endures,
seedtime and harvest,
cold and heat,
summer and winter,
day and night
will never cease.
(Gen. 8:22 NIV; cf. esp. Ps. 104:19b–23, 27)

In Genesis 9:8–17, YHWH's commitment to creation (cf. Ps. 104: 5, 9) is solemn (here we quote only vv. 9–11, but the ideas are repeated in the Genesis passage):

Understand that I am confirming My covenant with you and your descendants after you, and with every living creature that is with you – birds, livestock, and all wildlife of the earth that are with you – all the animals of the earth that came out of the ark. I confirm My covenant with you that never again will every creature be wiped out by the waters of a flood; there will never again be a flood to destroy the earth. (Gen. 9:9–11 HCSB)

Although, at one level, Konrad Schaefer is right to point out that Psalm 104 'makes no reference to Israel or her history',[76] the psalm's place in book 4 invites us to nuance this remark. Just as Genesis 1 – 11 cannot be separated from the remainder of that first book of Moses (and the Pentateuch) – the formula 'These are the progenies'[77] providing cohesion to the entire book – so too we must not divorce Psalm 104 from the two psalms that follow.[78] The God of Israel (Ps. 105) is the God of the universe (Ps. 104). The Creator must be obeyed, as the closing verse of Psalm 104 highlights; the Redeemer must be obeyed, as the closing verse of Psalm 105 highlights.

As we have seen, however, the Adamic lack of obedience needs to be remedied. God's choice of Abraham and Israel (on view in Ps. 105) is, in the flow of Genesis, set against the background of the escalation of the

[76] Schaefer 2001: 257.
[77] Which serves a cataphoric (forward-looking), introductory function. For a defence of this, see Ska 2000: 36–38.
[78] See n. 65 on p. 80.

sin problem which reaches its paroxysm with the Tower of Babel episode ('*union in pride*, the imperial sin'):[79] no element of 'mitigation or grace' is found in the narrative.[80] Patently, the flood does not resolve the sin problem (Gen. 9:20–29) and nor does the Noahic covenant (Gen. 11:1–9). Is it possible that this background in the first biblical book explains the imprecation in the concluding verse of Psalm 104 – that 'sinners be consumed from the earth' and 'the wicked be no more' (v. 35 ESV)? Eveson once again embraces a post-flood standpoint as he comments on this verse: 'This world is not the perfect world that was originally created and even the world that was renewed after the Flood was still inhabited by sinners.'[81] The Noahic covenant may constitute necessary bedrock for the solution, but the solution itself must deal with sin.

This leads us to the twin psalms 105 and 106.

Abrahamic covenant per se as insufficient solution (Psalms 105 – 106)

In Psalm 105, the Abrahamic covenant, corresponding to Genesis 12ff., is celebrated. Within the framework of this covenant, certain key historical moments, as far as Exodus 17 (followed by the beginning of the book of Joshua), are recalled.[82] Just as the Noahic covenant is described as 'everlasting' (Gen. 9:16; cf. 'for ever and ever' in Ps. 104:5), so also is the covenant with the patriarchs[83] (Ps. 105:10; cf. also v. 8). The parallelism across the four clauses[84] of verses 9 and 10 suggests that 'Israel' is as much a partner[85] and/or beneficiary of this covenant as Abraham, Isaac and Jacob were, and it is probable that we should understand 'Israel' as referring to the people (rather than being a quasi synonym for 'Jacob').[86]

---

[79] Blocher 1988: 200; emphasis original.

[80] As indicated by Clines's table (1997: 68) and his remark on the following page.

[81] Eveson 2015: 227.

[82] We have already noted that several incidents recorded in Exodus and Numbers feature in the following psalm (cf. Table 4.1 on p. 67). For a comparison between the historical account in Ps. 105 and that of the Pentateuch, see Broyles' analysis (1999: 403–404).

[83] In both cases, the phrase is *bĕrît 'ôlām*, 'everlasting covenant'.

[84] Verbless in two cases (verb-gapping being a characteristic device in Hebrew poetry).

[85] Cf. n. 48 on p. 75.

[86] The same preposition is employed for 'Israel' as for 'Isaac' and 'Jacob'. Where the name 'Israel' appears in the psalm (vv. 10, 23), it could be quasi-synonymous with 'Jacob', but the immediately following contexts (respectively vv. 12 and 24) speak of the people. It seems best to opt for a collective sense in these verses – similar to the usage we find in Ps. 81:4 (MT 81:5) (a context akin to that of Ps. 105:10) and Ps. 114:1 (a context akin to that of Ps. 105:23).

A particular promise is highlighted: that of the land (Ps. 105:11; cf. v. 44). This is peculiarly apposite given the historical context of the Babylonian captivity that is on view at the end of book 4 (Ps. 106:47): the exiles pray for restoration to their homeland.[87] This historical context also sensitizes us to the significance of YHWH's *remembering* of his covenant with Abraham.[88] Such remembering is what he did when his people were in Egypt (Ps. 105:42; cf. Exod. 2:24), and this is what he does 'for ever'[89] (v. 8). These are the realities – concerning YHWH's remembering – that the psalmist's audience is, in turn, called upon to remember (v. 5).[90] YHWH's[91] orchestrating of the events of the exodus testifies to his faithfulness to the Abrahamic covenant (cf. Gen. 15:13–14; Deut. 9:26–29).

The critical question for our purposes is whether this covenant constitutes the solution to the problems of Genesis 3 – 11.[92] The message that emerges from Psalms 105 – 106 (as also from the Pentateuch) is ambiguous. On the one hand, this covenant is unbreakable, proving to be permanently valid despite flagrant, abominable acts of rebellion. It provides the exiles with solid hope as they look to return to their country.[93] The Sinaitic covenant, which can be detected at the end of Psalm 105 with the mention of 'statutes' and 'laws' (v. 45), flows from the Abrahamic

---

[87] See pp. 61–64. Not that the other elements of the Abrahamic promise are absent from Ps. 105: (1) The notion of a privileged relationship between YHWH and his people is highlighted in v. 7a, as also by the terms in v. 6 (*bĕḥîrāyw*, 'his elect') and v. 15 (*mĕšîḥāy*, 'my anointed ones'). (2) The idea of a great multitude features in v. 24 ('And he made his people very fruitful'). (3) The blessing of all nations is presaged by v. 1b, particularly in the light of Pss 96, 98 and 100, which we examine below.

[88] Regarding the close connection between remembering and acting that we find in v. 5; cf. Childs 1962: 33–34.

[89] *lĕ'ôlām*.

[90] For the structural importance for the psalm of the verb *zākar*, 'remember', see Girard 1994b: 80–104, esp. 95.

[91] Girard draws our attention to the fact that 'the psalmist, without entirely leaving out Moses' name, reduces somewhat the key figure of the exodus to the role of obedient miracle worker (vv. 26–28), thereby obscuring his role as legislator and leader of the exodus . . . and presenting Yhwh himself as sole agent of the great act of liberation' (ibid. 103–104; cf. 86 n. 7). We may benefit from these observations, provided that we do not suggest that Ps. 105 is incompatible with the account in Exodus. Regarding the relationship between Pss 105 and 106, Broyles considers that they 'are so divergent, in fact, that one might call them contradictory' (1999: 405). In particular, he cites the contrast between Ps. 105:40 and Ps. 106:14–15. But the respective psalms provide *complementary* perspectives on the events in question (that YHWH should accede to the people's request does not imply that the request is virtuous).

[92] As might be suggested by the fact that the five occurrences in Gen. 3 – 11 of the root for 'curse', *'-r-r* (3:14; 3:17; 4:1; 5:29; 9:25), give way to five occurrences of the root for 'bless', *b-r-k*, in Gen. 12:2–3.

[93] As argued in our discussion of Ps. 106 at the start of this chapter.

covenant[94] but does not ultimately have the power to overturn the promise, as Psalm 106 shows.

On the other hand, the problems that Psalm 90 throws into sharp relief recur throughout the Israelites' history: nearly a thousand years[95] elapse between the time when Moses intercedes for the people at Mount Sinai (Pss 90:13; 106:23) and the time when the people pray to be gathered from among the nations (Ps. 106:47)[96] – and the period is considerably longer if it is traced as far back as the time of Genesis 3. Indeed, the cycle of human sin and divine wrath that is repeated so many times in Psalm 106 precludes our affirming that the Abrahamic covenant is the solution in and of itself. At most, we may recognize that it will become – or yield, or give rise to – the requisite solution. But the question arises (it may not be asked directly, but it is the 'elephant in the room'): how can the solution come about? What conditions need to be met in order for it to be realized?

'Pedagogy of failure' as anticipatory of superior mediation (Psalm 106)

Psalm 106 itself contains some pointers by way of response – thanks, in part, to the 'pedagogy of failure':[97]

> For all that Moses' and Phinehas' mediation was essential for keeping the Abrahamic promises alive, Psalm 106 highlights three ways in which it fell short: (1) it was only partially effective in keeping God's wrath at bay, for many Israelites were put to death; (2) it was only temporarily effective, for it needed to be repeated following each act of rebellion; and (3) the intercessors were themselves affected by the sin problem they were purporting to deal with (vv. 32–33; cf. Num. 20:7–12). Thus the Psalm 106 cycle contains an implicit call for a mediator who is greater than Moses.[98]

---

[94] For an extensive discussion of the relationship between the Abrahamic and Sinaitic covenants in the Pentateuch, see Hely Hutchinson 2022: 103–136.

[95] But see Ps. 90:4!

[96] Assuming that the exodus took place in the fifteenth century BC.

[97] This phrase is drawn from Blocher 2000: 126.

[98] Hely Hutchinson 2013b: 36.

Expressed in terms of its positive corollary, this 'greater-than-Moses'[99] figure – the mediator 'considered worthy of more glory than Moses'[100] – must be capable of intercession that is *total* in scope and *permanent* in duration, and he must himself be *morally perfect*. But Psalm 106 conveys still more information, albeit implicitly, regarding the shape of the solution, and this relates to the mediation of Phinehas.

Levitical covenant associated with the Davidic covenant (Psalm 106:30–31)

We have already noted, and commented extensively on, the importance of the Abrahamic covenant in Psalm 106,[101] including in relation to the Baal-Peor incident.[102] But this episode, as recounted towards the end of book 4 (Ps. 106:28–31), has additional importance for our purposes. Verse 31b ('from generation to generation, for ever') underscores the permanence of the effect of Phinehas' act and seems to refer to the setting-up of the covenant with him in Numbers 25:12–13. As is true of Abraham (and Noah), it is a *bĕrît 'ôlām* ('everlasting covenant') or, more precisely, a *bĕrît kĕhunnat 'ôlām* (Num. 25:13) – 'a covenant of a priesthood of perpetuity'.

The biblical data concerning this covenant are scant and enigmatic, and it is perhaps understandable that it should be neglected by most of the representatives of the various positions on the covenant-relationships spectrum we considered in chapter 2.[103] But what is at stake is the perpetuation of the priesthood. In the face of Israelite idolatry and sexual immorality, Phinehas intervenes, and God makes this pledge:

> Therefore tell him I am making my covenant of peace with him. He and his descendants will have a covenant of a lasting priesthood, because he was zealous for the honour of his God and made atonement for the Israelites.
> (Num. 25:12–13 NIV)

---

[99] This formula is employed in relation to the antitype of Solomon (Matt. 12:42; Luke 11:31).
[100] Heb. 3:3 HCSB.
[101] See pp. 65–75.
[102] See pp. 69–70.
[103] Progressive covenantalism being the exception (Gentry and Wellum 2018: 576–578). Palmer Robertson (covenant theology) also provides a sentence in a footnote (Robertson 1980: 27 n. 1).

Palmer Robertson states that '[t]he covenant with Phinehas (Num. 25:12, 13) appears as an adjunct to the Mosaic covenant, developing one specific aspect of the priestly legislation given to Moses'.[104] In a similar vein, though in the context of a more developed discussion, Paul Williamson asserts: '[The] priestly covenants (*sic*) serve the same general purpose as the Mosaic covenant with which they are so closely related . . . [T]he priestly and Mosaic covenants, while remaining distinct, run in parallel with one another'.[105] Peter Gentry follows in Williamson's footsteps in this regard.[106] Given the enigmatic nature of this matter, I share the hesitation that Williamson expresses[107] but end up proposing a different line.

Jeremiah speaks of a covenant 'with the Levites, the priests' (Jer. 33:21; cf. 33:22).[108] Given that the act of establishing a covenant with the Levites is nowhere clearly and expressly reported in the Old Testament,[109] the question arises as to what the prophet may be alluding to. The most promising candidate (and the one that features earliest in the biblical text) is not Numbers 25 (the covenant with Phinehas) but Numbers 18.[110] Speaking to Aaron, YHWH promises:

---

[104] Ibid.

[105] P. R. Williamson 2003: 152; cf. P. R. Williamson 2007: 105–106.

[106] Gentry and Wellum 2018: 576–578.

[107] P. R. Williamson 2003: 152; cf. P. R. Williamson 2007: 105–106.

[108] Regarding the question of whether the LXX, which does not include the equivalent of Jer. 33:14–26, predates the MT, we recognize the textual-critical difficulty. But the problem should not be overstated. As Emanuel Tov (1972: 191) writes, '[s]ince LXX and MT reflect two distinct redactional traditions, the critical study of the text of *Jeremiah* . . . should not consist of correcting the longer MT text by the shorter LXX text. Both traditions existed in Hebrew'; emphasis original. It is difficult to be sure of the precise dating of these recensions, but I subscribe to Sylvain Romerowski's view that both constitute the message of the prophet Jeremiah: '[A]lready at the time of the prophet, the history of his oracles' being written down was turbulent: a first collection, written in 605, was destroyed and then rewritten, though in augmented form. It is also possible that the two texts that we know correspond to two different compilations of Jeremiah's oracles produced during the prophet's lifetime. One of these would have been carried off to Babylonia, while the other would have followed the prophet to Egypt. It is not unthinkable that the prophet would have wanted to ensure that the two Jewish communities possess a written version of his prophecies' (Romerowski 2016: 71). In short, from the standpoint of our purposes in this book, I consider that Jer. 33:14–26 should be included and that it is not a late scribal addition. We may usefully bear in mind, as Shead (2012: 51) comments: 'Not only was [the Masoretic version] his last and final version, but its target audience, the exilic community in Babylon, was in Jeremiah's eyes the one group of people with a future in the divine plan of salvation. The seeds of the church were planted in Babylonian soil.' For the fact that the future belonged to the exiles in Babylon, cf. Jer. 24.

[109] But see the discussion in Verhoef 1987: 244–245; Baldwin 1972: 234.

[110] Another potential candidate, Deut. 33:9c ('For they have kept your word and they keep your covenant'), probably alludes to the golden calf incident (Exod. 32:25–29); cf. Craigie 1976: 396; McConville 2002a: 470; Block 2012: 792.

I give to you and to your sons and daughters all the holy contributions that the Israelites present to the LORD as a permanent statute. It is a permanent covenant of salt before the LORD for you as well as your offspring.
(Num. 18:19 HCSB)

Assuming that this is correct, the question then becomes how the covenant with Phinehas, set up subsequently, fits in with this Levitical covenant. The hypothesis that the two come to be closely tied squares with Malachi 2:1–9, a passage that deals at some length with YHWH's 'covenant with Levi' (vv. 4, 8[111]). The proximity between the Numbers 25 text and the Malachi 2 passage is suggested in particular by the fact that both speak of a covenant 'of peace' (Num. 25:12; Mal. 2:5 [cf. 2:6]).[112] Might the covenant with Phinehas not be a reaffirmation of the Levitical covenant that is centred on Phinehas' family line (Num. 25:13)?

Further, in the last part of the Hebrew canon, we come across the phrase 'the covenant of the priesthood and of the Levites' (běrît hakkěhunnâ wěhalěwîyim [Neh. 13:29]). This seems to be a hybrid of Numbers 25:13, 'a covenant of a priesthood' (běrît kěhunnat), and Jeremiah 33:21, 'my covenant . . . with the Levites' (běrîtî . . . wě'et-halěwîyim) (see Fig. 4.2). This

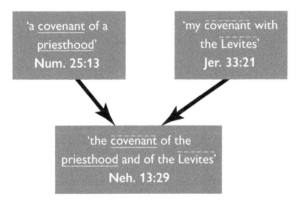

Figure 4.2 **The hybrid formation of the covenant phrase in Nehemiah 13:29**

---

[111] The construction in v. 8 is slightly different from that of v. 4.
[112] Douglas Stuart (1998: 1316) has drawn up a list of linguistic correspondences between the two passages and comments: 'The actual wording of verses 5–8 in reference to this covenant makes the connection with the Numbers 25 "covenant of peace" hard to miss . . . [T]he correspondences would have leapt out at Malachi's audience'.

is an additional argument in favour of the idea that the covenant made with Phinehas comes to be integrated with the Levitical covenant.

If our analysis thus far is correct, its importance for our purposes consists in its exhibiting the same characteristics as those of the Davidic covenant – as opposed to those of the Sinaitic covenant. This could already be suggested by the fact that these two covenants – and only these two – are described as a 'covenant of salt' (Num. 18:19; 2 Chr. 13:5). But it is more telling that the Levitical covenant, in common with the Davidic covenant, is both conditional and unconditional. On the one hand, its continuance depends on the Levites' behaviour: the prophet's aim in Malachi 2:3–4 is to stimulate repentance such that YHWH's covenant with Levi may be upheld (Neh. 13:29 also seems to reflect the conditionality of the covenant). On the other hand, its permanence is assured by the promises of Numbers 18 and 25 and, especially, by the very explicit declaration of Jeremiah 33:17–22:

'For thus says the LORD: David shall never lack a man to sit on the throne of the house of Israel, and the Levitical priests shall never lack a man in my presence to offer burnt offerings, to burn grain offerings, and to make sacrifices forever.'

The word of the LORD came to Jeremiah: 'Thus says the LORD: If you can break my covenant with the day and my covenant with the night, so that day and night will not come at their appointed time, then also my covenant with David my servant may be broken, so that he shall not have a son to reign on his throne, and my covenant with the Levitical priests my ministers. As the host of heaven cannot be numbered and the sands of the sea cannot be measured, so I will multiply the offspring of David my servant, and the Levitical priests who minister to me.'

(ESV)

This passage associates the Davidic covenant with the Levitical covenant in a remarkably tight way. On three occasions in the space of six verses, the covenant with David and the covenant with the Levites are spoken of as standing or falling together![113] A few verses later, we find the Davidic

---

[113] While I stress the intimate links between the Levitical and Davidic covenants, the ways in which they are *fulfilled* diverge. The former comes to be realized within the framework of a different priestly order (cf. our treatment of Ps. 110 in the next chapter [see pp. 139–141 and Heb. 7]).

and Abrahamic covenants also being spoken of in the same breath (Jer. 33:25–26). A further close connection needs to be noted, namely with YHWH's unbreakable covenant 'with the day and the night' (Jer. 33:20, 25). The latter is probably an allusion to the Noahic covenant in view of Genesis 8:22: 'day and night will never cease' (NIV).[114] It should be noted that the time horizon that Jeremiah is referring to is eschatological for him: he is looking forward to a *new*-covenant scenario that lies on the other side of the Babylonian exile.[115]

So, as Jeremiah looks forward to the new covenant, he anticipates a convergence of four unconditional covenants – the Noahic, Abrahamic, Levitical and Davidic – and he conceives of the latter two as being especially closely related.

What implications does this have for the end of book 4 of the Psalter? Bearing in mind that the final form of the Psalter dates to a later period than the book of Jeremiah and also that it is placed in a later section of the Hebrew canon, it seems that we may recognize the same covenantal configuration – even though it is not as explicit – as in Jeremiah 33. We have already discussed the Noahic (Ps. 104) and Abrahamic (Pss 105 – 106) covenants as being reaffirmed in relation to a post-exilic context. Psalm 106:30–31 has required us to reckon with the Levitical covenant, which also seems to be reaffirmed, and our examination of this covenant has led us to appreciate its kinship with the Davidic covenant. By implication, given that the Levitical and Davidic covenants not only exhibit the same characteristics but also – in Jeremianic perspective – stand or fall together, Psalm 106:31 may also be considered indirectly to suggest that the covenant with *David* is still valid. We recall that it is *that* covenant that had been called into question in Psalm 89. Just as Psalm 106 fashions the Psalter reader's expectations regarding a perfect intercessor whose ministry is totally and permanently effective, so also it indirectly reaffirms the promise of a permanent priesthood to which is *tied* the promise of a permanent kingship (Jer. 33:17–22).

I am not claiming more than 'indirectness' here. It should be stressed that a Davidic-covenantal perspective is far from being a key idea in Psalm 106 and does not even feature on the surface of the text. It is our particular

---

[114] The atmosphere of this passage in Jeremiah is similar to that of Isa. 54:9–10 where the permanence of the Noahic covenant is also on view.

[115] Hely Hutchinson 2005a: 101–105. We have already had occasion to note the background in Jer. 30 – 33; see e.g. p. 40.

enquiry regarding covenant relationships that leads us to make these intertextual observations. Yet these observations are methodologically and exegetically solid and useful for our purposes.[116]

Nor am I wanting to suggest that all the answers to the crisis of book 3 have been forthcoming. At this stage, the Psalter reader is not informed as to how the reiteration of the Levitical covenant and (indirectly) of the Davidic covenant can be squared with the harsh reality of the exile. Nor is there clarity, in relation to these two covenants, as to how their conditional and unconditional dimensions can be compatible with each other. The complete answer to the Psalm 89 perplexity is yet to emerge. But, by the end of book 4, the building blocks are in place. The Davidic covenant is still intact. It is as if the perspective of Psalm 78 is being given an underlining in a fresh and more optimistic setting than that of book 3. For that long salvation-historical psalm, in common with Psalm 106 which is so similar in the Psalter reader's mind, highlights God's grace in the face of repeated Israelite sinfulness – and ends with the choice of David.[117]

Thus far, we have considered the extremities of book 4. We have been led to note the unbreakable character of the *Abrahamic* covenant that implies also that a *Davidic*-covenant solution to the crisis of Psalm 89 is in prospect. This must await a *new*-covenant context. We have seen that the (unconditional) Noahic, Abrahamic, Levitical and Davidic covenants are all aligned in relation to that new covenant. We turn now to the middle of the book.

Typological structures recapitulated in the new-covenant solution (Psalms 93 – 100)

In 1998, Jerome Creach could speak of 'the already well-established theological affinity of Book Four and Isaiah 40–55'.[118] He demonstrates that, in addition, these two major units exhibit striking parallels at their beginnings and ends, with '[a]t least three theologically loaded terms[119]

---

[116] I owe the writing of this paragraph to a helpful discussion with Peter Orr and Robert Brown following the Moore College Lecture in August 2018 relating to this material.

[117] Cf. pp. 53–54.

[118] Creach 1998: 74.

[119] Human beings as 'grass' (*ḥāṣîr*), 'flower' (*yāṣîṣ/ṣîṣ*); the call for 'compassion'/'comfort' (*n-ḥ-m*) (ibid. 73); see the table (ibid. 74).

[appearing] both in Isaiah 40 and Psalm 90', and '[l]ikewise, Psalms 105–106 [sharing] at least four similarly significant words or phrases'.[120] The impressive list of lexical parallels between Psalms 93 – 100 and Isaiah 40 – 55 'reveals that generally [these two sections of biblical material] are at home on the same theological soil'; for example, 'both speak to the vicissitudes of the exile with the common conviction of Yahweh's hegemony over Israel'.[121]

These parallels should sensitize us to the *new*-covenant shape of the solution to the problem of Psalm 89 that book 4 implicitly sets forth. With regard to the theology of Isaiah 40 – 55, we have already discussed chapter 55 and the new covenant's encompassing of the Davidic covenant.[122] The new-covenant theme may also be seen clearly in Isaiah 42:6 (cf. Isa. 49:6), the suffering servant of Isaiah 42 – 53 being the new-covenantal key to the exiles' bright future. In addition, Isaiah 40 – 55 allows us to reinforce our findings regarding the foundational role played by the Abrahamic covenant in preparing the way for the post-exilic, new-covenant solution (Isa. 41:8; 51:2; cf. Pss 90; 105 – 106) and the concomitant reaffirmation of the Noahic covenant (Isa. 54:9a; cf. Ps. 104:5–9).

Further, the formula 'Give thanks to YHWH, for he is good, for his covenant loyalty endures for ever' anticipates new-covenant fulfilment;[123] we come across this formula twice in book 4, one instance of which comes at the end of the group of Psalms 93 – 100. What Jeremiah prophesied in the context of the first canonical occurrence of that formula (Jer. 33:11), namely a post-exilic restoring of the fortunes of YHWH's people (cf. Jer. 33:1–13), is in the background as that formula is replayed in Psalm 100. Further, this bright prospect is reinforced in that psalm, as also in Psalm 95, by another covenant formula which bespeaks the special relationship between YHWH and his people ('I will be your God and you will be my people'[124] and variants [Pss 95:7; 100:3]). Whether we are in the book 4 (esp. Pss 93 – 100) or Isaianic context, there is '[the good news of] salvation' to be 'preached' to the exiles (the verb *b-ś-r* [see Ps. 96:2; cf. Isa. 40:9; 41:27; 52:7]), and this comes in new-covenant form.

---

[120] 'Pity' (noun/verb); 'gather'; 'everlasting covenant'; 'joy' (*rinnâ*) (ibid.).
[121] Ibid. 68–69.
[122] See pp. 31–32 and 35.
[123] Cf. Hely Hutchinson 2005a.
[124] Jer. 7:23 NIV for this particular instance of the formula.

But what observations should be made about the characteristics of the new covenant that may be discerned in Psalms 93 – 100? As the definitive, eschatological (post-exilic) solution to the problem of the exile is presented, motifs relating to the history of the Israelites are redeployed. The Israelites' experience during the period between the Egyptian captivity and the Babylonian captivity is recapitulated on a superior plane and reworked in accordance with new circumstances. This is particularly so for the occasion when God's people left Egypt (the exodus). The reader who is versed in the book of Exodus will already find bells ringing on encountering (four times in this section[125]) the expressions 'It is YHWH who is king' (or '. . . who reigns' [*mālak*]) and (also four times in this section[126]) 'Sing to YHWH'. As David Mitchell rightly points out, 'the first reference in biblical history to the kingship of Yhwh' occurs in the Song of Moses that follows the exodus event: 'YHWH will reign [*yimlōk*] for ever and ever!' (Exod. 15:18). Regarding the second phrase, 'Sing to YHWH' (*šîrû la yhwh*), it appears for the first time three verses later (Exod. 15:21; cf. Exod. 15:1).[127] Psalm 98 portrays a new liberation (vv. 1–3) in the context of a glorious celebration (vv. 7–8). Psalms 95 and 100 employ the image of the shepherd, and, in the first case, we read that the flock of YHWH is that 'of his hand', a metaphor that bespeaks exodus (Pss 95:7; 100:3; cf. Exod. 14:31; Ps. 78:42). The Jeremiah 33 background to Psalm 100, already noted,[128] attunes us to the glorious character of the restoration that is in prospect for the exiles. Should we be tempted to think that the psalmist is *merely* recalling the first exodus out of Egypt, as opposed to anticipating a second or new exodus, we should note the warning given in Psalm 95:7d–11: the 'Meribah/Massah' rebellion must not be repeated!

A parallel in Ezekiel confirms the exactitude of our understanding. The key passage in this prophecy that sets forth the new exodus, namely 20:32–44, contains the only text in the book that affirms that YHWH is king[129] (v. 33) – which correlates with the emphasis on YHWH's kingship in the group of psalms that we are considering (Pss 93:1; 96:10; 97:1; 99:1). Moreover, the prophet ties this attribute to that of judge (Ezek. 20:33–36;

---

[125] Pss 93:1; 96:10; 97:1; 99:1.
[126] Pss 96:1–2; 98:1.
[127] Mitchell 1997: 284, 288, 295.
[128] In the preceding paragraph.
[129] In contradistinction to, for example, shepherd.

cf. Pss 94:2; 96:13; 98:9) and shepherd (Ezek. 20:37; cf. Pss 95:7; 100:3).[130]
We may add that the new-exodus theme is of major importance in the chapters of Isaiah that correspond to Psalms 93 – 100 (Isa. 40:3–4; 41:17–20; 42:14–16; 43:1–7, 14–21; 44:27; 48:20–21; 51:11; 52:11–12; 55:12–13): what is proclaimed as 'new' by the prophet (Isa. 42:9–10; 43:19; 48:6) anticipates the 'new song' of Psalms 96 and 98. The fact that the Isaiah and Ezekiel texts precede the Psalter (from both redactional and canonical perspectives) precludes our considering book 4 to be innovative in this regard: on the contrary, it perpetuates this motif that is developed by the Latter Prophets.[131] The Mount Sinai theophany is also recapitulated:

> Clouds and thick darkness surround Him;
> righteousness and justice are the foundation of His throne.
> Fire goes before Him
> and burns up His foes on every side.
> His lightning lights up the world;
> the earth sees and trembles.
> The mountains melt like wax
> at the presence of the LORD –
> at the presence of the Lord of all the earth.
> (Ps. 97:2–5 HCSB)

Once again we need to insist that this is not *simply* a throwback to the event recorded in Exodus 19 but also the presaging of a new event. This interpretation is required by the fact that YHWH's action gives rise to a joyful response on the part of 'Zion' (Ps. 97:8) – a metaphorical designation of the people that originates with a later stage than the time of the original Sinai theophany.

Assuming a certain consistency across these psalms, and given (once again) the Jeremiah 33 background, the reconfiguring of images for the new-covenant regime must extend beyond that of the exodus and Sinai – even if this is not immediately obvious. Does the interpreter not need to discern in Psalm 99 (vv. 2, 9) the *new* city of Zion (cf. Isa. 54:11–15), even if this is not developed so clearly and extensively as in Psalm 87? Should we not understand the 'gates' of Psalm 100:4 to be those of the *new* temple (cf. Pss 93:5; 96:6, 8; Ezek. 40 – 48)? Does the 'place of rest' of Psalm 95:11

---

[130] Zimmerli 1960: 217–221.
[131] For other texts in the Latter Prophets that evoke the new exodus, see Watts 2003.

not correspond to the *new* earth (cf. Isa. 11:6–9; 35; 65:17ff.)?[132] If we were to consider these to be no more than references to the city, temple and earth of the pre-exilic era, we would be inverting the parallels with Isaiah 40 – 55 that these psalms attest. It is, of course, the case that this prior epoch is evoked by these psalms, but the purpose of these reminiscences is to thrust the reader's mind forward to an eschatological era and a more glorious experience.

In this group of psalms, the king does not feature in this list of motifs that are recapitulated under the new covenant. This is intriguing, since Psalm 89 has put the question of the presence or absence of the Davidic king squarely on the agenda, and the Isaianic and Jeremianic backgrounds and parallels condition us to expect to see him in this particular psalmic context.

It is not that the last two books of the Psalter 'shift expectations away from the restoration of the human Davidic kings to the direct rulership of YHWH'.[133] What we should, however, note is that, in book 4, the re-affirmation of the Davidic covenant is not made in any explicit way.[134] This reflects:

1 the genius of divine pedagogy[135] which involves tension, suspense and progressive revelation;[136]
2 the fact that this is, after all, the 'Moses-book', and the theme of a coming messiah is not majored on in the Pentateuch;
3 the fact that the *building blocks* of the solution are being put in place here in book 4, and this means, as we have seen, emphasizing the Abrahamic covenant.

If the new exodus trumps the new temple in these psalms, this ties in with the absence of a fixed temple structure in the Pentateuch and the importance of the exodus in the Pentateuch. It also ties in with the fact that the exodus motif is fundamentally Abrahamic: YHWH liberates his people

---

[132] Perhaps Ps. 96:11–12 and Ps. 98:7–8 are also suggestive of the new creation.

[133] Wilson 2002b: 106.

[134] It is also true that, in Pss 93 – 100, YHWH's reign goes hand in hand with a clear monotheism (Pss 96:5; 100:3). Yet, if it is YHWH who is king (this is underlined by the syntax of the refrain of this section), the Psalter reader has known since the programmatic Ps. 2 that the rule of this one God is not incompatible with that of his anointed one.

[135] Nicole 1996.

[136] Cf. Hely Hutchinson 2015b.

because he remembers his promises to the patriarchs (Ps. 98:3; cf. Gen. 15:13–16; Exod. 2:24–25; Lev. 26:44–45).[137] By contrast, the temple was built after the setting-up of the Davidic covenant.

Further, the twin incidents of Meribah and Massah that are highlighted in Psalm 95 – and in this non-chronological order[138] – attest congruence with Psalm 106: on the one hand, the Meribah episode is directly cited in this closing psalm of the book (vv. 32–33), and, on the other, the Massah episode recalls Moses' intercession (Deut. 9:22–29). Likewise, if Psalm 99 underlines the importance of intercessors in God's bestowing of forgiveness upon his people – Moses, Aaron and Samuel are 'among those who call on [the] name' of the 'God who forgives' (vv. 6, 8) – this coheres with the fact that several of the theological emphases of these psalms square with the beginning and end of book 4.

In short, if, at this stage, the Davidic covenant is only hinted at, this should not be taken as an indication that it does not play an important part in the new-covenant regime.

Davidic-covenant solution connected to the new-covenant solution (Psalms 93 – 100 with Psalm 89)

That said, another hint that the Davidic covenant remains on the agenda may be gleaned from one of the themes of these psalms in the centre of the book, namely YHWH's exercising of dominion over creation, which harks back at several points to Psalm 89:5–18 (MT 89:6–19). In the context of the latter psalm, divine power over creation is presented with a view to celebrating the unshakeable nature of YHWH's commitment to David.[139] It would perhaps suffice, by way of demonstrating the intertextuality between Psalm 89 and Psalms 93 – 100 at this level, to compare the first psalm in the latter sequence, Psalm 93, which evokes particularly YHWH's majesty in relation to the waters, with Psalm 89:9 (MT 89:10) ('You rule over the surging sea; when its waves mount up, you still them' [NIV]). But it is useful to go further (see Table 4.5).[140] Given these echoes, it seems

---

137 Thus, Harman 1998: 326.
138 Cf. p. 68.
139 Cf. p. 48.
140 Lexical correspondences are indicated in bold.

Table 4.5 Intertextuality between Psalm 89 and Psalms 95 – 98

Ps. 89:7 (MT 89:8)	God is greatly feared in the council of the holy ones, more **awe** [= 'fear']-**inspiring** than **all** who surround Him. (HCSB)	Ps. 96:4	For the LORD is great and is highly praised; He is **feared** above **all** gods. (HCSB)
Ps. 89:11 (MT 89:12)	The heavens are Yours; the earth also is Yours. The world and everything in it – You founded them. (HCSB)	Ps. 95:4	The depths of the earth are in His hand, and the mountain peaks are His. (HCSB)
Ps. 89:12 (MT 89:13)	North and south – You created them. Tabor and Hermon **shout for joy** at Your name. (HCSB)	Ps. 98:8	Let the rivers clap their hands; let the mountains **shout** together **for joy** (HCSB)
Ps. 89:14 (MT 89:15)	**Righteousness and justice are the foundation of** Your **throne**; faithful love and truth go before You. (HCSB)	Ps. 97:2	Clouds and thick darkness surround Him; **righteousness and justice are the foundation of** His **throne**. (HCSB)
Ps. 89:17 (MT 89:18)	For You are their magnificent [= 'the **beauty** of their'] **strength**; by Your favor our horn is exalted. (HCSB)	Ps. 96:6	Splendor and majesty are before Him; **strength** and **beauty** are in His sanctuary. (HCSB)

that the Psalter reader should understand that, despite the last part of Psalm 89, YHWH remains powerful enough to bring about the realization of his promises to David. His perfect control of his creation serves as guarantee of his *ḥesed* and *'ĕmûnâ*, which had been called into question (Ps. 89:5, 8, 14 [MT 89:6, 9, 15]; cf. Pss 96:13; 98:3; 100:5).

The central group in book 4 (Pss 93 – 100) has further significance for our purposes. These psalms throw light on an important theme that is 'Abrahamic' (though absent from the extremities of the book): the salvation of the nations. We consider this now. We have already noted the importance of this theme of salvation for the nations in respect of book 2 where the 'Abrahamic' hue is clear[141] – though not as pronounced as here in book 4 – and of Psalm 87.[142] But how do Psalms 93 – 100 present the theme of blessing for all nations?[143]

New-covenant people drawn from all nations (Abrahamic covenant), on the basis of conversion, and not including all Israelites (Psalms 93 – 100)

Psalm 96 concerns the proclamation of YHWH's reign to all nations, and the psalmist does not hold back from appealing to the nations to submit to YHWH (vv. 1, 7, 8, 9). Since the peoples' gods are false (v. 5), and YHWH is coming to judge the peoples (vv. 10, 13), it is in the latter's interests to benefit from the salvation that is being announced to them (vv. 1–3). Psalm 98 has similar content to Psalm 96 in this respect: all the earth is called upon to sing to YHWH in view of the 'marvellous [salvific] things' he has performed (vv. 1–4). Verse 4a ('Give a resounding shout to the LORD, all the earth')[144] recurs at the beginning of Psalm 100; indeed, in the latter, short psalm, all seven imperatives are addressed to 'all the earth'.

This means that the psalmist envisages that the new-covenant formula ('Give thanks to YHWH, for he is good, for his *hesed* endures for ever' [cf. Ps. 100:4–5]) will undergird[145] the praise of YHWH *expressed by non-Jews*. It also means that it is envisaged that the nations, as well as Israelites, will enter the temple courts. Although there is significant continuity between the base text for the formula (Jer. 33:11) and its occurrence here, what we have here is a striking development relative to the prophet's perspective, namely the broadening of the scope of the formula to all nations.

This broadening is also a development relative to Psalm 95, which Psalm 100 clearly echoes. Whereas in Psalm 95 the first-person plural designates the Israelite people, as the reference to their disobedient

---

[141] See pp. 42–45.
[142] See p. 55.
[143] Cf. Zenger 1994: 157–170.
[144] Eveson 2015: 197.
[145] *kî* (beginning of v. 5) is explicative.

'fathers' requires (vv. 7d–11), it is unlikely that the referent here in Psalm 100 is so restricted. Commentators who adopt an explicit, clear-cut stance on the identity of the 'us'[146] and 'we'[147] of Psalm 100:3 are few and far between. It is possible to understand that the nations are being called upon to recognize *Israel* as the people of YHWH,[148] but a broader referent that encompasses *every worshipper* as part of the covenant people seems more likely.[149] Indeed, in this group, it is not possible to suggest that the worship offered up by the nations is in any way inferior to, or even different from, that offered up by Israel.[150] This may be seen by comparing Psalm 95:6 to Psalm 96:9, and Psalm 95:2 to Psalm 100:1, 4 (see Table 4.6).[151] In short, an important transposition comes about between Psalms 95 and 100: in Psalm 100:3, the declaration 'we are his people and the sheep of his pasture' is found on the lips of non-Israelites as well as Israelites. This psalm, the climax of the sequence, crowns the international perspective

Table 4.6 A comparison of the worship offered up by Israel (Psalm 95) and by the nations (Psalms 96 and 100)

Ps. 95:6	Come, let us **worship** and bow down; let us kneel before the LORD our Maker. (HCSB)
Ps. 96:9	**Worship** the LORD in the splendor of His holiness; tremble before Him, *all the earth*. (HCSB; emphasis added)
Ps. 95:2	Let us enter His presence **with thanksgiving**; let us **shout triumphantly** to Him in song. (HCSB)
Ps. 100:1, 4	A psalm of **thanksgiving**. **Shout triumphantly** to the LORD, *all the earth* ... Enter His gates **with thanksgiving** and His courts with praise. **Give thanks** to Him (HCSB; emphasis added)

---

[146] Pronominal suffix in *'ašānû*.

[147] Independent personal pronoun (*'ănaḥnû*).

[148] The position of, among others, Maclaren 1903: 79; Harman 1998: 330; Mitchell 1997: 291; Goldingay 2008: 136–137.

[149] Cf. Lohfink 1990; Zenger 1997b: 315–319; Weber 2003: 161–162, 163; Longman 2014: 348–350; Tucker and Grant 2018: 452–453.

[150] Tucker and Grant (2018: 453) express this point thus: 'All those who recognize Yahweh's cosmic kingship are called to join in this song of praise as full members of the covenant community (the sheep of Yahweh's flock).'

[151] Lexical correspondences are indicated by the bold type, but our main focus here is what features in italics.

of Psalms 96 and 98 by recognizing that the people of the new covenant encompasses all nations.

Such is what was provided for by the Abrahamic covenant, even if its realization is tied to the new covenant. We should recall that this theme of blessing for the nations is 'flagged' for the Psalter reader in the programmatic Psalm 2, for the parallel with Psalm 100 is remarkable. In the book of Psalms, an appeal, in the imperative, to serve YHWH occurs only in these two texts;[152] in both cases, it is addressed to the nations[153] (and, further, in both cases, there is a call to joy) (see Table 4.7).[154]

Table 4.7 A parallel appeal to serve YHWH in Psalms 2 and 100

Ps. 2:11	**Serve the LORD with** fear, and rejoice with trembling. (KJV)
Ps. 100:2	**Serve the LORD with** gladness; come before Him with joyful songs. (HCSB)

Three additional comments need to be made regarding the definition of the people of YHWH under the new covenant. First, as the call to conversion – particularly in Psalm 96 – implies, not every individual member of the nations is included in the covenant people: the universal appeal does not imply a universal*ism* of principle or of practice. Only those who enter the temple courts benefit from YHWH's salvation (here I combine the ideas of Ps. 96:2 [plus 98:2] and Ps. 100:4); such people are not subject to the righteous judgment of YHWH (Pss 96:13; 98:9).

Second, not all Israelites are beneficiaries of salvation. Psalm 95 insists that only those who heed YHWH's voice will enter the place of rest: the new crossing of the desert does not ultimately apply to those whose hearts are wayward. The people whom YHWH does not abandon are those who are upright in heart (Ps. 94:12–15). In addition, we should note that Psalm 91, which lies outside the group we have been considering but which is not unconnected to it,[155] underlines the importance of putting one's trust in YHWH as the place of protection: this is the only criterion for salvation.

Third, the parallels with Isaiah 40 – 55 require us to reckon with the importance of the work of the servant of YHWH, raised up (1) to 'restore

---

[152] Cf. Gerstenberger 2001: 203.
[153] As indicated by the preceding verse in each case.
[154] Lexical correspondences are indicated in bold.
[155] E.g. Howard 1993.

the preserved ones of Israel' and (2) so that YHWH's salvation 'may reach to the end of the earth'[156] (Isa. 49:6 NASB; cf. Isa. 42:6). The new-covenant people of God, drawn from Israel and the nations, are the fruit of the servant's suffering (Isa. 50 – 55). Once again, we find ourselves coming back to the figure of the king,[157] although, once again, only indirectly (as far as book 4 is concerned).

I do, however, believe that it is appropriate to discern the presence of the king in Psalm 101 – and even the figure of the suffering servant in Psalm 102. My convictions in relation to these two psalms are probably more speculative than what I have advanced hitherto, but they are not critical to our overall project, and they are, for the most part, anticipatory of themes that I take to be more clearly presented in book 5 (and to which we will return).

Sinaitic-/Davidic-covenant conditions satisfied by the eschatological king (Psalm 101)

For reasons set out in appendix 4, it appears necessary to take 'Of David' in a post-Psalm 72:20 context to mean 'relating to an eschatological David'. Although, as Kirkpatrick asserts, Psalm 101 'may be regarded as the expression of David's solemn resolution to prepare himself and his city for Jehovah's coming to dwell in their midst', its placement in book 4 may be designed to 'suggest how [Jehovah's] kingdom might be made a reality for Jerusalem under the sway of a true ruler, some second David, whose kingdom would be based on the principles of the Divine government'.[158]

For our purposes, what we need to note is this king's integrity and determination to put into practice the requirements of the law of Moses. We also need to observe the correlation between his aspirations and the conditions of the Davidic covenant that we set out in the previous chapter;[159]

---

[156] The formula here is not especially close to that of Ps. 2:8, even if the idea is. In Ps. 2, the context is of judgment, which, in common with salvation, is a global phenomenon.

[157] For the relationship between the suffering servant and the king, see e.g. Webb 1996: 233–234.

[158] Kirkpatrick 1901: 590. The second of these quotations is found in McKelvey 2010: 177–178 n. 21. Kirkpatrick writes many decades before the rise of editorial criticism!

[159] See pp. 49–50. Harman (1998: 331) mentions the 1 Kgs 9 text.

Table 4.8 The conditions of the Davidic covenant (1 Kings) fulfilled by the ideal Davidic king (Psalm 101)

1 Kgs 2:4	If your sons keep their **way**, to **walk** before me in truth, with all their **heart** and all their soul . . .
1 Kgs 9:4	if you **walk** before me as David, your father, **walked**, with **integrity of heart** . . . to perform according to all that I commanded you, if you keep my statutes and my judgments . . .
Ps. 101:2*	I will pay attention to the **way** of **integrity**. When will You come to me? I will live [= '**walk**'] with a **heart of integrity** in my house. (HCSB)

* Note also the recurrence in v. 6b of three key terms from this verse. One of the occurrences of 'integrity' is a noun, the other an adjective; it is the noun that features in 1 Kgs 9:4. The phrase 'heart of integrity' is almost identical to 'integrity of heart' in 1 Kgs 9:4.

we reproduce two of them in Table 4.8.[160] By virtue of these links with the 1 Kings texts that draw attention to the conditional dimension of the Davidic covenant, Psalm 101 sensitizes the Psalter reader to the importance of finding a king who fits the bill of obedience. Should this king materialize, the anguished questioning of Psalm 89 can be answered, and it can be seen that the conditionality of 1 Kings is not ultimately at variance with the radically unconditional formulation of the Davidic covenant in Psalm 89.

Verse 1 plays a key role in this regard. In a throwback to Psalm 89, the king sings 'of *ḥesed* and justice'. Here, it is probably not these attributes as found in YHWH (contra NIV).[161] To be sure, the Psalter reader might readily believe, with Christopher Seitz, that the start of Psalm 101 is affirming precisely those perfections of YHWH that had been called into question at the end of Psalm 89.[162] If, however, such is the case, it is only via an indirect route, for we need to begin with the observation from the succeeding verses that the psalmist is concerned with his *own* character and behaviour.

Indeed, the primary intertextual import of Psalm 101:1 relates to the conditionality of the Sinaitic covenant. Those covenant conditions can be met only in the *new*-covenant king whom Psalm 89 anticipated by means

---

[160] Lexical correspondences are indicated in bold.
[161] '[Y]*our* love and justice'; emphasis added.
[162] Seitz 1998: 164.

of its portrayal of David.[163] As he sings 'of *ḥesed* and justice', the (human) king expresses his resolve to deliver on YHWH's moral expectations[164] – to be his 'stand-in', 'the exact reflection of the divine power'.[165] Since this first verse calls to mind Psalm 89:14 (MT 89:15) ('Righteousness and justice are the foundation of your throne; steadfast love and faithfulness go before you' [ESV]), the king of Psalm 101 is depicted as 'making the grade' of the perfect divine standards. Further, the first half of Psalm 89:14 (MT 89:15) is picked up word for word in Psalm 97:2 in relation to YHWH, as we have already had occasion to note;[166] this only reinforces our conclusion that the Psalm 101 king needs to be seen as being on a par with YHWH – in line with what we began observing regarding the new-covenant king in our consideration of Psalm 2.[167] As Raymond Jacques Tournay[168] expresses it, here we have a 'portrait of the ideal king . . . that describes in advance' the one whom YHWH calls 'my servant David'. The superior recapitulation of 'David' lies with one who satisfies the conditionality of the covenant established with the son of Jesse.[169]

New-covenant (and Abrahamic-covenant) fulfilment enabled by a suffering servant (Psalm 102)

That Psalm 101 ends with the king apparently residing in the 'city of YHWH' (v. 8) seems to be significant in relation to the psalm that follows.[170] For Psalm 102 is concerned with the rebuilding of the city, and the themes

---

[163] Cf. pp. 51–53; Dumortier 1972: 193.

[164] Cf. Mic. 6:8. Allen usefully points out the juxtaposition of these two virtues in Ps. 119:149 (1983: 2, though not in the updated 2002: 10). In this verse in Ps. 119, the virtues are predicated of YHWH rather than the psalmist.

[165] Cf. p. 52.

[166] See p. 98.

[167] See pp. 28–29.

[168] Tournay 1988: 180.

[169] Gundersen's arguments and my own are similar here, and he usefully appeals to close ties between this psalm and Ps. 18 as well as Ps. 15 (2015: 182–184). 'Ultimately, Psalm 101 reveals that the unbearable tension and covenantal dissonance marking Psalm 89 will be resolved' (ibid. 186). For our treatment of Ps. 18 and the way in which it anticipates the perfect king, see pp. 36–37.

[170] That Ps. 102 also links up with the succeeding Ps. 103 squares with the presence in both these psalms of Ps. 90 related themes; for a list of them in relation to Ps. 102, see Wilson 1985: 218.

of king and city are tied[171] in the preceding book (Ps. 78:68–70),[172] as also in the programmatic Psalm 2. It may be correct to argue that the speaker in Psalm 102 is the king of Psalm 101,[173] but we should be careful not to let complementarity spill over into fusion,[174] lest the specificities of each psalm be stifled.

Psalm 102 portrays the fulfilment of the new covenant beyond the exile (vv. 12–16 [MT vv. 13–17]):[175]

> But you, O LORD, are enthroned for ever;
> you are remembered throughout all generations.
> You will arise and have pity on Zion;
> it is the time to favour her;
> the appointed time has come.
> For your servants hold her stones dear
> and have pity on her dust.
> Nations will fear the name of the LORD,
> and all the kings of the earth will fear your glory.
> For the LORD builds up Zion;
> he appears in his glory
> (ESV)

The construction of the new city of Zion goes hand in hand with the realization of the Abrahamic covenant: verse 22 (MT v. 23) speaks of the time '[w]hen the peoples are gathered together, And the kingdoms, to serve the LORD' (Ps. 102:22 NASB; cf. Ps. 2:11; 100:2). These events come about thanks to the prayer of one who 'pours out his complaint before YHWH' (heading [MT v. 1]). Indeed, the 'outcome of the drama and anticipation of thanksgiving' in verses 15–22 (MT vv. 16–23) echoes the supplication of verses 1–2 (MT vv. 2–3).[176]

But who is the supplicant? It seems to be an 'individual whose destiny is profoundly tied to that of the city'[177] as also to the people. Commentators

---

[171] Cf. Howard 1997: 200 n. 1.

[172] Perhaps the juxtaposition of Ps. 86 (king) and Ps. 87 (city) should also be viewed in the same light.

[173] Witt 2012.

[174] As in Witt's phrase 'the afflicted king', used in relation to Ps. 102 (ibid. 600, 603, 604); or Zenger's '"kingly" petitioner' ('[d]er "königliche" Beter' [1994: 171]).

[175] These verses tie in with what we have noted regarding the exilic setting that underlies book 4 (Ps. 106:47, discussed at the beginning of this chapter). Cf. Wenham 2001: 95.

[176] Girard 1994b: 31.

[177] Ibid. 36.

are justifiably intrigued by the movement between the individual and corporate perspectives in the psalm.[178] 'The prayer of an afflicted one' in the heading (MT v. 1) is transposed into 'the prayer of the destitute' in verse 17 (MT v. 18), 'destitute' ('*ar'ār*) being a collective noun, as the plural suffix attached to the verse's second occurrence of 'prayer' indicates, parallel with the first.[179] Again, the afflicted individual's 'groaning' in verse 5 (MT v. 6) recurs in verse 20 (MT v. 21) as a symptom of the 'prisoner' ('*āsîr*) – to be understood collectively, as the plural in the parallel ('sons of death') demonstrates.[180] The individual perspective returns towards the end (vv. 23–24 [MT vv. 24–25]), but the psalm concludes with the perspective of the (plural) 'servants' of YHWH (v. 28 [MT v. 29]; cf. v. 14 [MT v. 15]).

Would it be fanciful to infer from these data that the 'afflicted one' represents the people who are 'destitute', 'prisoner', 'sons of death' – in exile? Might he not even be the *substitute* of these 'servants' of YHWH? For we need to recognize that his sufferings recall those of Psalm 90:7–11 – the wrath of YHWH comes upon him (Ps. 102:3–4, 10–11, 23 [MT 102:4–5, 11–12, 24]). Here is the one whose heart is 'struck' (v. 4 [MT v. 5]; the root *n-k-h*), whose strength has been 'broken' (v. 23 [MT v. 24]; the root '-n-h), who suffers 'because of [the] indignation and [the] wrath' of YHWH (v. 9 [MT v. 10]). Might he not hold the key to the liberation of the captives?

Other things being equal, the theology of book 4 would lead us to assume that this individual has sinned against YHWH and needs an intercessor in order to find forgiveness (cf. Pss 90; 99; 103; 106). Yet the information in the psalm does not sit well with this. He is simply an 'afflicted one' who is 'weak' (heading [MT v. 1]); and, although the prayers of others are associated with his (v. 17 [MT v. 18]), there are no indications of any need for a mediator. '[N]o specific sins are mentioned. He seems a Job-like figure,' writes Geoffrey Grogan.[181] Might he not be the one who intercedes on behalf of the people? Bearing in mind the background of Isaiah 40 – 55 that features abundantly in book 4, I suggest that the 'afflicted one' of Psalm 102 corresponds to the suffering servant of YHWH

---

[178] Cf. the summary in Allen 2002: 16–19.

[179] Four French translations opt for a singular here ('sa prière', 'his/her prayer'). This is understandable given the context and highlights the problem the interpreter needs to grapple with. But, despite the LXX, the plural, 'their prayer', is textually secure.

[180] The words are not identical, but '*anḥâ* (v. 5 [MT v. 6]) and '*ănāqâ* (v. 20 [MT v. 21]) are phonetically and semantically close.

[181] Grogan 2008: 171.

who is 'smitten by God, and afflicted' (Isa. 53:4 ESV; the roots *n-k-h* and *'-n-h* respectively – the same as those noted above for Ps. 102). He is 'numbered with the transgressors', bears 'the sin of many, and makes intercession for the transgressors' (Isa. 53:12 ESV). I am not alone in this stance; Erich Zenger also affirms that '[t]he . . . petitioner . . . bears features of the suffering servant of Isaiah'.[182]

If I am right to discern allusions to the Fourth Servant Song of Isaiah 52:13 – 53:12, this fourth book of the Psalms takes us a long way in our search for a solution to the problems of Genesis 3. Although I want to avoid fusing the perspectives of Psalms 101 and 102, the prophecy of Isaiah enables us to understand that the king and the suffering servant prove to be one and the same figure.[183]

One key book 4 psalm remains to be considered before we can offer a concluding synthesis of our findings.

Convergence of Abrahamic, Davidic and new covenants in providing the solution to the Adamic problem (Psalm 103)

'Psalm 103 offers multiple correspondences with Psalm 90',[184] and I have shown elsewhere that there are good reasons to view Psalm 103 as the answer to Moses' prayer in Psalm 90.[185] This means[186] that there are also good reasons to consider Psalm 103 to be the answer to the perplexity of Psalm 89. It is not, however, necessary to subscribe to a precise manner of accounting for the links between Psalms 90 and 103 in order to recognize that the latter substantially responds to the crisis of book 3. For our (covenant-relationships) purposes, what is the shape of this response? I outline five aspects below.

---

[182] Even if the demonstration is lacking (Zenger 1994: 171). See also Hensley 2018: 263.

[183] See n. 158 in this chapter.

[184] Vesco 2008b: 944.

[185] Hely Hutchinson 2013b: 37 n. 25. For a similar appreciation, see Vesco 2008b: 944–945. This does not mean that I exclude the idea of preliminary answers to the Psalm 90 prayer earlier in the book. Pss 91 and 92 may well serve that function. It seems that the two verses that close Ps. 91 (vv. 15–16) respond both to Ps. 89:46–49 (MT 89:47–50) and to Ps. 90:13–17. Ps. 92 celebrates attributes of YHWH that were called into question in Ps. 89: his covenant loyalty (*ḥesed* and *'ĕmûnâ* [v. 2 (MT v. 3)]) and his uprightness, dependability and absence of injustice (v. 15 [MT v. 16]).

[186] For reasons developed extensively in the early part of this chapter.

1. We should note that the forgiveness of sins heads the list of 'benefits' which need to be remembered (vv. 2–3) and that this forgiveness applies both to the individual (vv. 3–5) and to the community (vv. 6–18);[187] it even has repercussions for the entire cosmos (vv. 19–22).[188] Do we not have here, in this key idea in Psalm 103, the answer to the problems of Genesis 3 – 11?

2. The personification of the cosmos in verses 21–22 recalls the same phenomenon that we find in the central group of Psalms 93 – 100 (Pss 93:3; 96:11–12; 98:7–8). As we have seen in this chapter, the context in which the latter feature is eschatological – that of the fulfilment of the new covenant. This sensitizes us to the possibility of a new-covenant fulfilment for Psalm 103 as well. This seems to be confirmed by the strong hue of Isaiah 40 – 55 that colours Psalm 103,[189] as also by the fact that the psalm corresponds, to a considerable extent, to a commentary on the last[190] part of the new-covenant formula ('for his covenant loyalty endures for ever'): *ḥesed* ('covenant loyalty') reverberates, at more or less regular intervals, through the psalm,[191] while *'ôlām* ('for ever') also plays a significant role.[192] These two terms echo Psalm 89.

3. As we might, by now, expect in this book 4 context, the new-covenant solution to the Adamic problem does not bypass the realization of the Abrahamic covenant. This can be seen in the fact that the ('Abrahamic') golden calf episode is, once again, indirectly evoked here (Ps. 103:8; cf. Exod. 34:6).[193] The Abrahamic 'all nations' theme is also present: the expression 'those who fear [YHWH]' (vv. 11, 13, 17) – referring to the

---

[187] The number of beneficiaries of YHWH's work shifts: compare vv. 3–5 with vv. 10–14.

[188] Forgiveness is not mentioned in the last part of the psalm, but it would seem that this climactic section nonetheless reflects both of the psalm's preceding parts (cf. Rev. 5:9–14: the response of all creation to the redemption accomplished by the Lamb).

[189] Kidner (1975: 365–366) mentions these links: Isa. 40:30f. (Ps. 103:5); Isa. 55:6–9 and 49:15 (Ps. 103:11–14); Isa. 40:6–8 (Ps. 103:15–18). One could add, in relation to vv. 15 and 16 of the psalm, Isa. 40:24 and 51:12. See Michaud (1993: 663) regarding exegetes' considering that the psalm is influenced by Isaiah and not vice versa.

[190] The term 'good', which belongs to the first part of the formula, also features in the psalm (v. 5), although it is used here as a noun and with a sense that differs from that of the adjective in the formula.

[191] Vv. 4, 8, 11, 17.

[192] Featuring once in v. 9 and twice in v. 17.

[193] See p. 56 and our extensive discussion towards the start of the present chapter. Sakenfeld (1978: 227) comments that 'Ps. 103:6ff. almost seems to be an extended comment on the conflated formulaic tradition of Ex. 34:6–7' (her demonstration covers vv. 8, 9, 10–14, 17–18).

beneficiaries of forgiveness in the psalm – is a general phrase that can accommodate non-Israelites,[194] in keeping with the redefinition of the people of God that emerges through the sequence that runs from Psalm 95 to Psalm 100.[195]

4. If our appreciation of the meaning of 'Of David' (*lĕdāwid*) in post-Psalm 72 contexts is correct,[196] the heading of Psalm 103 (MT v. 1a) requires us to tie the solution to an eschatological king from David's line (the one who has been on view in Ps. 101). The reminiscences of Isaiah 40 – 55 that we find in Psalm 103 probably have the same effect: the mind of the careful reader of the Scriptures is drawn to the Davidic-covenant promise of Isaiah 55:3 (*ḥasdê dāwid*).[197]

5. The beneficiaries of forgiveness are not without precepts to put into practice; they may even be said to 'keep [YHWH's] covenant' (v. 18). Patently, this cannot mean 'keep perfectly the law of Moses within the framework of the Sinaitic covenant', for otherwise there would be no need for the forgiveness of sins which Psalm 103 majors on, and this psalm presents an Abrahamic–Davidic–new-covenant solution. It does, though, mean that YHWH's new-covenant beneficiaries are characterized by the concern to obey specific commandments. We will return to this question as we tackle the theme of law in our penultimate chapter.

Summary

We have focused on the theological heart of the Psalter (book 4). As was the case at the end of our previous chapter, there is much material to synthesize. I trust that the headings provided along the way do much of this summarizing for us. Here is a reminder of the key 'take-home' points as they feature in the headings, though organized in a somewhat different order for the sake of serving the purposes of our enquiry.

We were taken back to the beginning of Scripture to see the fundamental problem of sin:

---

[194] We interact in the next chapter (pp. 122–123) with the debate regarding the meaning of this phrase in Pss 115 and 118.
[195] See pp. 99–101.
[196] See appendix 4.
[197] See pp. 31–32.

1 the Adamic problem is exposed (Ps. 90:3–11);
2 the remedy for the exile will be a consequence of the remedy for Adamic sin (Ps. 90:12–17).

The solution, also set forth in Genesis, cannot bypass the Noahic covenant but essentially lies with the Abrahamic covenant:

3 the Noahic covenant is an indispensable part of the solution (Ps. 104);
4 the Abrahamic covenant is the basis for the exiles' prayer (Ps. 106:45–47);
5 the Abrahamic solution is to be applied to the exile (Pss 89 – 90).

Yet other covenants are also required:

6 the Abrahamic covenant per se is insufficient as a solution (Pss 105 – 106);
7 a Davidic-covenant solution is intimately connected to the Abrahamic-covenant solution (Pss 93 – 100 with Ps. 89);
8 the Levitical covenant is associated with the Davidic covenant (Ps. 106:30–31).

There needs to be superiority relative to the Israelites' experience on a number of levels:

9 the 'pedagogy of failure' anticipates superior mediation (Ps. 106);
10 the typological structures are to be recapitulated in a new-covenant solution (Pss 93 – 100).

What, specifically, do we learn regarding the relationship between the Davidic and the new covenants?

11 The conditional dimension of the Davidic covenant is implicitly reaffirmed; the Sinaitic–Davidic-covenant conditions are to be satisfied by the eschatological king (Ps. 101).

And what do we learn regarding the relationship between the Abrahamic and the new covenants?

12 The new-covenant people are drawn from all nations (Abrahamic covenant), on the basis of conversion, and do not include all Israelites (Pss 93 – 100).

13 New-covenant and Abrahamic-covenant fulfilment will be enabled by a suffering servant (Ps. 102).

Overall, we may talk especially in terms of:

14 the convergence of Abrahamic, Davidic and new covenants in providing the solution to the Adamic problem (Ps. 103).

We should conclude our chapter by putting flesh on those bones and drawing the various threads together.

How does book 4 answer the perplexed calling into question of the durability of the unconditional promises to David (notably in Ps. 89)? In this 'Moses-book', the fundamental answer lies not with the Mosaic (Sinaitic) covenant but with the Abrahamic covenant. That God will not renege on his promises to Abraham implies that the means whereby those Abrahamic promises reach fulfilment have not been set aside. This means that, ultimately, the Davidic covenant must come to be realized.

Yet it must be understood that the Davidic covenant has a conditional dimension and that the fundamental problem that needs to be resolved is not the exile but sin (Pss 90; 106). The Noahic covenant does not deal with sin, but it does provide for the stability of the creation (Ps. 104). The Abrahamic covenant will give rise to the solution, although it does not, in and of itself, equate to this solution (Pss 105 – 106). What is required is a (superior) antitype of the structures of Israel's history (Pss 93 – 100; 106): a greater mediation, exodus, city, temple, earth (cosmos) . . . and king. It appears that fulfilment of the Levitical covenant remains on the agenda (Ps. 106), and this must also mean that the Davidic covenant will reach fulfilment (cf. Jer. 33).

Indeed, such a new-covenant scenario is in prospect on the other side of the exile. YHWH is powerful enough to bring this about (Pss 93 – 100)! People from all nations will figure among the beneficiaries of this covenant, on the basis of conversion (Pss 95 – 100; 102 – 103). It seems that the key to its realization lies with an eschatological king who will satisfy the conditions of the Sinaitic and Davidic covenants and who is also a suffering servant – the people's representative and substitute (Pss 101 – 102). Sins will be forgiven (Ps. 103).

If we have come a long way in our enquiry, the Psalter reader seeks greater clarity at this stage regarding the new-covenant scenario that must come about. And so we must turn to the concluding book of the Psalter in our next chapter.

5

The outworking of the answer in book 5

Introduction

We continue our quest to understand the newness of the new covenant, relative to the Davidic covenant, as it emerges from the Psalter. We have seen that five covenants are lined up in their fulfilment: the Noahic, Abrahamic, Levitical, Davidic and new (cf. Jer. 33:14–26). In book 5 and the Psalter's concluding doxology, we see this alignment underlined, although it is *particularly* the Abrahamic, Davidic and new covenants that are in evidence here. This is relatively unsurprising once we realize that the new-covenant formula ('Give thanks to YHWH, for he is good, for his *ḥesed* endures for ever'), rooted in Jeremiah 33:11, is the refrain of this final book.[1] And this is what constitutes the key answer to the psalmist's perplexity: the convergence of the Abrahamic, Davidic and new covenants in their fulfilment.

Convergence of Abrahamic and new covenants in their fulfilment (Psalm 107:1–3)

As even an editorial-critical sceptic can readily acknowledge,[2] there is a clear link between the end of book 4 and the beginning of book 5 (see Table 5.1).[3] Indeed, Psalm 107 shows us the answer to the exiles' prayer in Psalm 106:47:

---

[1] Cf. Hely Hutchinson 2005a.
[2] Cf. Goldingay 2008: 249.
[3] Lexical correspondences are indicated in bold.

Table 5.1 The answer to the exiles' prayer: the link between the end of book 4 and the start of book 5 of the Psalter

Psalm 106:47	*Psalm 107:1–3*
Save us, Yahweh our God, and **gather** us from the nations, so that we may **give thanks** to Your holy name and rejoice in Your praise. (HCSB)	**Give thanks** to the LORD, for He is good; His faithful love endures forever. Let the redeemed of the LORD proclaim that He has redeemed them from the hand of the foe and has **gathered** them from the lands – from the east and the west, from the north and the south. (HCSB)

The description in v. 2 relates to a 'second exodus,' the restoration from exile. It assumes that the promises in Isaiah have been fulfilled. The people who experienced this restoration are the ones who should take up that conventional declaration in v. 1, given that they are in a position to affirm that it is not merely a conventional declaration but something they have proved to be true.

That is even clearer in v. 3. Psalm 106:47 pleaded with Yhwh to 'gather us from the nations,' in effect praying for the fulfilment of the promise in Isa. 60:4. Verse 3 presupposes that this has happened[4]

This is important for our purposes, since, in line with these observations, what is termed here a 'conventional declaration' bespeaks new-covenant fulfilment (cf. Jer. 33:11). We have already had occasion to comment on this important formula several times,[5] but here in book 5 it takes on particular significance, for it reverberates through the book in a crescendo pattern (cf. Pss 118; 136) and may be considered the book's refrain. Irrespective of the precise structure one discerns in the book,[6] the prominence of this formula strikes the Psalter reader. In other words, the notions of the return to the land and the realization of the new covenant – which are two sides of the same coin – pervade this final book of the Psalter.[7] This observation that new-covenant fulfilment is to the fore in book 5 is given emphasis if, as is my conviction, Psalm 107 is programmatic

---

[4] Goldingay 2008: 249.

[5] See pp. 3, 93, 99, 108.

[6] Snearly (2016: 57–78) summarizes the major proposals. My own point of view is set forth in Hely Hutchinson 2013b: 37–38; 2015b: 137–138.

[7] At least as far as Ps. 136.

for the book.[8] Since this point of view is not generally found in the literature,[9] I do not set store by it in the discussion that follows.

By this stage in our study, we are mindful that new-covenant fulfilment goes hand in hand with Abrahamic-covenant fulfilment and even that the Abrahamic covenant gives rise to the new covenant.[10] Indeed, we should not lose sight of the fact that Psalm 106:45 (which speaks of YHWH's remembering his covenant in line with his *ḥesed*) is in the immediately preceding context of Psalm 107:1. This means that the *ḥesed* of the opening verse of book 5 (and the book's refrain) has Abrahamic-covenant connotations, for, as we have seen extensively,[11] in Psalm 106:45 the parallel term *běrît* alludes to the promises to Abraham. If the people are now back in the land and praising YHWH for his faithfulness to his 'good word' according to the new covenant regarding the end of the exile (cf. Jer. 33:14), this is also because he has proven faithful to prior promises to Abraham.

In this chapter, we are going to find our conclusions from previous chapters reinforced: as book 5 sets forth the outworking of the solution to the anguished questioning of book 3, we will find that new-covenant fulfilment converges with Abrahamic-covenant fulfilment and Davidic-covenant fulfilment (and even, though less prominently, Noahic-covenant fulfilment and Levitical-covenant fulfilment). The covenant God proves to be *faithful*: such is the denotation of *ḥesed* in the context of the new-covenant formula that is all-important in book 5.[12]

The bulk of the first part of this chapter will be taken up with a consideration of two psalms, along with their immediately preceding context, that showcase the new-covenant formula (Pss 118; 136). But, first, further observations from Psalm 107 are also relevant to our enquiry.

'Sons of Adam' and 'all nations' included in the new exodus (Psalm 107)

It is instructive to interact with the reasons why two particular commentators question the idea that Psalm 107 evokes a post-exilic return. First, Dahood considers that the phrase 'those redeemed by Yahweh' (v. 2) refers

---

[8] Hely Hutchinson 2013b: 38.

[9] Weber (2003: 209) touches on this idea.

[10] See the summaries at the end of the two preceding chapters.

[11] See pp. 65–75.

[12] For further discussion of the meaning of this term in the context of the new-covenant formula, see Hely Hutchinson 2005a: 104–106, including nn. 8 and 11.

to the redemption from Egypt, the verb *g-'-l* being used, for example, in Exodus 6:6[13] and 15:13.[14] Second, Motyer remarks that '[i]t is quite common to link the psalm with the return from exile in Babylon but this does not accord with the worldwide view the psalm takes of the gathered people (v. 3)'.[15]

I reply to both exegetes by appealing to the psalmist's skilled use of metaphors to a variety of ends. On the one hand, just as we have also seen in Psalms 93 – 100,[16] he draws on Isaiah, particularly chapters 40 – 55, to portray a return from exile that is *patterned after* that of the exodus from Egypt; I refer to the work of others in this area,[17] and, in order to provide

Table 5.2 Roffey's analysis of intertextuality between Psalm 107 and Isaiah 40 – 55

Common imagery and language	Psalm 107	Isaiah
The desert turning fertile	35–36	41:17–18; 43:19–21; 44:3
The drying-up of the fertile	33–34	44:27; 50:2
The way through the desert	4–7, 40	40:3–4; 43:19–21 et al.
Affliction, offering and healing	17–20	51:21; 53:10–12; 54:10
Imprisonment and deliverance (note distinct parallel)	10–14 16	42:7, 22; 45.2b; 49:9–12 (45:2b)
The control of the sea, of chaos (*tōhû*)	23–30 40	43:16; 50:2; 51:10, 15; 54:11 (45:18)
YHWH as redeemer (*gĕ'ûlê yhwh*)	2, 3 2	43:1 et al. (62:12)
Redemption and sea	2–3, 23–30	51:10, 11, 15
From the north and from the sea (*miṣṣāpôn ûmiyyām*)	3	49:12

Adapted from Roffey 1997: 72–73. © J. W. Roffey 1997; 'Beyond Reality: Poetic Discourse and Psalm 107', in Eugene E. Carpenter, *A Biblical Itinerary: In Search of Method, Form and Content, Essays in Honor of George W. Coats*, Sheffield Academic Press, used by permission of Bloomsbury Publishing Plc.

---

[13] Dahood cites Exod. 6:8, but it appears that he is referring to 6:6.

[14] Dahood 1970: 81.

[15] Motyer 1994: 557.

[16] See pp. 92–97.

[17] Regarding the background in Isaiah, see Delitzsch 1889: 139–147; Kissane 1954: 178–180; Jacquet 1978: 167–173; Beaucamp 1979: 173; Goulder 1998: 117–125; Broyles 1999: 408; Goldingay 2008: 249–260; Vesco 2008b: 1030.

a ready idea of the intertextuality involved, I reproduce John Roffey's table (see Table 5.2).[18]

On the other hand, and at the same time, the psalmist presents this return from exile from a particular angle – that of the redemption of human beings at a general and international level. This needs a little exploration.

According to the refrain of the psalm (vv. 8, 15, 21, 31), the beneficiaries of the 'wonderful deeds' are the 'sons of Adam'. The phrase *běnê 'ādām* recalls Psalm 90:3 (its most recent occurrence for the Psalter reader, and the only one in book 4) and draws attention to the fact that the redemption spoken of in the psalm corresponds to the remedy for the sin problem of Genesis 3 – 11.[19] This phrase also occurs in Psalm 89:47 (MT 89:48). As we demonstrated in the previous chapter,[20] the juxtaposition of Psalms 89 and 90 binds together the Israelites' exile problem with humanity's sin problem. Against this background, it is unsurprising that the captives' plight in Psalm 107:10 is explained (*kî*, 'for') in the following verse by their rebellion 'against the words of God' (Ps. 107:11). Again, we read that '[f]ools suffered affliction because of their rebellious ways and their sins' (Ps. 107:17 HCSB). The sin that gave rise to the exile owing to the breaking of the (conditional) Sinaitic covenant needs to be bracketed with the sin of Adam recorded in Genesis 3; and the testimony of the last two books of the Psalter is that the solution to the exile (the new covenant) and the solution to the fall (announced, in the first instance, in the Abrahamic covenant) also go hand in hand.

The 'sons of Adam' who are redeemed include people drawn from all nations. The key that unlocks the meaning of verse 3 is its Isaianic background, chiefly 43:5–6 and 49:12, but we quote other, related texts in Table 5.3.[21] In context, these Isaianic texts combine the themes of new exodus (Isa. 11:15–16; 43:2, 16–20; 48:20–21; 49:10–11) and the salvation of the nations (Isa. 11:10; 42:6; 48:19; 49:1, 6) effected thanks to the work of the messiah (Isa. 11:1–5) and the servant (Isa. 42:1–7; 49:1–6).[22] According to the theology of the prophet, the return from exile is to be understood figuratively inasmuch as its participants include non-Israelites who were

---

[18] Roffey 1997: 72–73; table adapted.

[19] See the exegesis of Ps. 90 in the previous chapter (esp. pp. 79–80).

[20] See p. 76.

[21] Lexical correspondences are indicated in bold. 'Land' and 'earth' reflect the same Hebrew term: *'ereṣ*.

[22] The convergence of the Isa. 11 and 49 texts, including the 'banner' motif, constitutes an additional reason to recognize that the Messiah (Isa. 11) and servant (Isa. 49) are two functions of the one figure. Cf. chapter 4, n. 158, and Oswalt 1998: 310.

Table 5.3 The Isaianic background to Psalm 107:3

Ps. 107:3	and has **gathered** them from the **lands** – from the **east** and the **west**, from the **north** and the **south**. (HCSB)
Isa. 11:11–12	On that day the Lord will extend His hand a second time to recover – from Assyria, Egypt, Pathros, Cush, Elam, Shinar, Hamath, and the coasts and islands of the **west** – the remnant of His people who survive. He will lift up a banner for the nations and **gather** the dispersed of Israel; He will collect the scattered of Judah from the four corners of the **earth**. (HCSB)
Isa. 43:5–6	Do not fear, for I am with you; I will bring your descendants from the **east**, and **gather** you from the **west**. I will say to the **north**: Give them up! and to the south: Do not hold them back! Bring My sons from far away, and My daughters from the ends of the **earth** (HCSB)
Isa. 49:12	See, these will come from far away, from the **north** and from the **west**, and from the **land** of Sinim. (HCSB)
Isa. 49:22	This is what the Lord GOD says: Look, I will lift up My hand to the nations, and raise My banner to the peoples. They will bring your sons in their arms, and your daughters will be carried on their shoulders. (HCSB)

never exiled from Canaan as such. To be sure, the texts cited above (and especially the two with which Ps. 107:3 resonates most directly) do not immediately suggest that the nations will be converted, and it is possible to interpret Isaiah 43:6 and 49:12 as referring only to the Israelites. But the verse that precedes the first text, namely Isaiah 11:10, is clearer in speaking of salvation for the nations:

> On that day the root of Jesse
> will stand as a banner for the peoples.
> The nations will seek Him,
> and His resting place will be glorious.
> (HCSB)

The 'banner for the peoples' image is taken up in Isaiah 49:22, and it seems likely that the latter text also implies that the nations will be saved.[23] This means that non-Israelites participate in the new exodus, and it seems reasonable to suggest (in relation to the other two Isaianic texts) that those who come 'from afar', 'from the end of the earth', 'from the north', 'from the west' encompass members of the nations.[24] In brief, this 'Abrahamic' theme of blessing for the nations is evoked in the introductory psalm of book 5 where we must recognize, once again, the inextricable link between new-covenant fulfilment and Abrahamic-covenant fulfilment.

So, in tandem with bespeaking new-covenant fulfilment, Psalm 107 depicts a return from exile in which 'sons of Adam', drawn from all nations, participate. That this is so seems peculiarly apposite in the light of the psalm's conclusion. The significance of the closing verse 43 should not be overlooked ('Whoever is wise, let him attend to these things; let them consider the steadfast love of the LORD' [ESV]). The importance of this verse is signalled by several factors:

1 it is set apart from the rest of the psalm by virtue of its appeal (via jussives) to the reader;
2 its call to heed the content of the psalm, and meditate on it, lends weight to the forty-two verses that precede it;
3 it provides a wisdom lens through which to interpret the psalm: as in the case of Psalm 78,[25] Psalm 107 contains lessons to be learned.

Who, in particular, is being addressed in this final verse? The answer chimes in with the general Adamic / 'all nations' theme of the psalm: 'whoever is wise' (v. 43) applies to non-Jews as well as Jews.

New-covenant fulfilment not yet experienced in the post-exilic period (Psalm 107:43)

Psalm 107:43 also goes some way to orientating us with regard to the timing of the fulfilment of the new covenant. If the original recipients

---

[23] That Isa. 49:22–23 speaks of the submission of the nations to Israel is not incompatible with the salvation of the nations: Van Winkle 1985: 446–458; H. G. M. Williamson 1998: 127.

[24] This idea of participation by the nations in the new exodus gains some prominence in the closing section of Isaiah (60:3–4, 6–7, 9; 62:2, 10–12).

[25] Cf. our remarks on this psalm in chapter 3 (see pp. 53–54).

of the Psalter were post-exilic Jews[26] needing to meditate on this psalm, verse 43 alerts us to the possibility that they were *not* already grasping the covenant faithfulness of YHWH (*ḥasdê. . .* [v. 43]). In other words, they were not automatically part of the group of 'YHWH's redeemed' (v. 2) or 'sons of Adam' who were celebrating 'his wonderful deeds' (vv. 8, 15, 21, 31).

Does this not mean that the return from exile, such as portrayed in the psalm, had not yet taken place – that the new exodus in question needs to be understood as not having been fulfilled under Zerubbabel, Ezra and Nehemiah? As the original readers were challenged to heed Psalm 107:43, did they not need to understand that the salvation of which the psalm speaks does not apply in any automatic way to Jews? These suggestions certainly square with the reading of the psalm that we have proposed, as also with what we saw in the last chapter regarding the composition of the people of God under the new covenant.[27] It also fits with what we know of the post-exilic period from the testimony of the last three Latter Prophets.[28] One need only reflect on the people's priorities according to Haggai 1:2–4 – their 'panelled houses' as opposed to the house of YHWH[29] – or the prophecy of Zechariah, who *forecasts* the new exodus as a future event (10:8–10), and also forecasts the blessing of all nations (2:15; 8:20–23; 14:16).[30] 'Promises such as those in Isa. 40–55 saw partial fulfillment in the events that followed the fall of Babylon in 539, but only very partial fulfillment.'[31] The new-covenant recapitulation that we find in Psalm 107, including with respect to the return to the land, is eschatological, even from the point of view of the circumstances that prevail on the other side of the Babylonian exile.

Davidic covenant indirectly reaffirmed by virtue of intertextuality (Psalm 107:43)

The closing verse of Psalm 107 calls on the reader to meditate on the '*ḥasdê yhwh*'. It is significant that the only other place in the Psalter in which this

---

[26] For our presuppositions concerning the dating of the Psalter, see p. 7.

[27] See pp. 99–102.

[28] For further discussion, covering Ezra–Nehemiah, see Hely Hutchinson 2022: 225–228.

[29] Or, later, the catalogue of sins listed in Mal. 3:5.

[30] Similarly, Zechariah speaks of a new temple to come (1:16; 6:12–13), whereas Ps. 107:22 seems to presuppose its present existence.

[31] Goldingay 2008: 260. We do not concur with Goldingay in his comments in the paragraph that follows (ibid. 260–261); he understands Ps. 107 to find fulfilment in that post-exilic period.

phrase occurs is the very start of Psalm 89; other than the superscription, these are the opening words of that final psalm of book 3. Yet this is the very covenant faithfulness – regarding the promises made to David – that is called into question in the closing part of Psalm 89 as the psalmist voices his perplexity. As book 5 opens, the Psalter reader is now called upon to understand that YHWH's covenant faithfulness is visible in the shape of the new exodus of which Psalm 107 speaks. 'Whoever is wise' (Ps. 107:43) must grasp the fact that the Davidic covenant remains valid. The authors of other book 3 psalms that had appealed to the God of the exodus from Egypt were wise (cf. Pss 74; 77): the fifth book of the Psalter showcases the new exodus by way of response to the crisis of book 3. The eschatological return from exile that is on view in Psalm 107 is testimony to YHWH's covenant faithfulness – not only that which had been pledged to Abraham, and which is displayed in the realization of the new covenant, but also that which had been promised to David. The Abrahamic, Davidic and new covenants converge in their fulfilment.

Convergence of Abrahamic-, Davidic- and new-covenant fulfilment confirmed (Psalm 118 and immediately preceding context)

New covenant fulfilled (Psalm 118)

The next occurrences of the new-covenant formula frame Psalm 118 (vv. 1, 29). In addition, its short form is repeated three times (*kî lĕʿôlām ḥasdô*), in each of verses 2, 3 and 4. We are familiar with the fact that the formula harks back to Jeremiah 33:11 and thus connotes a return to the land in line with the new covenant;[32] the Psalter reader's mind is all the more filled with this perspective since the use of the formula at the beginning of the opening psalm of book 5 has already underlined this. The new-exodus motif also seems to emerge from the rest of the psalm. Indeed, we should note how Exodus 15:2 is picked up, verse 14 quoting the first half of the verse word for word[33] and other verses also echoing it (see Table 5.4).

---

[32] See pp. 3, 93, 99, 108, 114.
[33] Kidner 1975: 414–415; Schröten 1995: 88; Auwers 2000: 67 n. 210.

Table 5.4 Intertextuality between Exodus 15:2 and Psalm 118

Exod. 15:2	The LORD is my strength and my song; He has become my salvation. This is **my God**, and I will praise Him, my father's God, and **I will exalt** Him. (HCSB)
Ps. 118:14	The LORD is my strength and my song; He has become my salvation. (HCSB)
Ps. 118:28	You are **my God**, and I will give You thanks. You are my **God**; **I will exalt** You. (HCSB)

Further, the salvific action of 'the right hand of YHWH', a phrase which features three times in the psalm (vv. 15–16), calls to mind the same idea in the Song of Moses: 'LORD, Your right hand is glorious in power. LORD, Your right hand shattered the enemy' (Exod. 15:6 HCSB); 'You stretched out Your right hand, and the earth swallowed them' (Exod. 15:12 HCSB).[34]

Abrahamic covenant fulfilled (Psalms 115 – 118)

Themes that are characteristic of the fulfilment of the Abrahamic and Davidic covenants are also present in the psalm. I believe that the group in verse 4 that celebrates YHWH's covenant loyalty, 'those who fear YHWH', encompasses non-Jews. The scholarly debate regarding the referent of this phrase continues.[35] For many, it designates the totality of Israelites – or godly Israelites – without alluding to proselytes. In view of the use of the phrase elsewhere (Ps. 22:23 [MT 22:24]; cf. Ps. 34:7 [MT 34:8]), this may be right.[36] It is, however, probable that, at this point in book 5, the referent is broader and that the links with preceding ('Egyptian Hallel') psalms[37] (Pss 113 – 118) clarify the matter.

The trio that is the object of the exhortation in Psalm 118:2–4 ('Israel', 'house of Aaron', 'those who fear YHWH') features twice in Psalm 115 (vv. 9–11; vv. 12–13).[38] The latter psalm begins (v. 1) by highlighting the

---

[34] The Hebrew term for 'right hand' is *yāmîn* in all these cases.

[35] For a summary of the debate, see Goulder 1998: 170.

[36] Eveson 2015: 297.

[37] For remarks concerning the coherence of this group, see Kidner 1975: 401; cf. also Berder 1996: 92–95 (to his list could be added the transcendence of God in Ps. 113:4 and Ps. 115:3); Prinsloo 2006. Hayes (1999: 148) rightly mentions the strikingly high density of the use of terms for God in this group (more than one occurrence per verse on average).

[38] The syntax of Ps. 115:13 may not strengthen my position. If the second part of the verse, 'small and great alike', explicates 'those who fear YHWH', it needs to be admitted that it does so without specifying a universal dimension.

faithfulness (*ḥesed*) and loyalty (*'ĕmet*) which should inspire praise of YHWH (cf. vv. 15–18). The shortest psalm in the Psalter (Ps. 117), which constitutes the context that immediately precedes the verses that we are considering at the start of Psalm 118, issues an appeal to the nations to praise YHWH for his faithfulness (*ḥesed*) and loyalty (*'ĕmet*), thus echoing Psalm 115 and suggesting to the Psalter reader that the nations should be included among the trio of Psalm 115. By the time we reach Psalm 118:1–4, whose appeal is similar to that of Psalm 117, the matter is settled in the Psalter reader's mind. When, in addition, one notes the links that bind Psalms 116 and 118 at the level of content,[39] thus further supporting the unity of the sequence from Psalm 115 to Psalm 118, it becomes clear that the burden of proof lies with those who would exclude the nations from 'those who fear YHWH' in Psalm 118:4. Finally, we should observe that Psalm 117 echoes Psalm 100, a psalm which also presupposes the salvation of the nations, as we have seen. There is even a strong case to be made for understanding the referent of the first-person plural in Psalm 117:2 to encompass non-Jews ('for great is his *ḥesed* towards us'), in line with what we concluded for the equivalent phenomenon in Psalm 100. Since, however, this vexed question is not critical to our thesis regarding the identity of 'those who fear YHWH' in Psalm 118:4, it need not concern us at this point. We cover it in appendix 5.

In short, the 'Abrahamic' 'all nations' theme is indeed present in this group of psalms: to revisit the perspective of Psalm 107:43, we may affirm that representatives of the nations are among those who prove to be wise in heeding the faithfulness of YHWH – and this means that they participate in the new exodus. Although it is ancillary to our demonstration, we submit that this is precisely what the juxtaposition of Psalms 114 and 115 also suggests. In this book 5 context, mention of Israel's exodus from Egypt (Ps. 114:1) serves not simply to recall that event but also to thrust the Psalter reader's mind forward to its antitype, the new exodus, in which (all) 'those who fear YHWH' (Ps. 115:11, 13) take part.

Davidic covenant fulfilled (Psalm 118)

It remains to be demonstrated that the fulfilment of the Davidic covenant is also a feature of Psalm 118. The psalm 'sets forth a figure who has been

---

[39] In both psalms, a sacrifice of praise/thanksgiving is offered at the temple following an occasion of deliverance, in the face of death, that is orchestrated by YHWH.

delivered from death, having been in the grip of the nations' (vv. 5–21).[40] The people as a whole benefit from this salvation (vv. 2–4, 22–27). Indeed, the individual's affirmation that Yah(weh) 'has become for me salvation' (v. 14) seems to give rise to a collective reaction: 'The voice of joy and salvation is in the tents of the righteous' (v. 15). Later in the psalm, we hear the people again, gathered at the temple (v. 26); they express their joy at something 'wonderful' (v. 23), namely that '[t]he stone the builders rejected has become the cornerstone' (v. 22 NIV). In keeping with what we have already seen, the 'day' for rejoicing (v. 24) corresponds to the time when the new covenant finds fulfilment in the event of the new exodus, and the 'wonderful' thing evokes the refrain of the opening psalm of book 5 (the 'wonderful deeds' of Ps. 107:8, 15, 21, 31).[41]

So, although I do not want to suggest that this psalm is free of exegetical difficulty, it does seem to associate the new exodus with salvation that is attained for the individual figure and the people. The individual seems to represent the nation and is welcomed as its saviour – even as 'the one who comes in the name of YHWH' (v. 26) and whose victory over 'all nations' has been absolute (vv. 10–12). It is difficult not to discern here a Davidic king. At the same time, this figure undergoes rejection and distress – extreme difficulties that are interpreted as severe punishment[42] administered by YHWH (vv. 7, 12, 18, 22). In verse 18, it is possible that we are meant to detect an allusion to the suffering servant whose punishment[43] benefits the people. Our essential point is this: Psalm 118 drives us to consider that the Davidic king will play a key role in the fulfilment of the new covenant. The people are saved thanks to his victory and suffering.[44] And so, in context, the divine faithfulness (*ḥesed*) that is mentioned five times in the psalm (vv. 1–4, 29) amounts to an eloquent response to the perplexity of the end of book 3: YHWH has not abandoned the dynastic promise.

At our next staging post for the new-covenant formula (Ps. 136), the same scenario may be observed, except that the emphasis is greater: the

---

[40] Hely Hutchinson 2013b: 40.

[41] The form of the verb *p-l-ʾ* in Ps. 118:23 is slightly different from that of Ps. 107; see Delitzsch 1889: 215 for analysis.

[42] The severity is suggested by the construction in v. 18 (verb preceded by a reinforcing infinitive absolute of the same root).

[43] The noun *mûsār* of the Fourth Servant Song (Isa. 53:5) is cognate with the verb employed twice in Ps. 118:18.

[44] This ties in with the NT perspective on the psalm which we discuss in Hely Hutchinson 2021a.

fulfilment of the new covenant in the event of the new exodus entails the fulfilment of the Abrahamic and Davidic covenants.

Convergence of Abrahamic-, Davidic- and new-covenant fulfilment confirmed (Psalm 136 and immediately preceding context)

New covenant fulfilled (especially Psalm 136)

In Psalm 136, the full form of the formula is found only once, in the opening verse, but its short form subsequently appears in every verse of the psalm. In other words, YHWH's eternal *ḥesed* is celebrated with remarkable insistence and vigour. The cause for this celebration includes his lordship and work in creation and providence (vv. 2–9, 25), but it is the exodus that takes pride of place – not only the departure from Egypt but also the arrival in Canaan (vv. 10–22).

As one might expect at this stage, it is the *new* exodus and *post-exilic* return to the land that we should have in mind. To be sure, the historical survey in the psalm ends with the first arrival in the land. But we need to take account of (1) the refrain of the psalm, part of the new-covenant formula which we have repeatedly commented on as providing for a permanent solution to the crisis of the exile;[45] (2) the fact that the Psalter reader is conscious of a new return to the land from the opening of book 5; (3) the particular role played by verses 23–24 in suggesting this recapitulation. For here, the first-person plural bursts into the psalm, taking over from the third-person singular. This is the voice of a later generation, and all the signs point to its being the post-exilic generation.[46] Indeed, this is the same phenomenon as the one we have already seen at the end of Psalm 106, a historical psalm that exhibits affinities with Psalm 136: third person (referring to YHWH and the people) gives way to the first-person plural of the prayer 'Save us' (Ps. 106:47; cf. Ps. 106:6). We have already seen that these are the people who experience the new exodus of Psalm 107.[47]

---

45 See pp. 3, 93, 99, 108, 114, 121.
46 Cf. Goldingay 2008: 596.
47 See p. 113.

Further, it is instructive to observe how a second refrain in Psalm 107 connects with Psalm 106 and anticipates Psalm 136. We read four times: 'And they cried to YHWH in their distress (*baṣṣar lāhem*)' (Ps. 107:6, 13, 19, 28) 'and he delivered them (*yaṣṣîlēm*)' (Ps. 107:6 ESV). This recalls Psalm 106:44 ('he looked upon their distress [*baṣṣar lāhem*]'[48] [ESV]) which refers to the 'many times' when YHWH 'delivered them (*yaṣṣîlēm*)' (v. 43). Not only do these observations reinforce the parallel between the new exodus and the prior deliverances but they also invite us to discern a similar recapitulation in Psalm 136: '[YHWH] freed us from our adversaries (*miṣṣārênû*)' (v. 24; the word for 'adversary' is a homonym of the word for 'distress' used in Pss 106 and 107),[49] just as he had done at the time of the exodus from Egypt (vv. 10–15). Again, '[h]e remembered us (*zākar lānû*) in our low estate' (Ps. 136:23 NIV), just as he had previously done many times, including during the exodus from Egypt (we should note the use of *zākar* in this context in Ps. 105:8, 42; cf. Ps. 106:45).

The context that precedes Psalm 136 confirms this interpretation. The 'concatenation' (or chain-linking) that runs through the sequence of Psalms 134 – 136 is striking and impressive[50] and serves to point up the tightness of connection between the Songs of Ascents (Pss 120 – 134) and the two psalms that follow. The exhortation to praise Yah(weh) in Psalm 135 – 'for YHWH is good' (v. 3), in accordance with the new-covenant formula – is grounded in essentially the same truths as in Psalm 136: his lordship, including over creation (vv. 5–7, 15–18), and especially his delivering of his chosen people in the exodus (vv. 4, 8–14). It should be noted that the beginning and end of the psalm (vv. 1–2, 21) throw the spotlight on the presence of YHWH in the temple and the presence of worshippers in Jerusalem.

Psalm 135 'replays' the short preceding psalm, the last Song of Ascents (Ps. 134), in these regards. In this book 5 setting, the Psalter reader cannot understand 'house of YHWH' (Pss 134:1; 135:2; cf. Ps. 122:9) as simply designating a pre-exilic structure. For the Songs of Ascents present Zion

---

[48] This collocation is found only in these five verses and Hos. 5:15.

[49] BDB 865.

[50] And uncontroversial, as quick inspection of the psalms would suggest. Even if there were only the mention of 'servants of YHWH' standing 'in the house of YHWH' in successive psalms (Pss 134 – 135) or only 'Sihon, king of the Amorites' and 'Og, king of Bashan' in successive psalms (Pss 135 – 136), that would be enough for the Psalter reader to be struck. See Hely Hutchinson 2013b: 38 n. 26.

as the terminus of a journey,[51] or probably several journeys, whose starting point is not Egypt. Rather, these journeys begin in Meshek and Kedar (Ps. 120:5), which are both far from Jerusalem and far from each other: the former is to the north-west and the latter to the south and east.[52] It makes sense to understand these places in terms of a merism that metaphorically conveys the totality of faraway locations where exiles[53] are scattered 'among the nations' (Ps. 106:47). But they undertake the journey to their homeland, and they end up arriving in Zion, ultimately 'gathered in from the lands, from the east and from the west, from the north and from the south' (Ps. 107:3 ESV).

Abrahamic covenant fulfilled (Psalm 135)

What indications are there that the new exodus on view in Psalm 136 encompasses non-Jews, in line with the Abrahamic covenant? In Psalm 135:20, we come across the phrase 'those who fear YHWH' (*yir'ê yhwh*). The people in question are called upon to bless him, 'for YHWH is good' (v. 3), and so they need to be seen as being of a piece with those who are called upon to praise YHWH, 'for he is good', two verses later, at the beginning of the twin psalm that follows (Ps. 136:1). We have already commented on the phrase *yir'ê yhwh* in its Psalm 115 and 118 contexts: non-Israelites are incorporated in the referent. Since several verses of Psalm 115 fetch up in Psalm 135,[54] we would need to have a good reason to exclude non-Israelites from the scope of the phrase here. In Psalm 115, the psalmist exhorts 'those who fear YHWH' to put their trust in him (v. 11) and declares that YHWH 'will bless those who fear YHWH' (v. 13), whereas, in Psalm 135, this group is exhorted to 'bless' YHWH (v. 20; the same verb *b-r-k*). Expressed in terms of the logic of the two psalms that immediately precede Psalm 135, they should bless YHWH because they themselves are beneficiaries of YHWH's blessing (Ps. 134:1–3; the verb *b-r-k* is found in each verse), that blessing (*habběrākâ*) being 'life (*hayyîm*), for ever ('*ad-hā'ôlām*)' (Ps. 133:3).

Bearing in mind the chain-linkage in the sequence running from Psalm 133 to Psalm 136,[55] and the fulfilment of the new covenant that is evoked

---

[51] This seems to emerge particularly from Pss 120 – 122; cf. Beaucamp's reading (1979: 252–253). Considerations of movement in the Songs of Ascents are put forward by Prinsloo (2006).

[52] Cf. Delitzsch 1889: 263; Kidner 1975: 430–431; Motyer 1994: 572; Goldingay 2008: 452.

[53] The use of the verb *g-w-r* ('to sojourn') in 120:5 indicates that the psalmist is not at home.

[54] Compare Ps. 115:4–14 with Ps. 135:15–20.

[55] In addition to the striking concatenation across Pss 134 – 136, this link between Pss 133 and 135 is worth noting: they both exhibit parallelism (133:1; 135:3) between *tôb* ('good') and

by the return to Zion, we need to recognize that 'those who fear YHWH' are included in the 'brothers' of Psalm 133:1.

Sinaitic conditionality observed (Psalm 133)

In Psalm 133, a number of covenantal strands come together, and, for our purposes, a consideration of this psalm is peculiarly illuminating. What lies behind the language and concepts of verse 1 is Israelite obedience to the Sinaitic covenant as set forth in Deuteronomy.[56] That covenant required the Israelites to choose 'life (*haḥayyîm*) . . . blessing (*habbĕrākâ*)' (Deut. 30:19). This life is synonymous with YHWH himself, and the blessing is identified with the realization of the Abrahamic promise concerning the land; but 'life . . . blessing' could be attained only if YHWH's commandments were kept:

> I call heaven and earth to witness against you today, that I have set before you life and death, blessing and curse. Therefore choose life, that you and your offspring may live, loving the LORD your God, obeying his voice and holding fast to him, for he is your life and length of days, that you may dwell in the land that the LORD swore to your fathers, to Abraham, to Isaac, and to Jacob, to give them. (Deut. 30:19–20 ESV)

This is precisely what was out of reach for the Israelites under the Sinaitic covenant. Owing to their rebellion, the people could not obtain 'life' and 'blessing': patently, with the advent of the exile, the Abrahamic promise concerning the land was far from being fulfilled. As indicated in the previous chapter,[57] Deuteronomy 30 does, however, specify that, in the event of exile, a return to the land would still be in prospect and, once circumcised of heart, the people would live and enjoy blessing.

Psalm 133 depicts the unity of all who receive 'blessing, life' (*habbĕrākâ ḥayyîm*) from YHWH at Zion (v. 3).[58] It presupposes a return from exile. Unlike the first experience of occupying the land, this scenario is permanent ('*ad-hā'ôlām* [v. 3]). This implies both that the Abrahamic

---

(note 55 *cont.*) *nā'îm* ('pleasant'). We find this parallelism in only one other place in the Psalter (Ps. 147:1) and in one other verse (Job 36:11).

[56] Leow 2017: 193–194 (incl. n. 38).

[57] See pp. 73–74.

[58] It is possible that 'there' (v. 3) refers to the unity of which v. 1 speaks, but the following psalm enables us to understand that the blessing of YHWH comes from Zion.

promises find fulfilment, which includes blessing for the nations (Gen. 12:3; 18:18; 22:18; 26:4; 28:14), and that the Sinaitic conditionality is observed (or, at least, no longer an obstacle). To be sure, the psalm does not spell out a link between the unity it celebrates and circumcision of the heart. But Psalm 119, which immediately precedes the Songs of Ascents, seems to presuppose this spiritual circumcision[59] predicted in Deuteronomy 30 and reiterated by the prophets Jeremiah (31:33) and Ezekiel (11:19–20; 36:26–27) in relation to the new covenant.[60]

New covenant fulfilled in stages (Psalms 119 – 136)

We should not, however, avoid the complexities of the long Psalm 119. It cannot be said of this psalm that it amounts to a wholesale fulfilment of the new covenant, since its author is exposed to persecution (e.g. vv. 81–88). In fact, the psalmist seems to represent the believer who undertakes the journey portrayed by the Songs of Ascents:[61] at the beginning of the psalm (the 'way' [v. 1]) and at the end (the straying, like a lost sheep [v. 176]), his attitude to the *tôrâ* is expressed in terms of movement.[62]

Yet the circumstances envisaged by Psalms 133 – 136 are those of the journey's end, in Zion (cf. Ps. 128:5). The new-covenant formula of Jeremiah 33 and book 5 is found on the lips of those who have arrived 'there'

---

[59] Vv. 2, 10, 11, 34, 36, 58, 69, 80, 111, 112, 145 and 161 enable us to understand that the author of Ps. 119 is committed to keeping YHWH's commandments with all his heart, recalling Deut. 30:6. Other data tie up with this observation; e.g. the psalmist describes YHWH's commandments as his 'delight' (vv. 24, 77, 92, 143, 174; these are the only occurrences in the Psalter of the plural noun *ša'ăšū'îm*).

[60] Hos. 14:4–8 (MT 14:5–9) may be considered an instructive parallel to Ps. 133 in certain respects: YHWH is the source of life-giving blessing in a new-covenant context that presupposes his prior action in the lives of the people: 'I will heal their backsliding' (DBY). This final chapter of the prophecy echoes the first three chapters, which present the same scenario as that which is on view in the Psalter: the Abrahamic, Davidic and new covenants converge in their fulfilment (cf. Hely Hutchinson 2022: 215–219).

[61] Regarding the meaning of the title for this group of psalms (usually *šîr hamma'ălôt*, 'song of the ascents'), Allen has compiled the range of interpretations (2002: 193–195). The use of *ma'ălâ* in Ezra 7:9 (cognate with the verb '*-l-h* which features in a similar context in Ezra 2:1) fits well with our understanding of book 5 of the Psalter: a 'going up' (DBY) or 'journey' (NIV) is undertaken by the exiles in Babylonia. That this could be viewed as a pilgrimage, as might be suggested by the use of the verb '*-l-h* in Isa. 2:3 ('Come, let us go up' [NIV]), need not be ruled out, but the idea of a liturgical procession does not sit well with the new exodus on view in book 5.

[62] For details on the use of this metaphor in Ps. 119, see Brown 2002: 32–34. Nielsen (2001) points up the importance of the juxtaposition of Ps. 119 with the Songs of Ascents and also comments on the use in Ps. 119 of metaphors for the 'way' (but her conclusions seem speculative).

(Ps. 133:3)[63] and who have even come to the 'house of YHWH' (Jer. 33:11; Pss 134:1; 135:2): 'for his covenant faithfulness endures for ever' (throughout Ps. 136).

In keeping with the sequence of Psalms 120 – 134, it seems that we can affirm that the new exodus, to which the journey seems to correspond, is not realized in a punctiliar fashion, but is staggered over a period during which the former exiles' condition is ambiguous. Indeed, it seems necessary to speak of a 'restoration of the fortunes' for the land and the people in a Jeremiah 30 – 33 sense,[64] which is first inaugurated and subsequently consummated. We see this tension between interim and final fulfilment in Psalm 126: Zion's fortunes have been restored (v. 1), yet prayer is made for further restoration of fortunes (v. 4). Or, again, in Psalm 130 terms, forgiveness has been attained (v. 4), but Israel must nurture the hope of 'plentiful redemption' still to come (vv. 5–8).

During this ambiguous period, fulfilment of both the Abrahamic covenant and the new covenant is in progress and on track. This means that more and more people drawn from the nations learn of YHWH: proclamation of YHWH's great acts is made among the nations during this period (cf. Ps. 126:2). It also means that these representatives of the nations make the journey to Zion. Indeed, the Psalter reader who is immersed in the theology of the Latter Prophets may react to Psalm 122:1 ('Let us go to the house of YHWH') by recalling Isaiah 2:3 and Micah 4:2: the prophets had predicted that the nations would stream to Jerusalem following the exile and, in particular, that they would express their intention to go to the temple (*hālak* in these three texts).

Davidic covenant fulfilled, with conditionality satisfied (Psalm 132)

Psalm 136 also evokes the fulfilment of the Davidic covenant. The preceding context is, again, important here. Five of the Songs of Ascents (Pss 122; 124; 127; 131; 133) contain a title whose approximate meaning is 'relating to a recapitulated (/new/eschatological) David/Solomon'.[65] More

---

[63] The attentive Psalter reader is struck by the contrast between the 'there' (*šām*) of this verse, designating Zion, and the same word that features twice in Ps. 137 (vv. 1, 3) to speak of the exilic setting 'by the rivers of Babylon'. But see also the remark in n. 58 above.

[64] For the use of the expression *šûb šĕbût* in that section of Jeremiah, see Hely Hutchinson 2005: 101–105.

[65] See appendix 4.

directly, Psalm 132 refers to the Davidic covenant. This psalm stands out within the Songs of Ascents: in the context of this group, its peculiar length and content strike the reader.[66] At the same time, it coheres with the rest of the group by virtue of its concern for the city of Zion as YHWH's desired dwelling place (v. 13) and the locus of his blessing (vv. 15–16; cf. Pss 133:3; 134:3). Indeed, if the above analysis is correct, this psalm precedes a sequence of four that present the final fulfilment of the new covenant (and the Abrahamic covenant) as going hand in hand with the end of the journey. Psalm 132:7–8 anticipates the arrival in Zion:

> Let us go . . .
> Arise, O LORD, and go to your resting-place,
>   you and the ark of your might.
> (Ps. 132:7–8 ESV)

These verses are a throwback to the transfer of the ark of the covenant from Kiriath-jearim to Jerusalem, narrated in 2 Samuel 6; a few verses later, in Psalm 132:11, we read of the dynastic promise, corresponding to one chapter further on in the Samuel narrative (2 Sam. 7):

> The LORD has sworn to David
> A truth from which He will not turn back:
> 'Of the fruit of your body I will set upon your throne . . .'
> (Ps. 132:11 NASB)

It seems that YHWH's commitment to Zion as his own dwelling place needs to be closely associated with this promise (cf. 2 Sam. 7:13a); 'for ever' ('ădê-'ad) in verse 12, referring to the Davidic throne, finds a parallel in verse 14 where the same phrase refers to YHWH's resting place. From the standpoint of this psalm, the permanent establishment of Zion as YHWH's dwelling is thus indissolubly linked to the permanent establishment of David's throne. Given, as we have seen, that Psalms 133 – 136 present the culmination of the new exodus and resultant state of affairs in Zion by way of definitive response to the exile, and given, therefore, that YHWH's presence in Zion is perpetual (cf. Ps. 133:3), it follows that these psalms also presuppose the parallel reality, namely that the oath sworn to David is fulfilled.

---

[66] For its unique characteristics, see Auwers 1996: 558.

Indeed, these four psalms probably reflect the realization of the promises in the closing verses of Psalm 132. We should consider, in this regard:

1 verse 14: 'here I will dwell' (ESV; cf. Pss 133:3; 134; 135:2, 21);
2 verse 15: 'I will abundantly bless her provisions' (ESV; cf. Pss 133:3 [*habbĕrākâ*, 'blessing']; 134:3 [*yĕbārekĕkā*, 'May he bless you . . . !']);
3 verse 16: 'her godly ones (*ḥăsîdêhā*) will sing aloud for joy' (NASB; cf. the refrain of Ps. 136 which celebrates YHWH's *ḥesed*);
4 verse 18: 'His enemies I will clothe with shame' (ESV; cf. Pss 135:8–11; 136:10, 17–20).

Even if there is no explicit linkage between verse 17 and the four psalms that follow, it would not be possible to understand that the promise of this verse – concerning 'a horn for David . . . a lamp for [YHWH's] messiah' – could be set aside. Perhaps, though, there is an implicit parallel that the Psalter reader should discern between the 'there' of the end of Psalm 132 and the 'there' of the end of Psalm 133 (*šām* in both cases, designating Zion in both cases[67]) (see Table 5.5). If this is right, the messiah may be considered the channel that YHWH employs to bestow the blessing (cf. Gen. 12:2–3).[68] Either way, the praise to which worshippers of YHWH are called in Psalm 136 does not bypass the realization of the Davidic covenant.

Table 5.5 A possible parallel between the endings of Psalm 132 and Psalm 133

Psalm 132:17	*Psalm 133:3b*
There I will cause a horn to sprout up for David; I have prepared a lamp for my anointed one. (NRSV)	For **there** the LORD has commanded the blessing, life for evermore. (ESV)

It will be recalled that the conditional dimension of the Davidic covenant is not mentioned in Psalm 89.[69] Psalm 132 does include it:

If your sons keep my covenant
and the statutes I teach them,

---

[67] Although recall the possibility mentioned in n. 58 above.
[68] Cf. our discussion of this theme in relation to Ps. 21 (see p. 37).
[69] Cf. Table 3.5 on p. 49 and discussion on pp. 47–51.

then their sons shall sit
> on your throne for ever and ever.
(Ps. 132:12 NIV)

This 'if' has the power to explain the exile and thus roll back some of the perplexity of the psalmist at the end of book 3. But the preceding verse 11b must remain valid: 'Of the fruit of your body I will set upon your throne . . .' (NASB): YHWH has sworn an oath in this regard, irrevocably (v. 11a). The juxtaposition of these two verses implies that the dynastic promise, though inviolable, will reach fulfilment only in a messiah who upholds the stipulations of the Sinaitic covenant (cf. Ps. 101 and the character of the new David as presented in book 5 and discussed below). Psalm 132:17 corroborates our reading by virtue of its allusion to Jeremiah 33:15 (see Table 5.6).[70]

Table 5.6 An allusion in Psalm 132 to the messianic promise in Jeremiah 33:15

Psalm 132:17a	Jeremiah 33:15*
There I will **cause** a horn **to sprout up for David** (NRSV)	In those days and at that time I will **cause** a Righteous Branch **to sprout up for David**, and He will administer justice and righteousness in the land. (HCSB)

* Cf. also 2 Sam. 23:5 (although the sense is not immediately obvious); Jer. 23:5 (although the verb *q-w-m* is used); Ezek. 29:21 (although the link with David is not explicit).

Psalm 132 thus indicates how two apparently contradictory notions can be reconciled. The Sinaitic conditionality (that we find, for example, in Ps. 78)[71] and the Davidic unconditionality of Psalm 89 are not, ultimately, at variance with each other. Although new-covenant newness is partly defined relative to the Sinaitic covenant, whose conditionality is removed for a people who could never observe it, that conditionality is not taken away as such. On the contrary, without its being satisfied, the new covenant would never prove to be fulfilled. It is imperative that the law be kept. Only a perfectly obedient messiah will suffice. Psalm 132,

---

[70] The bold items in the table are identical between the two passages, although the syntax is slightly different.
[71] See pp. 53–54.

which responds to Psalm 89 more directly than any other individual psalm,[72] ends on the confident note that the Davidic crown (*nēzer*), though 'defiled . . . in the dust' at the exile (Ps. 89:39 ESV [MT 89:40]), will be restored (Ps. 132:18).[73]

If it be asked why the king should be only *implicitly* present in Psalms 133 – 136, the answer may lie with the aim that the redactor–compiler of the Psalter has in mind in relation to his post-exilic readership. For these recipients of the Psalter had access to the temple in Jerusalem, but there was no king. Although Psalms 133 – 136 bespeak the final fulfilment of the new covenant, the post-exilic community would have been able to appropriate the content of these psalms ahead of time: they would have been in a position to seek to put into practice the ideal set forth in Psalm 133 and the calls to praise in Psalms 134 – 136. That would mean that Psalms 119 – 136 would have a similar aim to that of Chronicles in terms of inciting the post-exilic returnees to seek the consummation of the kingdom against the background of a rebuilt temple but a messiah whose arrival needed to be anticipated.[74]

That said, we should not shy away from the fact that Zion and messiah are *twin* concepts in Psalm 132. Nor should we underestimate the imposing 'presence' of the new David in book 5. We move on to consider how the 'Of David' psalms in this closing book function.

David recapitulated in a superior antitype (Psalms 108 – 110; 138 – 145)

There are two groups of *lĕdāwid* ('Of David') psalms that frame book 5 (Pss 108 – 110; Pss 138 – 145). We have already signalled that the Psalter reader is led to focus on an eschatological David and not simply the David of the generation immediately following Jesse.[75] The absence of historical information relating to that David of 1000 BC is noteworthy given the number of book 5 psalms that carry *lĕdāwid* in the title. It is all the more striking since these psalms echo the sufferings and achievements of David, son of Jesse, especially as presented in book 2 psalms, many of whose titles *do* contain historical notes relating to the life of the king. Psalm 140, for

---

[72] Veijola (1982: 49, 72–75) notes twenty-eight points of contact between the two psalms.
[73] Cf. Gosse 2002: 196.
[74] See appendix 3.
[75] See appendix 4.

example, recalls five Davidic psalms from book 2,[76] and substantial parts of Psalms 57 and 60 come together to form Psalm 108.[77]

Victory, judgment and suffering intensified

It is instructive to study these 'reworkings' in their new context. Psalm 57 is picked up not only in Psalm 108 – the opening 'Of David' psalm in book 5 – but also in Psalm 142. If the latter were to be considered without reference to Psalter context, it could be taken to be an exception to the rule that historical information relating to David, son of Jesse, is absent from the titles of book 5. Indeed, we are told that this psalm concerns the time 'when he was in the cave' (Ps. 142 heading [MT 142:1]). Given, however, that this title echoes that of Psalm 57, which itself undergoes a transposition in the first Davidic psalm of book 5, and is also picked up in subsequent *lĕdāwid* psalms in this book,[78] the Psalter reader is sensitized to the need to interpret Psalm 142 intertexually.

We start by considering how the transposition in Psalm 108 works. This psalm essentially combines Psalm 57:7–11 (MT 57:8–12) and Psalm 60:5–12 (MT 60:7–14). Thus, five of Psalm 57's verses (out of eleven, or twelve including the heading) are quoted in Psalm 108. By omitting the other verses, Psalm 108 removes all reference to individual distress,[79] retaining only the notes of confidence and victory.[80] As Longman states:

> While Psalm 57 is an individual lament and Psalm 60 a corporate
> lament, Psalm 108 is a psalm of assurance that reapplies the previous

---

[76] Regarding Ps. 140:3 (MT 140:4): cf. Pss 52:2 (MT 52:4); 57:4 (MT 57:5); 58:4 (MT 58:5); 64:3 (MT 64:4). Regarding Ps. 140:4 (MT 140:5): cf. Ps. 71:4 (the preceding Ps. 70, to which Ps. 71 is tied, is *lĕdāwid*). Regarding Ps. 140:5 (MT 140:6): cf. Pss 57:6 (MT 57:7); 64:5 (MT 64:6). In a similar vein, I discuss Ps. 144 below. 'Perhaps Pss 118 and 135 could be added to this list, although they contain fewer allusions to other psalms' (Hely Hutchinson 2013b: 41 n. 34). We also consider Ps. 138 below (see p. 137).

[77] Regarding Ps. 108, Kidner (1975: 387) remarks: 'The fact that the term *God* is used by itself frequently in this psalm, but in only one other place in this Fifth Book of the Psalter (Ps 144:9), makes it clear that the present psalm is the borrower from the other two, not the lender, since Book II, in which they occur, strongly prefers this title to "the Lord"'; emphasis original. Beaucamp (1979: 180) comments similarly (although I do not subscribe to his late dating of Pss 42 – 83).

[78] Ps. 138:8, cf. Ps. 57:2 (MT 57:3); Ps. 140:3 (MT 140:4), cf. Ps 57:4 (MT 57:5); Ps. 140:5 (MT 140:6), cf. Ps 57:6 (MT 57:7).

[79] As Broyles remarks (1999: 411). Likewise, as Broyles also mentions (ibid.), the lament of Ps. 60 does not fetch up in Ps. 108.

[80] There is one verse in Ps. 57 among those that are omitted by Ps. 108 whose outlook is positive (v. 5 [MT v. 6]), but it corresponds to the refrain that recurs in v. 11 (MT v. 12) and is picked up in Ps. 108:5 (MT 108:6).

psalms to produce a prayer 'for Yahweh's final, eschatological "day of vengeance" when he establishes his lordship among the nations.'[81]

Indeed, in Psalm 108, 'David' celebrates YHWH's faithfulness (*ḥesed*) and loyalty (*'ĕmet*) and thus reaffirms what had been called into question in Psalm 89 regarding the dynastic promise. He proclaims these realities among the nations, a move which lies in the trajectory of the fulfilment of the Abrahamic promise of blessing for all nations (vv. 2–4 [MT vv. 3–5]). At the same time, to the extent that the nations are his adversaries, this king will crush them and lay claim to their territories (vv. 7–13 [MT vv. 8–14]).

By contrast, in Psalm 142, we encounter distress of an intensity that is, in places, comparable to that of Psalm 88 ('my spirit grows faint within me . . . no one is concerned for me. I have no refuge; no one cares for my life' [Ps. 142:3–4 NIV (MT 142:4–5)]). This distress outstrips that of the psalm of David 'in the cave' (Ps. 57 heading [MT 57:1]) from book 2. Thus the recapitulation operates on a higher plane relative to the experience of the David of 1000 BC and does so in both directions: in Psalm 108 total victory over the enemies is envisaged, while in Psalm 142 the distress is magnified.

By this stage in our study, it is unsurprising that there should be such an escalation between the David of books 1–2 and the David of book 5. Indeed, it seems significant that the mention of Saul in the title of Psalm 57 does not fetch up in the title of Psalm 142. This chimes in with our understanding that the historical episode in the cave that David (immediate son of Jesse) experienced has been recast for a new context in which the 'David' of book 5 exhibits features of the antitype. For this new David – who is tied, according to the context of this final book, to the new exodus and the new covenant – the victory takes on a new dimension, but so too does the suffering. So, inasmuch as Psalm 142 sets forth a recapitulated David, antitype of the David of the generation immediately following Jesse, this psalm is no exception to the rule that book 5 does not present historical information in the titles.

Given that the recapitulation of original historical events entails an intensification or a move into a superior sphere, it is not incidental that the strongest imprecations are found in book 5 (Pss 109; 137). Although

---

the latter is not a *lĕdāwid* psalm, it is attached[82] to a group of Davidic psalms that contain imprecations (Pss 139:19; 140:8–11 [MT 140:9–12]; 141:6[83]). It should be recognized that, under the new covenant, not only is the new-exodus salvation more glorious than the deliverance from Egypt but also – and this is the other side of the coin – YHWH's judgment of his enemies is more terrifying. We have already noted the promise that YHWH will clothe the king's enemies with shame (Ps. 132:18) and the realization of this promise in Psalms 135 – 136; it is appropriate that in Psalm 109 we hear the David of the new covenant[84] calling down divine curses on his adversaries,[85] for this is one of the roles he fulfils as messiah (Ps. 110:6; cf. Ps. 2:6–9). Indeed, this presages the fulfilment of the covenant with Abram: 'I will bless those who bless you, and him who dishonours you I will curse' (Gen. 12:3 ESV). It may be that Psalm 109:28 alludes to this verse: 'Let them curse, but you will bless!' (ESV).[86] We should also notice the vocabulary of the new covenant that underlies the prayer offered up by the new David: 'because your steadfast love is good [*kî ṭôb ḥasdĕkā*], deliver me!' (Ps. 109:21 ESV; cf. v. 26).

The first *lĕdāwid* psalm of the second (and larger) 'David' group of book 5, Psalm 138, strikingly reinforces the perspective of the first *lĕdāwid* psalm of the first group that we have already considered (Ps. 108). It borrows from a number of David psalms from books 1 and 2 (as well as from other psalms).[87] The psalmist gives thanks to the name of YHWH in view of his faithfulness (*ḥesed*) and loyalty ('*ĕmet*), expressing his desire that 'all the kings of the earth' should similarly give thanks after hearing YHWH's words (vv. 2, 4). The last verse contains an echo of the new-covenant formula that plays such an important part in this final book of the Psalter: 'YHWH, your *ḥesed* is for ever' (*yhwh ḥasdĕkā lĕ'ôlām* [v. 8]).

King combined with righteous suffering servant

Book 5 stands out from books 1 and 2 in another important respect: we are not told that David suffers as a result of his sin. In book 1, David's sin

---

[82] See Hely Hutchinson 2013b: 38 n. 27.

[83] Strictly speaking, this verse constitutes a prediction rather than a prayer. The same is true of Ps. 143:12.

[84] I do not, however, affirm that in every *lĕdāwid* psalm in book 5 the new David is the speaker. Patently, this is not the case for Ps. 110 (cf. Mark 12:36–37).

[85] Cf. Berthoud 2001.

[86] Cf. Harman 1995: 67.

[87] The book 1 and 2 psalms on Schaefer's helpful (2001: 324) list are (allowing for one or two typographical adjustments) 5:7 (MT 5:8); 9:1 (MT 9:2); 23:4; 57:2 (MT 57:3); 68:32 (MT 68:33).

problem emerges explicitly in a section seemingly delimited by the alphabetic acrostics Psalms 25 and 34[88] (see Pss 25:7, 11, 18; 32) and becomes more sustained and pronounced in the final section of that book (Pss 38:1–5, 18 [MT 38:2–6, 19];[89] 39:1, 8, 11 [MT 39:2, 9, 12]; 40:12 [MT 40:13]; 41:4 [MT 41:5]). In book 2, the problem is further accentuated from the outset as David the adulterer and murderer appears in the first lĕdāwid psalm (Ps. 51). But the David of book 5 calls to mind the David–Solomon of the first two books who is a moral paragon (Pss 18; 45; 72).[90] Certain texts might suggest (at most) that he could, in principle, have sinned against YHWH (Pss 139:24; 141:3–4; 143:2), but even these verses form part of the picture of a David who is concerned to be beyond reproach, and none of these psalms indicates that he is guilty, despite his suffering.

It is true that 'no one living is righteous before [YHWH]' (Ps. 143:2 NIV), but this figure belongs nonetheless to the category 'righteous' (cf. Pss 140:13 [MT 140:14]; 142:7 [MT 142:8]). He is loving towards enemies who attack him gratuitously (Ps. 109:2–5). He looks to know the will of the God he worships so as to put it into practice, being led by YHWH's 'good Spirit' (Ps. 143:10). The Psalter reader's mind is drawn to the righteous David of Psalm 18:20–24 [MT 18:21–25]; indeed, 'the David of Psalm 18'[91] comes to be on display in Psalm 144 (to which we will return) as book 5 draws to a close.[92]

Taking account of the fact that he is described four times as the servant ('ebed) of YHWH (Pss 109:28; 143:2, 12; 144:10),[93] might it not be right to discern here – in the righteous David who suffers unjustly – the suffering servant figure who has already emerged from our study of Psalm 102? The combination of king and servant that we detected in Psalm 118[94] is apparently not an isolated case in book 5.

---

[88] Hely Hutchinson 2013b: 29 n. 12. This theme may already be present in Ps. 6, by deduction from v. 1 (MT v. 2). See following note.

[89] It is worth noting the echo of Ps. 6:1 (MT 6:2) that we find in Ps. 38:1 (MT 38:2). Given that the vocabulary of these two opening verses is almost identical, the Psalter reader is invited to compare the two psalms. The idea that David has sinned may underlie Ps. 6, but it does not feature on the surface. By contrast, in Ps. 38 David's sin is vividly spelled out. This datum ties in with the broader observation that the sin problem becomes clearer as book 1 unfolds.

[90] See p. 36.

[91] Kidner 1975: 477.

[92] I take Ps. 145 to be simultaneously the concluding psalm of book 5 and the appropriate transition to the concluding doxology of the Psalter represented by the last five psalms. Cf. Wilson 1985: 189, 193–194.

[93] The presence of this title per se is not a major component of our demonstration. Pierre Grelot (1962: 378) is right to point out that the term has a broad usage.

[94] See p. 124.

Levitical covenant fulfilled by a superior priesthood – combined with kingship (Psalm 110)

The psalms that conclude these 'Of David' groups (Pss 110; 144 – 145) appear to have climactic significance and are of particular importance in terms of elucidating the newness of the new covenant. Their placement coheres with that of other psalms that are structurally prominent and that are royal and/or deal with matters of covenant relationships (see our treatment of Pss 2; 45;[95] 72; 89; 103 – 106).[96]

In keeping with the perspective of Psalm 2,[97] the king of Psalm 110 rules in Zion, and is absolutely victorious over his enemies, crushing kings on the day of wrath (vv. 2, 5–6). The ambiguity in verse 5 (whose wrath – that of YHWH or the king?) recalls, again, Psalm 2 and other portraits of the new-covenant king:[98] the clear distinction between YHWH and the psalmist's 'lord'[99] is evident in verse 1 but not in verses 5–6.[100] While these two figures operate in harmony, ultimate authority lies with YHWH: it is he who delegates power to the king and instals him as priest for ever (*lĕ'ôlām*) – by an irrevocable oath (v. 4; cf. Ps. 132:11).[101]

---

[95] It is true that Ps. 45 is not the first psalm in book 2, but it is the first psalm to follow the crisis with which book 2 opens (Pss 42 – 44).

[96] This observation regarding the strategic placement of psalms that deal with covenant relationships is a reminder that our quest in this book is not peripheral to the Psalter's design. Cf. our remark to this effect, tied to Ps. 2's introductory role, towards the beginning of chapter 3 (see p. 26).

[97] One may be tempted to follow the numerous exegetes who discern in the last word of verse 3 an echo of Ps. 2:7 ('I have begotten you', as opposed to MT's 'your youth'); there is even considerable external support for this (including many Hebrew manuscripts and LXX). Aside from the danger of being influenced by Ps. 2 (cf. Coppens 1955: 10), on my understanding of the structure of the psalm (see n. 100 below) it is unlikely that YHWH is the speaker in v. 3: his declarations are limited to vv. 1 and 4.

[98] Cf. our discussion of this theme in chapter 3 (see pp. 29–30) and appendix 2.

[99] The enhanced clarity afforded by the NT (cf. Calvin 1960: 446 [*Inst*. II.X.20]) reveals that the king of Ps. 110 is David's Lord (Mark 12:36–37). This is in line with my contention in this chapter that book 5 sets forth the antitype of David, son of Jesse – a new, superior David.

[100] I presuppose that the referent of 'my/the lord' (*'ădōnî/'ădōnāy*) is constant between vv. 1 and 5 – as is also his position at the right hand of YHWH. The third-person singular thus designates the king throughout the last three verses of the psalm. According to this reading, the king is addressed concerning YHWH after the first oracle (vv. 2–3) and YHWH is addressed concerning the king after the second oracle (vv. 5–7). This squares with our view that it is the son's wrath that is spoken of in Ps. 2:12 (cf. Ps. 110:5: 'on the day of his [sc. the king's] wrath'). For a discussion of other interpretations of Ps. 110, see Allen 2002: 117.

[101] There is much to stimulate readers in Emadi's recent study of this psalm. Since, however, I believe that Psalter context drives us to see the king on view in this psalm as being tied to

In our discussion of Psalm 106, we highlighted the need (which emerges from the relentless repetition of the cycle of human sin followed by divine wrath) for intercession that is total in its scope, permanent in its effectiveness and sin-free in its administration.[102] We also noted that Psalm 106 reaffirms the Levitical covenant which provides for a perpetual priesthood.[103] With a greater or lesser degree of directness, these themes come together in Psalm 110.[104] Here is the mediator who is superior to Moses and Phinehas. The significance of the new order of priesthood, that of Melchizedek, is not spelled out, but YHWH's oath does draw attention to its permanence (v. 4). That this priest obtains total forgiveness for the people is an idea consistent with the fact that he is simultaneously the king who fulfils a key role in the new exodus, for the link between total pardon and the new exodus is established by Psalm 130:

If you, O LORD, should mark iniquities,
    O Lord, who could stand?
But with you there is forgiveness,
    that you may be feared.
(Ps. 130:3–4 ESV)

O Israel, hope in the LORD!
    For with the LORD there is steadfast love,
    and with him is plentiful redemption.
And he will redeem Israel
    from all his iniquities.
(Ps. 130:7–8 ESV)

Under the old (Sinaitic) covenant, it was unthinkable that the two offices of Davidic king and Aaronic priest could be combined in the one person (cf. 2 Chr. 26:16–23).[105] This perpetual priesthood forms part of a radically

---

[102] See pp. 86–87.

[103] See pp. 87–92.

[104] The irreproachable character of the king is not directly indicated in Ps. 110 itself.

[105] Blocher (2002: 245) points out that '[f]rom the time of the official institution of the priesthood, and then of the monarchy ... the two offices were only ever confused by dint of transgression of the *Tôrâ*'.

(note 101 *cont.*) the new covenant (as we have been seeing in this chapter), I do not share his view (2022: 112–123) that we need to work out how and when YHWH swore the oath of verse 4 to *David*, son of Jesse. On my analysis, the parallels with Ps. 2 to which he draws attention (cf. his table [ibid. 99]) reinforce my stance, since I believe that Ps. 2 sets forth new-covenant theology (cf. my pp. 26–35).

new regime that appears both to fulfil and to transcend the exigencies of the Levitical-covenantal order. The problem of sin (of Gen. 3 – 11) which, according to book 4, is bound together with the problem of the exile,[106] finds its solution as David's seed (*zeraʿ*) combines the functions of priesthood and kingship. The Levitical covenant needs to reach fulfilment alongside that of the Davidic covenant, exactly as our reading of book 4 indicated.[107] The structurally prominent Psalm 110 does seem to respond to the concerns of the structurally prominent Psalm 106 which in turn has already paved the (Abrahamic) way towards a solution to the crisis of Psalm 89.

Yet Psalm 110 does not bear the full weight of this king-priest theme within the Psalter. In addition to the intercessory role carried out by the servant of Psalm 102 (who is also the king of Ps. 101), and the way in which the 'pedagogy of failure' device of Psalm 106 anticipates the superior priesthood,[108] it may well be that the end of Psalm 132 points to a sacerdotal role for the messiah. The use of the rare verb *ṣûṣ* in relation to the crown (*nēzer*) of the Davidic king (Ps. 132:18) recalls the use of the cognate noun *ṣîṣ* in relation to the turban worn by the high priest.[109] This golden object, perhaps resembling a flower, was attached to the turban (Exod. 28:36–37), equating to a 'holy crown' (*nēzer-haqqōdeš* [Exod. 39:30; Lev. 8:9]) and bearing the inscription 'Holy to YHWH'. Further, in the narrative of Numbers 17:1–13 (MT 17:16–28), YHWH demonstrates the divine origin of the authority of the high priest in the 'contest of the staffs' (Num. 17:8 [MT 17:23]):[110] 'On the next day Moses went into the tent of the testimony, and behold, the staff of Aaron for the house of Levi had sprouted and put forth buds and produced blossoms (*wayyāṣēṣ ṣîṣ*), and it bore ripe almonds' (ESV).

These associations between the root *ṣ-w-ṣ* and the authority of the high priest align well with the context of Psalm 132:18 in which YHWH promises to clothe the messiah's enemies with shame. We conclude that it is appropriate to see here in Psalm 132 the same confluence of royalty and priesthood that Psalm 110 sets forth more directly.

---

[106] See pp. 76–78.
[107] See pp. 87–92.
[108] See pp. 86–87.
[109] Cf. Eveson 2015: 413.
[110] Cf. Kidner 1975: 452.

Priesthood democratized (Psalms 118; 134 – 135)

Under this new regime, it seems that the priesthood is democratized. I recognize that this is less clear in book 5 than other aspects of the Melchizedekian order, but there are several data that need to be reckoned with. These are outlined below.

1. Already in book 4, in Psalm 100, the nations are invited to enter the temple courts (v. 4; cf. Ps. 117), apparently enjoying the same status as Jews – and even Levites.

2. What group of people is present in the temple in Psalm 118:26b? Could it not encompass 'those who fear YHWH' (v. 4)? Do they not penetrate 'as far as the horns of the altar' (v. 27)?

3. Who are the 'servants of Yahweh who stand in the house of Yahweh, in the courts of the house of [their] God' (Ps. 135:1–2 HCSB)? Do they not include 'those who fear YHWH' (v. 20)? Indeed, we should note that the phrase 'his servants' (*'ăbādāyw* [v. 14]) stands in parallel with 'his people' (v. 14), bearing a broad connotation by virtue of its being defined over against the 'servants' of Pharaoh (*'ăbādāyw* [v. 9]).

4. In the preceding psalm, some[111] consider that 'servants of YHWH' (Ps. 134:1) refers to the Levites who needed to carry out their particular duties 'during the nights'. There are, however, several factors that point in the direction of a wider referent here: the chain-linking between Psalms 134 and 135;[112] the seemingly broad designation of the same phrase 'servants of YHWH',[113] and in a similar context, in Psalm 113:1 (which is a parallel text to Ps. 135:1, already considered);[114] the inclusion of the word 'all' before '[the] servants of YHWH' in Psalm 134:1; the fact that this

---

[111] Including the great scholars Calvin (1859: 511), Delitzsch (1889: 319) and Kidner (1975: 454).

[112] See p. 126.

[113] The data of the psalm itself do not suggest a limited referent, and our reading, above, of the group of psalms of which it forms a part (related to the new exodus) implies that the 'servants' correspond to the people of YHWH in general.

[114] The differences between the two verses are minimal: compare 'Hallelujah! Praise, ye servants of Jehovah, praise the name of Jehovah' (Ps. 113:1 DBY) with 'Hallelujah! Praise the name of Jehovah; praise, ye servants of Jehovah' (Ps. 135:1 DBY).

concluding 'Ascents' psalm is associated with the climax of the journey to Zion which is undertaken by every servant of YHWH.[115]

So what does it mean for 'all the servants' to be in the temple 'during the nights' (Ps. 134:1)? I find it hard to resist the conclusion that this alludes to the democratization of the priesthood under the new covenant. Whereas the privilege of drawing near to God belonged to Levites under the old regime, it seems that the permanent priesthood 'after the order of Melchizedek' (Ps. 110:4 ESV), taken on by the messiah in this new regime, provides for such access to be granted to all worshippers of YHWH.

Blessings democratized (Psalm 144)

It will be recalled that in Psalm 18 the *historical David* enjoys some considerable measure of the fulfilment of promises that apply to his *son* and that ultimately go hand in hand with the realization of the *new* covenant.[116] Psalm 18 has pride of place among the psalms that are picked up in Psalm 144.[117] Given the new-covenant outlook of book 5, this is, perhaps, unsurprising. But here in book 5, a transposition occurs. Despite some ambiguity, the data of Psalm 18 required us to view that book 1 psalm as anchored in the Davidic covenant: as we mentioned, it does not, for example, reflect the democratization relative to the Davidic covenant that characterizes the new covenant of Isaiah 55 or Psalm 2. Here, however, in Psalm 144, that democratization is clearly on view. Having given 'salvation to kings' and, in particular, to 'David, his servant', YHWH recapitulates his salvific action on behalf of the speaker (v. 11), the new David (Ps. 144 heading [MT 144:1]), which gives rise to covenant blessings for the community of YHWH's people (vv. 12–15).[118] The latter verses, with which the psalm climaxes, evoke the blessings of the Sinaitic covenant as enumerated in Leviticus 26 and Deuteronomy 28.[119] These blessings proved to be

---

[115] If our comments above regarding the juxtaposition of Ps. 119 with the Songs of Ascents are on target, it is instructive to note the recurrence (fourteen times) of the term 'servant' in Ps. 119. The psalmist of Ps. 119, a servant of YHWH, corresponds to the believer of Pss 120 – 134 who undertakes the new-exodus journey.

[116] See pp. 36–38.

[117] Cf. Hamilton 2021c: 486–488.

[118] It would seem that there is a causal link between the individual's prayer and the community's being blessed. The syntax of the beginning of v. 12 is not without difficulty (cf. Gerstenberger 2001: 430; Terrien 2003: 901), but *'ăšer* (v. 12) seems to fulfil a final/purpose function (Joüon §168f, p. 519) or consecutive/result function (Joüon §169f. 521); cf. Kidner 1975: 479 n. 2.

[119] Thus, *inter alia*, Beaucamp 1979: 297–298; Goldingay 2008: 689; VanGemeren 2008: 987; Hossfeld and Zenger 2012: 182; Eveson 2015: 474; Bullock 2017: 543; Hamilton 2021c: 491.

unattainable under that regime, but the new covenant provides the solution. Significantly, there is no danger of a return to the curses of the Sinaitic covenant: a second exile is ruled out, as we read in verse 14 ('no breach, no going out': *'ên-pereṣ wě'ên yôṣē't*).[120]

Book 5 thus concludes (ahead of its doxology in the following psalm) with the perspective of the fulfilment of the new covenant, the people enjoying the blessings of prosperity and security. Verses 12–14 have a different character from the rest of the psalm but are reminiscent of texts such as Amos 9:11–15, Psalm 72:16 and Psalm 132:13–15 which reflect the convergence between the fulfilment of the Abrahamic and Davidic covenants.[121] The double use of 'happy' (*'ašrê*) in verse 15 takes on a new-covenant flavour, and, in the light of its counterpart at the other end of the Psalter (Ps. 1:1 with Ps. 2:12),[122] ties in with our interpretation of Psalm 2 that those who take refuge in the son are beneficiaries of the new covenant.[123] Perhaps we should even discern in the last clause of the psalm an equivalent, appropriate for a psalm-praise context, of the pan-scriptural covenant formula 'I will be your God, you will be my people'[124] (e.g. Gen. 17:7–8; Exod. 6:7; Lev. 26:12; Jer. 31:33; Ezek. 36:28; 37:27; Hos. 2:23 [MT 2:25]): 'Happy are the people who have YHWH as their God!' (Ps. 144:15).[125]

---

[120] In other words, the inverse of the threat of exile: compare the language of Amos 4:3 (*ûpĕrāṣîm tēṣe'nâ*: 'And you shall go out through the breaches' [ESV]). Cf. Delitzsch 1889: 392; Dahood 1970: 333; Ziegler 1973; Tournay 1984: 522; Broyles 1999: 503; Goldingay 2008: 690; Grogan 2008: 223 ('national security against foreign invasion'); Vesco 2008b: 1335; Eveson 2015: 474; Ross 2016: 903; Bullock 2017: 543; Ash 2018: 281.

[121] Regarding Ps. 72, cf. pp. 42–45; regarding Ps. 132, cf. pp. 130–134. Regarding Amos 9, v. 11 refers to the Davidic covenant, while v. 12 echoes the Abrahamic promise of Gen. 22:17 (cf. also Acts 15:14–19).

[122] For other ways in which 'Psalm 144 recollects Psalm 2', see Snearly 2016: 166.

[123] Further, it confirms the fact that meditating on the *tôrâ* in the sense that we advocate for Pss 1 – 2 (as the introduction for the Psalter) leads to new-covenant blessing. See Hely Hutchinson 2013b: 25–28 (and cf. the double 'happy' [*'ašrê*] in Ps. 119:1).

[124] Which we have had occasion to note in relation to Ps. 50 (cf. chapter 3, n. 97, and Ps. 100 (p. 93).

[125] If I underline the new-covenant 'democratization' of the blessings relative to the Davidic covenant, it should be apparent that I do not mean, contra Auwers (1996: 552, citing Wellhausen) that the 'messiah' of Ps. 132:10 corresponds to the post-exilic community. Nor, though, do I follow those who see in this verse a pre-exilic successor to David. Against the background of 2 Sam. 7: 21, 25–26, David prays in the light of the promises of 2 Sam. 7:11b–16, referring to himself in the third person. The meaning of Ps. 132:10 is as follows: 'For the sake of the promise made to David, do not reject his prayer!' We find the same parallelism between 'David' and 'messiah' in v. 17 – which highlights the perspective of his prayer being answered.

YHWH's 'Abrahamic' *ḥesed* reiterated in the last 'David' psalm (Psalm 145)

Psalm 145, which closes book 5 by way of doxology, spotlights the Abrahamic covenant as a reason for ascribing praise to YHWH, the one who is 'great and most worthy of praise' (v. 3). The psalm celebrates the rule of YHWH over his entire creation, and his providence in this regard. Yet allusions to his intervention in redemptive history are also apparent: YHWH is the saviour of 'those who fear him' (v. 19) and the destroyer of 'all the wicked' (v. 20). It is verse 8 that alludes most clearly to the covenant with Abraham: YHWH is 'gracious and compassionate, slow to anger and great in' *ḥesed* (HCSB). This formula recalls, once again, Moses' intercession for the people at the time of the golden calf episode (Exod. 34:6) and at Kadesh-barnea (Num. 14:18–19); Psalms 90 and 106 have already drawn the Psalter reader's attention to the importance of this mediation, grounded in the promises to Abraham, in terms of offering hope to the wayward exiles.[126] We may recall too that the Exodus 34:6 formula also features in Psalm 103 which corresponds to the answer to Moses' prayer in Psalm 90.[127] We even came across this formula in Psalm 86 where the Psalter reader can begin to glimpse a brighter future than the exile for YHWH's people.[128] That book 3 psalm is also the one that requires the Psalter reader to consider what 'David' might refer to in a post-David-son-of-Jesse context.[129] At this stage in the progressive revelation of the Psalter, it would be difficult to read the *ḥesed*-affirming Exodus 34:6 formula in any way other than in terms of a response to the crisis of the exile.

It turns out that the psalmist's perplexity regarding the apparent absence of YHWH's *ḥesed* in Psalm 89 is answered in this *Abrahamic* formula as found in the last *Davidic* psalm of *each of the last three books of the Psalter* (Pss 86; 103; 145).

We have been observing, again and again in book 5, that the Abrahamic, Davidic and new covenants converge in their fulfilment. This is also what we find in the Psalter's concluding doxology (or 'Final Hallel' [Pss 146 – 150]),[130] to which we now turn.

---

[126] Cf. our discussion in chapter 4 (see pp. 71–72).

[127] See chapter 4, p. 108, including n. 194.

[128] See pp. 55–56. For an extensive discussion of this formula in the Psalter, see Hensley 2018: 209–254.

[129] See appendix 4.

[130] Snearly (2016: 173) explains that '[t]he most popular proposal is that Psalms 146–150 are the conclusion to the Psalter'. He provides a defence for the cohesion of this group (ibid. 171–184).

Convergence of Noahic-, Abrahamic-, Davidic- and new-covenant fulfilment confirmed (Psalms 146 – 150)

These 'Final Hallel' psalms seem to express praise to YHWH from the standpoint of a people who have been gathered into a Zion that is at least partially rebuilt (Pss 146:10; 147:2–3, 12–13; 149:1–2; 150:1). This, then, is a new-covenant scenario, and indeed the blessings envisaged by Psalm 144:12–15 have come to a certain degree of fruition (Ps. 147:13–14). But arrival in Zion does not always equate in a simplistic fashion to the terminus of the new exodus, for here, at least, the *ultimate* goal has not yet been reached (to couch this in the typological terms of these psalms, the rebuilding of Zion must go on through to completion). In particular, the final judgment – the 'judgment decreed' (Ps. 149:9 HCSB) in, for example, Psalm 2:8–9[131] – still lies in the future. Psalm 149 informs us that all YHWH's 'godly ones' (v. 9; cf. vv. 1, 5) will take part in this judgment: royal responsibilities are to some extent democratized under the new covenant (vv. 6–9) – as also appears to be the case for priestly responsibilities (already discussed).[132]

Who are these 'godly ones' (*ḥăsîdîm*)? Some of the data point in the direction of the '[sons of] Israel', so named as the privileged recipients of his special revelation (Ps. 147:19–20), the people who are 'near to him' (Ps. 148:14). Indeed, the judgment of Psalm 149 is executed *against the nations* (vv. 7–9). By this stage, it is, however, difficult for the Psalter reader to cast aside all the information regarding the identity of the new-covenant people that has been set forth; we are attuned to the possibility that the language of the type (in this case, ethnic Israel) is being used to designate its antitype. Thus, we understood the 'godly ones' of Psalm 132:16 (*ḥăsîdêhā*) to be those who had undertaken the new-exodus journey.[133] Other data in this concluding doxology reinforce the perspective that we have seen in books 2, 4 and 5 by way of realization of the Abrahamic covenant: the people of God are drawn from all nations. Thus we read that 'the LORD takes pleasure in those who fear him, in those who hope in his' *ḥesed* (Ps. 147:11 ESV), loving the righteous, protecting the foreigners, but

---

[131] See also Pss 96:13; 98:9, in line with Allen 2002: 400–401.
[132] See pp. 142–143.
[133] See p. 132.

bringing the wicked down to the ground (Pss 146:8–9; 147:6). Further, in Psalm 148, the injunction to praise YHWH is addressed to, among others, 'kings of the earth and all peoples, princes and all judges of the earth' (Ps. 148:11 HCSB). The latter verse echoes Psalm 2:2, 10; we should recall that that introductory and programmatic psalm recognizes 'all' those among the nations who repent as being 'happy' (*'ašrê*) in a salvific sense (Ps. 2:12; cf. Ps. 144:15).[134]

Regarding the Davidic covenant, the structure of this concluding group of psalms is instructive. While we should certainly view Psalm 150 as the Psalter's climax-of-the-climax, a good case can be made for considering Psalm 148 to be the centre of a concentric structure across the five psalms and thus of particular prominence and importance. Here, I reproduce Zenger's table (see Table 5.7). Sensitivity to this structural feature throws into sharper relief what is already (on any account of the shape of the Final Hallel) climactic in this long psalm, namely the reasons for praising YHWH

Table 5.7 Zenger's analysis of the concentric structure of Psalms 146 – 150

146	147	148	149	150
Creation theology (allusions to Gen. 1:3, 9)	Creation theology	Creation theology (allusions to Gen. 1 – 2)	Creation theology	Creation theology (allusions to Gen. 1)
	Israel 'Children of Zion' *'nwjm* *rṣh* *mšpt*	Israel	Israel 'Children of Zion' *'nwjm* *rṣh* *mšpt*	
2 x *hll* 1 x *zmr*	Many verbs of praise	Only *hll*	Many verbs of praise	Only *hll*
	thlh	*thlh*	*thlh*	

Adapted from Zenger 1997a: 18. Adapted with permission of Brill; © E. Zenger 1997; '"Daß alles Fleisch den Namen seiner Heiligung segne" (Ps 145,21): Die Komposition Ps 145–150 als Anstoß zu einer christlich-jüdischen Psalmenhermeneutik', *Biblische Zeitschrift* 41: 1–27; permission conveyed through Copyright Clearance Center, Inc.

---

134 For other suggestions of links between Pss 2 and 149, consult Hossfeld and Zenger 1993: 51.

as stated in the closing two verses: 'his name alone is exalted' (Ps. 148:13 ESV) and 'He has raised up a horn for his people' (Ps. 148:14 ESV).[135]

With regard to this 'horn' metaphor, Tremper Longman asks: 'Does this refer to the strength of the people, or to God's choice of an individual who would exercise strength on behalf of his people?'[136] There can be no doubting which answer the Psalter reader gives. The construction is a throwback to Psalm 132:17, 'I will cause a horn to sprout up for David' (NRSV) (in both cases, a hiphil-conjugated verb with YHWH as subject is followed by the noun 'horn', and then by the preposition 'for', followed by another noun indicating the beneficiary). In addition, the expression in Psalm 148:14 echoes the hope expressed regarding David in Psalm 89:24 (MT 89:25) ('his horn will be exalted')[137] – hope that the psalmist feared had been dashed by the Babylonian exile. It is, of course, the case that 'horn' does not always designate a royal figure. But these intertextual links are of considerable importance in the design of the Psalter, and this interpretation, though in the minority,[138] is most 'satisfying':[139] the culmination of the book of Psalms showcases the messiah and calls upon 'the choir of creation'[140] to praise YHWH for him (Ps. 148; cf. Ps. 150:6). As this climactic note is sounded, the Psalter reader knows that the definitive solution to the crisis of Psalm 89 has been provided and cannot but be caught up in the expression of praise.

There are, however, significant distinctions between Psalm 132:17 and Psalm 148:14. In context, the former ('I will cause . . . to sprout up' [NRSV]) is promissory and the latter ('He has raised up' [ESV]) declarative and retrospective;[141] the former speaks of the dynastic promise as it will be fulfilled, the latter of the same promise following its fulfilment; the former expresses the theology of the Davidic covenant as a future contributor to new-covenant circumstances, the latter the theology of the Davidic covenant as it coincides with new-covenant circumstances. In the former

---

[135] The phrase 'horn of his people' (KJV, DBY) would more naturally be conveyed by a straightforward genitival construction, without the preposition.

[136] Longman 2014: 474.

[137] The same verb *rûm*, though in the qal conjugation.

[138] See, in its favour, Kidner 1975: 488; Harman 1998: 451; Eveson 2015: 495; Hamilton 2021c: 518–519.

[139] Eveson's term (2015: 495). Ross (2016: 948) asserts that there is 'no internal support', within the psalm, for the allusion to a king. But it seems to me that Psalter context cannot be set aside in this case.

[140] Kidner's phrase (1975: 487).

[141] I am not leaning on a notion of 'tense' in Hebrew, although it happens that a *qātal* form is attested here in a past context and a *yiqtol* in a future one.

case, the beneficiary of the 'horn' can be described as 'David', whereas, in the latter case, the beneficiary is the people.[142] In other words, what was promised to David is ultimately (under the new covenant) of benefit to all YHWH's people. This fits with what we noted in relation to Psalm 72.[143]

We should notice that Davidic- (and new-)covenant fulfilment is partly predicated on the stability of the created order (Ps. 148:5–6). It would be unthinkable that YHWH should raise up a horn for his people without also undertaking not to destroy the earth. Verse 6 may allude to the covenant with Noah,[144] the necessary bedrock for covenants established thereafter: with regard to the 'waters above the heavens' and other created elements of the heavens, YHWH 'established them for ever and ever; he gave a decree, and it shall not pass away' (Ps. 148:4, 6 ESV). This may recall the equivalent allusion in Psalm 104, the stability of the creation being the indispensable condition for the theology of Psalms 105 – 106.[145]

The links, which are widely acknowledged,[146] between the end of Psalm 148 and the beginning of Psalm 149 (notably the recurrence of 'praise' and 'godly ones') require that we discern in the 'king' of Psalm 149:2 the same referent as the 'horn' of Psalm 148:14. Thus the 'new song' (Ps. 149:1) with which the people praise YHWH concerns the messiah's rule. Although full and final fulfilment of the programme of Psalm 2 is still future from the perspective of the Psalter's conclusion, the messiah has been installed on Zion (cf. Ps 2:6), and this is chief among the 'mighty deeds' (Ps. 150:2) that give rise to praise on the part of 'everything that has breath' (Ps. 150:6).[147]

Summary

As for the previous two chapters, it is appropriate that we 'zoom out' at this concluding stage to take in the essential findings, beginning with the key headings whose order we reorganize for the sake of serving our enquiry.

---

[142] It should not, however, be suggested that the faithful people *become* the house of David (contra Auwers, who quotes 2 Macc. 2:17 (2000: 120, including his n. 20).

[143] See Fig. 3.2 on p. 45.

[144] Cf. Goldingay 2008: 731, and, less directly, Eveson 2015: 494.

[145] Cf. our earlier discussion of Ps. 104 (pp. 80–84).

[146] E.g. by Kidner 1975: 489; Auwers 2003: 12, incl. n. 30; Weber 2003: 383; Vesco 2008b: 1365–1366; Hossfeld and Zenger 2012: 895; Snearly 2016: 178.

[147] Brueggemann (1988: 92) considers that Ps. 150 does not present reasons to praise YHWH. For a brief discussion and critique of his position, see Hely Hutchinson 2005b: 92, 96.

The overarching theme that we saw in book 5 is:

1 the convergence of Abrahamic-, Davidic- and new-covenant
  fulfilment (Pss 107; 118 and immediately preceding context;
  136 and immediately preceding context; 145; 146 – 150[148]).

With regard to the relationship between the Davidic and the new covenants, which is our particular focus, we also noted that:

2 the conditionality of the Davidic covenant is satisfied (Ps. 132).

And regarding the relationship between the Abrahamic and the new covenants, we observed that:

3 'sons of Adam' and 'all nations' are included in the new exodus
  (Ps. 107).

We were enabled to ascertain much regarding the shape of the new-covenant regime:

4 David is recapitulated in a superior antitype (Pss 108 – 110;
  138 – 145): victory, judgment and suffering are intensified, and the
  role of king is combined with that of righteous suffering servant;
5 the Levitical covenant is fulfilled by a superior priesthood –
  combined with kingship (Ps. 110);
6 the priesthood is democratized (Pss 118; 134 – 135);
7 blessings are democratized (Ps. 144).

All this presupposes that:

8 Sinaitic conditionality is observed (Ps. 133).

With regard to the timing of new-covenant fulfilment, we learned that:

9 new-covenant fulfilment is not yet experienced in the post-exilic
  period (Ps. 107:43);
10 the new covenant is fulfilled in stages (Pss 119 – 136).

---

[148] Also Noahic-covenant fulfilment (Ps. 148).

Thus the data of book 5, as well as those of the Psalter's concluding doxology, reinforce those of book 4, but they also lend greater clarity and precision to the picture of how covenants relate. The perplexity voiced in Psalm 89 is answered by a new-covenant regime that establishes the conditions which provide for the fulfilment of the Abrahamic and Davidic covenants. Accordingly, relative to the Davidic covenant, the new covenant is new both temporally and in its capacity to bring together, in the context of a new exodus, these two covenants that had been established previously. It is also predicated on the stability of the creation guaranteed by the Noahic covenant.

The realization of the Davidic covenant presupposes the satisfaction, achieved under the new covenant, of the conditions that were stipulated under the Sinaitic covenant; forgiveness is assured that is total in scope and permanent in efficacy. Such fulfilment rests with the eschatological son of David. This king proves also to be a righteous suffering servant as well as a permanent priest in whom the Levitical covenant finds its fulfilment within the context of a new (Melchizedekian) order. His victory and sufferings are heightened relative to those of his ancestor David.

Although the new covenant – which thus encompasses the Davidic covenant – constitutes a definitive response to the exile (there will be no further deportation!), the new exodus does not occur in an instant. The democratization of blessings won by the Messiah's victory presupposes the presence of a people at a rebuilt Zion and the final judgment of the nations. This judgment is more terrifying than what befell Pharaoh; the enemies of the people of Abraham are cursed in line with the promise of Genesis 12:3.

This new-covenant people, who will enjoy royal and priestly responsibilities not afforded during the Sinaitic regime, is made up of Jews and non-Jews. By raising up a 'horn . . . for David', YHWH also raises up a 'horn for his people', which includes those from among the nations who 'fear' him, fulfilling the promises to Abraham. Such beneficiaries of the solution to the sin problem, showered with privileges and blessings, will praise YHWH, along with the entire created order, 'for he is good, for his covenant faithfulness endures for ever'.

6

The law and the new-covenant believer's ethical life

We have seen how the psalmist's perplexity is answered: the Davidic covenant remains on the agenda and is to be fulfilled within the framework of the new covenant. We are nearly in a position to conclude our study on new-covenant newness in the Psalter. Before we draw together the key findings of our enquiry and offer an evaluation of our seven models, we need to address a residual question, relating to the law of Moses, that those models raise. That is our concern in this penultimate chapter.

Mosaic law (or a part of it) applied to the new-covenant believer?

It is important to stress that our aim in this chapter is not to give a complete account of the Psalter's perspective on the law of Moses. The only question that we are seeking to answer is the main one that our covenant-relationship models have put on the agenda for us: does the law of Moses regulate the new-covenant believer's ethical life?

We have argued in favour of a new-covenant outlook in book 5. In relation to the long Psalm 119, we observed that the law is in the believer's heart,[1] and we also discerned in the previous chapter that the psalmist's new-exodus journey was inaugurated without being consummated.[2] We do not have to read far in this psalm to realize that the psalmist's ethical life is of major importance and that there are particular commandments that he aspires to keep. Is it possible to work out the 'particulars' of these particular commandments?

---

[1] Cf. chapter 5, n. 59.
[2] See pp. 100–101.

Thesis: permanence of Mosaic (moral) law (Psalm 111:9; Jeremiah 31:33; Psalm 119)

Correlative with Psalm 119 is Psalm 112:1 where we read: 'Happy (*'ašrê*) is the man who fears the LORD, taking great delight in His commands' (HCSB). But, again, we ask: which commands? We must take account of the preceding psalm, Psalm 112's twin acrostic. Psalm 111:9 speaks of the exodus ('He sent redemption to his people' [ESV]), followed, it seems, by the establishment of the covenant at Sinai ('he has commanded his covenant for ever' [ESV]).[3] This would suggest that, other things being equal, the divine stipulations that need to be put into practice are those that YHWH revealed to Moses in the context of that Sinaitic covenant.

Indeed, commenting on the prophecy concerning a law in the heart in Jeremiah 31:33 and parallel texts, Pierre Buis finds no indication in favour of the idea of a new law.[4] Or, again, Walter Kaiser argues:

> Clearly, Jeremiah 31:33; Ezekiel 11:20; 36:27, make it plain that in the new covenant God will place his *tôrâ* ('law') 'in their minds and write it on their hearts,' so that his people would be able to follow *ḥuqqây* or *ḥuqqotây* ('my statute' or 'my decrees') and *mišpāṭây* ('my laws' or 'my judgments'). The burden of proof is not on those who say this is the same law as the one that God gave to Moses; rather, it is squarely on those who have some other law in mind than the one to which these words ordinarily point in this document.[5]

> God's *tôrâ* appears as part of the new covenant and the so-called 'Zion Torah' of the last days (Isa. 2:3; 42:4; 51:4, 7; Jer. 31:33; Ezek. 11:20; 36:27; Mic. 4:2) ... [I]t would be an eisegetical fallacy to import a meaning such as 'law of Christ' or a 'transformed *tôrâ*' into the meaning packages of these eschatological texts.[6]

---

[3] Cf. Calvin 1859: 344; Delitzsch 1889: 179; Briggs and Briggs 1907: 383; Kidner 1975: 398; Michaud 1993: 737; Mays 1994: 356–357; Allen 2002: 125–126; Weber 2003: 227; Estes 2019: 350.

[4] Buis 1968: 5.

[5] Kaiser 1996c: 304.

[6] Kaiser 1996b: 398.

So he maintains that it is the law of Moses (and not another law) that YHWH writes on the heart of the new-covenant believer: 'The New Covenant *Tôrâ* is the Same as the Mosaic Law';[7] 'Surely, it is the same "law" God revealed to Moses that is to be put on the hearts of all who believe in the new covenant.'[8]

Kaiser does, however, argue for 'the priority and the precedent-setting nature of the moral law, which stems from the character and nature of God'. It is this moral law that is 'abiding' and permanent.[9] In this regard, he appeals to Psalm 119 which speaks of laws established perpetually. He cites verses 91, 89, 160 and 144:[10] 'The law did not originate with Moses; it came from the mouth of God (Ps. 119:13, 71[11]). God's "laws endure to this day" (v. 91), are "eternal ... in the heavens" (vv. 89, 160) and "are forever right" (v. 143[12]).'

In favour: Mosaic law as implicitly subdivisible, with an appeal to the heart (Psalms 40; 50 – 51)

From the perspective of the book of Psalms, we may value Kaiser's arguments to the extent that it does seem possible – even necessary – to distinguish laws that may be described as 'moral' from those that may be described as 'ceremonial' within the Mosaic law.[13] In Psalm 51, following the act of adultery committed by David (a 'moral' matter), we know that what God delights in is not animal sacrifices (which, in any case, could not be offered under these circumstances)[14] but a 'heart' (vv. 16–17 [MT vv. 18–19]). It is not that God never approves of sacrifices, as the following two verses of that psalm make clear, but that, as the previous psalm has already spelled out, formal, ceremonial worship is unacceptable if the Decalogue is being flouted (as we have already seen from Ps. 50).[15]

---

[7] His heading in Kaiser 1996c: 304.

[8] Kaiser 1996a: 189.

[9] Ibid. 197–198.

[10] Kaiser 1996c: 308.

[11] It appears that this should be v. 72.

[12] It appears that this should be v. 144.

[13] My point here should not be confused with an argument in favour of a tripartite structure for the Mosaic law (the idea that it contains moral, ceremonial and civil subgroups).

[14] See chapter 3, n. 103.

[15] See pp. 45–46.

Psalm 40:6c (MT 40:7c) goes so far as to say that YHWH did not ask for 'burnt offering or sin offering' – a Semitic formula that highlights, again, the superior relative value of obedience. YHWH seeks worshippers for whom the law is in the heart (cf. Ps. 40:8 [MT 40:9]).

Against: 'qualified newness' suggested by the Psalter

These data are not, however, sufficient to allow us to argue for continuity between the law of Moses and the law that applies under the new covenant (whether of the whole code or only a 'moral' subset of it). Indeed, we need to proceed with caution for several reasons, outlined below.

1 Recapitulation expected

We have grown accustomed, in our consideration of books 4 and 5, to the recapitulation of old-covenant notions, with allusions to exodus, city, temple, earth and kingship serving to bespeak their corresponding transposed, antitypical realities. The idea of a new law, analogous to the Mosaic legislation but transposed for the new covenant, would cohere with our understanding of the other phenomena that feature in Israel's history and serve as types of new-covenant realities. It would even be surprising if the Sinaitic commandments were adopted wholesale and in a straight line, without any transposition, under the new regime.

2 Abrahamic covenant referred to in Psalm 111:9

Before we embrace the argument from Psalm 111, we should be sensitive to the character of the covenant in question, namely its being commanded *lĕ'ôlām* ('for ever'); this is syntactically prominent in verse 9 ('he commanded, for ever, his covenant'). In the light of the unfolding of the last three books of the Psalter, it would be surprising if *lĕ'ôlām* were describing the Sinaitic covenant: we have learned to associate this phrase with the covenants with Abraham (Ps. 105:8) and David (e.g. Ps. 89:28 [89:29]) and the new covenant (e.g. Ps. 107:1) but not with that of Sinai. The first of these references is particularly relevant given the affinities between it and Psalm 111:9: with 'word' in parallel to 'his covenant' in Psalm 105:8, YHWH 'commanded his covenant' in both texts.

Further, the phrase 'his wonderful deeds' (*niplĕ'ōtāyw*) in Psalm 111:4 recalls the refrain of Psalm 107 where the 'wonderful deeds' (*niplĕ'ōtāyw*) refer to the return to the land – a return that connotes new-covenant ful-filment (vv. 8, 15, 21, 31).[16] The second half of that same verse ('YHWH is gracious and compassionate') undoubtedly echoes Exodus 34:6 and hence (as we have had repeated occasion to discuss)[17] the Abrahamic covenant which is at the root of the new covenant.[18] Again, the following verse ('he remembers, for ever, his covenant' [Ps. 111:5b]) evokes Psalms 105 – 106 and the Abrahamic covenant (Pss 105:8; 106:45).[19] This interpretation seems to be confirmed by the probable allusion to the crossing of the desert in verse 5a[20] and by the allusion to the taking of the promised land in verse 6b – in other words, by the evidence of YHWH's faithfulness to the Abrahamic covenant as signalled by the psalmist in the immediate context.

Finally, the lexical and syntactical parallelism between verse 5b (*yizkōr lĕʿôlām bĕrîtô*, 'he remembers, for ever, his covenant') and verse 9b (*ṣiwwâ lĕʿôlām bĕrîtô*, 'he commanded, for ever, his covenant') is striking and provides additional support for the idea that the covenant to which the latter alludes is the Abrahamic.[21] On this understanding, the second line of verse 9 does not relate the continuation of the history (any more than the third line of the verse does) but explains the theological founda-tion for the redemption mentioned in the first line.

3 Broad range of notions encompassed by 'law' (and synonyms) in Psalm 119

We should be aware of the broad range of notions that are encompassed by the term *tôrâ* and the various other words employed quasi-synonymously with it in Psalm 119. As Jean-Luc Vesco asserts:

The divine instruction designated by this series of terms that Psalm 119 uses as synonyms is not the Mosaic law, or the Pentateuch,

---

[16] See pp. 113–115.

[17] See pp. 55–56, 71–72, 108, 145.

[18] Hensley (2018: 107) correctly identifies the Exod. 32 – 34 background but then associates this chiefly with the Sinaitic covenant. As we demonstrated extensively in our treatment of book 4, YHWH's grace in the face of the golden calf rebellion is grounded in the *Abrahamic* promises.

[19] Hamilton (2021c: 301) makes similar observations.

[20] Cf. e.g. Delitzsch 1889: 178; Kissane 1954: 198; A. A. Anderson 1972b: 774; Estes 2019: 349; Hamilton 2021c: 301.

[21] In line with the views of Jacquet 1978: 237; Williams 1987: 310; Harman 1998: 364; VanGemeren 2008: 821–821.

or the book of Deuteronomy, or the canon of Scripture fixed later, but the totality of revelation viewed as a guide . . . to salvation.[22]

As Jerome Creach points out, 'Psalm 119 speaks of trust in *tôrâ* like other psalms refer to seeking refuge in Yahweh'.[23] The psalmist holds firmly to the *tôrâ* as promise and/or source of life,[24] salvation,[25] protection,[26] proximity with YHWH,[27] compassion,[28] faithfulness (*ḥesed*).[29] If the psalmist is conscious of his failings (v. 176), he leans on the 'word of truth' (v. 43) for grace (vv. 29, 58, 132, 135),[30] mindful that God is good (*ṭôb* [vv. 65, 68]).[31]

This is all of a piece with the new-covenant formula which plays such a key role in book 5 and which brackets the preceding Psalm 118 (vv. 1, 29). We are not denying the association of '*tôrâ*' and synonyms with the Sinaitic legislation,[32] still less backtracking on the importance of obedience to specific commandments for the new-covenant believer. But, in keeping with Leslie Allen's conclusion,[33] we should take account of the significant range of meanings that '*tôrâ*' can cover.[34]

Kaiser's appeal to Psalm 119 as an argument in favour of the continuing validity of part of the law of Moses is further weakened by the observation that this long psalm develops Psalm 1 inasmuch as the psalmist meditates on[35] the *tôrâ*, delighting in it[36] and recognizing its full sufficiency[37] –

---

[22] Vesco 2008b: 1142, quoted by Wenham 2012: 88.

[23] Creach 1996: 71.

[24] Vv. 25, 37 (although there is no *tôrâ*-related term in this verse, as is also true of v. 90), 40, 50, 77, 88, 93, 107, 109(?), 116, 144, 149, 154, 156, 159, 175.

[25] Vv. 41, 81, 117, 123, 154–155, 166, 170, 174.

[26] V. 114.

[27] V. 151.

[28] Vv. 82, 156.

[29] Vv. 41, 64(?), 76, 88, 124, 149, 159.

[30] Qal masculine singular imperative of *ḥ-n-n*, with first-person singular suffix, except in the last case which is closely tied to the second-last reference by virtue of the evocation of Num. 6:24–26.

[31] Cf. Kidner's discussion of the qualities and benefits of Scripture according to Ps. 119 (1975: 419–422).

[32] The terms *mišpāṭ*, *ḥōq*, *miṣwâ*, *ʿēdâ* and *dābār* feature in various combinations in Deuteronomy.

[33] He considers that '"Torah," as Yahweh's written revelation seems to embrace both Deuteronomy and at least Isaiah, Jeremiah and Proverbs' (Allen 2002: 184).

[34] Ps. 119:89–91 draws our attention to the role of the word of God in creation and providence. We may usefully note that Ps. 78:1 attests another meaning of '*tôrâ*', namely an account of salvation history that yields lessons for subsequent generations.

[35] E.g. v. 97.

[36] Vv. 72, 97, 103.

[37] The psalm's eightfold acrostic form suggests this; cf. vv. 92, 114, 116, 149.

unlike the wicked. This evocation of the opening psalm is suggested as early as the first two verses:

How happy ['ašrê] are those whose way is blameless,
who live according to the LORD's instruction!
Happy ['ašrê] are those who keep His decrees
and seek Him with all their heart.
(Ps. 119:1–2 HCSB)

Psalm 1's introductory role for the Psalter militates against a narrow understanding of 'tôrâ'; we have elsewhere argued that, although allusions to the law of Moses are encompassed by its usage in the first psalm, the 'instruction' in question needs to be understood in close association with the content of Psalm 2 and the Psalter as a whole.[38]

Psalm 112:1 recalls this opening psalm. In Psalm 1, the 'man' (hā'îš) is 'happy' ('ašrê) by virtue of his godly conduct, tied to the fact that 'his delight' (ḥepṣô) is in the 'tôrâ of YHWH' (Ps. 1:1–2). According to Psalm 112:1: 'Happy ('ašrê) is the man ('îš) who fears the LORD, taking great delight (ḥāpēṣ) in His commands' (HCSB). In neither case should we restrict the referent to the Sinaitic legislation (or a part of it).

4 Sabbath not featured in Psalm 119, but wisdom motifs present

Gordon Wenham rightly remarks that the importance of observing the sabbath is all but absent from the Psalter.[39] Given the length of Psalm 119, this observation should reinforce our suspicion that the corpus of legislation which the new-covenant believer is meant to obey does not correspond, in any direct or straightforward way, to the law of Moses. Similarly, it is worth noting that bĕrît ('covenant') which is found in parallel with 'the ten words' in Deuteronomy 4:13,[40] does not feature in Psalm 119,[41] further undermining the idea that the 'law' of this psalm overlaps closely with the Decalogue. We are not suggesting that there is no overlap at all with the Ten Commandments, but, in our understanding of the tôrâ of Psalm 119, we need to be able to accommodate Vesco's

---

[38] Hely Hutchinson 2013b: 25–28.
[39] Wenham 2005: 183.
[40] Cf. also Deut. 9:9.
[41] Cf. Levenson 1987: 564.

observation: 'The psalm makes no mention of any particular statutory provision of the legal texts and never alludes to Moses.'[42]

As if to make the picture more complex, we should be attuned to some similarities between Psalm 119 and the book of Proverbs,[43] notably with the emphasis on the theme of life and death (Ps. 119:25, 37, 40, *passim*; cf. Prov. 1:12; 5:5; 7:27; 9:18). Jon Levenson asks:[44]

> What are the commandments that the author of Psalm 119 insists he has always observed? To those who see the author as devoted to the Pentateuch, the answer is obvious: he is speaking of the Pentateuchal laws, for example, the Sabbath, love of one's neighbour, the dietary laws, the pursuit of justice. But, if so, then why does he never mention any specifics? Why does he not insist, with Moses and Samuel, that he has never misappropriated property, or, with Ezekiel, that he has never eaten forbidden food? The utter lack of concreteness and specificity in his discussion of commandments is further evidence against the assumption that the Pentateuch is uppermost in his mind. Instead, the usage in Psalm 119 is closer to that of Proverbs, where *miṣwâ* (and its synonyms) indicates the counsel of a sage rather than juridical or cultic norms.[45]

Levenson goes on to cite Proverbs 13:13–15 and 28:4–5.

Levenson's questions are apposite. We should, however, beware of embracing a dichotomy between 'the counsel of a sage' and 'juridical and cultic norms'. The book of Proverbs overlaps to some extent with the Pentateuchal laws. For example, 'He who justifies the wicked and he who condemns the righteous are both alike an abomination to the LORD' (Prov. 17:15) is a Proverbial expression of commandments found in Exodus 23:6–7 and Deuteronomy 16:18–20. Again, the reality that '[t]he LORD detests dishonest scales, but accurate weights find favour with him' (Prov. 11:1 NIV; cf. 16:11; 20:10; 20:23) has roots in Leviticus 19:36 ('Use honest scales and honest weights').[46] It would also seem that in Proverbs 10:8,

---

[42] Vesco 2008b: 1142.

[43] Ps. 1, whose similarities with Ps. 119 have already been touched on, is clearly a wisdom psalm, exhibiting affinities with the book of Proverbs.

[44] Levenson 1987: 566–567.

[45] Cf. Freedman's similar remarks (1999: 89).

[46] The same is true for boundary stones (Prov. 22:28; 23:10; cf. Deut. 19:14). See also Prov. 6:16–19; 8:13; 11:6. To 'fear' YHWH (a key notion in Proverbs) includes not sinning against him (Exod. 20:20; cf. Deut. 10:12; 1 Pet. 1:17).

13:13 and 19:16, *miṣwâ* should be understood as being at least partially 'Pentateuchal'.

Thus the Proverbial wisdom that we find in Psalm 119 should not be *opposed* to the law of Moses. The Mosaic code is, after all, divine wisdom too (Deut. 4:5–8)! Further, the widely recognized[47] evocation of Deuteronomy in Psalm 119 should guard us against viewing the *tôrâ* of Psalm 119 as being entirely discontinuous with the *tôrâ* of Moses. These reminiscences of Deuteronomy extend well beyond the term *tôrâ* and several of the related words, already noted.[48] 'The centrality of *learning* (l-m-d), and *keeping* (š-m-r) the law, and of doing so *with one's whole heart* (Deut. 4:29, 6:5, etc.) are again Deuteronomic'.[49]

Perhaps, too, the characteristics of the righteous man in Psalm 112 imply that, in certain respects, the new law lies in the trajectory of the law of Moses. As one 'who fears the LORD, taking great delight in His commands' (v. 1 [HCSB]), he 'conducts his business fairly' (v. 5 [HCSB]).

5 Newness underlined by virtue of Isaianic background

We should join Stephen Dempster in considering the parallel between Psalms 119 – 134 and Isaiah 2:2–5 / Micah 4:1–5:

> These pilgrimage psalms are probably placed here to show that the reason for the return from exile is to go up to hear the Torah in all its wonder and to worship the Lord . . . Israel's ascent can thus point the way to the nations (Zech. 8:23).[50]

Indeed, we have already noted the inclusion of the nations in the new exodus.[51] What body of legislation are the nations expected to observe once they arrive in Zion (cf. Isa. 2:3)? Even if Dempster's hypothesis is hard to prove, we have regularly appealed to the Isaianic background to the Psalter, and it makes sense to do so again here in Psalm 119.[52]

---

[47] Including by Levenson (1987: 563–564). See also e.g. Deissler 1955: 270–272; Goulder 1998: 204–206; Ross 2016: 461; Tucker and Grant 2018: 704.

[48] See n. 32 in this chapter.

[49] Goulder 1998: 205; emphasis original.

[50] Dempster 2003: 200.

[51] See pp. 115–119.

[52] For links between Isaiah and Ps. 119, see Deissler 1955: 275–276.

Dempster's passage, Isaiah 2:2–4, is picked up in the First Servant Song, Isaiah 42:1–9. In both passages, we come across '*tôrâ*' (Isa. 2:3; 42:4), the root *š-p-ṭ* ('judge' [Isa. 2:4; 41:1, 3, 4]) and the idea of just rule for the nations (Isa. 2:4; 42:3–4, 6); and it is implicit that this rule concerns those who recognize YHWH's lordship (Isa. 2:3; 42:8). This parallel informs our understanding of the new-covenant context in which the '*tôrâ*' applies. Specifically, in Isaiah 42, the servant of YHWH is presented as a new Moses: he will be 'a covenant for the people[53] and a light to the nations' (Isa. 42:6 HCSB); it is 'his *tôrâ*' that is the object of these nations' hope (or expectation [v. 4]).[54] This new Moses is set within the framework of a new regime of which the nations are beneficiaries:

'Behold, the former things have come to pass,
    and new things I now declare;
before they spring forth
    I tell you of them.'

Sing to the LORD a new song,
    his praise from the end of the earth,
you who go down to the sea, and all that fills it,
    the coastlands and their inhabitants.
(Isa. 42:9–10 ESV)

It is not that the *tôrâ* in question is peculiar to the nations, if by that one were to mean that the Israelites would be called upon to obey a different body of legislation. Indeed, the following Servant Song (that of Isa. 49:1–7)[55] exhibits several parallels with the first[56] and makes it clear that the servant's role involves taking salvation not only to the ends of the earth but also to a remnant within Israel (v. 6). It is true that Isaiah does not

---

[53] Whatever the precise meaning of 'covenant of the people' (*bĕrît 'ām*) in Isa. 42:6, this phrase stands in parallel with 'light of the nations', and, given the unity of Isa. 40 – 55, the covenant in question cannot be separated from that of Isa. 55:3 which we considered in chapter 3 (see pp. 31–32, 35). The work of the suffering servant (Isa. 42 – 53) acts as the keystone for the establishment of the new covenant: he 'will justify many' (Isa. 53:11 NIV) – drawn from among Jews and non-Jews (Isa. 55:1–5; cf. Isa. 54:1–3).

[54] Piel of *y-ḥ-l*.

[55] We should also note its continuation as far as v. 13, esp. v. 8: the servant is, again, presented as a new Moses (and we again encounter the phrase 'covenant of the people', *bĕrît 'ām*; cf. n. 52 above).

[56] Motyer 1993: 383–384.

spell out the content of the *tôrâ* in question. But the newness of covenant, partner (with the inclusion of non-Israelites), mediator (new Moses) and location (Zion) combine to suggest the likelihood of needing to reckon with some degree of newness in the area of law too.

We should also take account of Isaiah 51:4–8 which contains significant parallels with the First Servant Song[57] as also with 2:2–5; other than in chapter 42, the only occurrences of '*tôrâ*' in Isaiah 40 – 55 (or even Isa. 40 – 66) are to be found here. YHWH, Zion's comforter (v. 3), will promulgate his '*tôrâ*', a development which seems to go hand in hand with the advent of salvation for the Israelite people and for the nations, and also with the establishment of a just administration which will attract the nations (vv. 4–7). As in 42:4, '*tôrâ*' and '*mišpāṭ*' ('judgment') feature in parallel (v. 4). There are also some transpositions relative to chapter 42 that highlight the convergence between YHWH's intervention and the servant's role in bringing about salvation: here, it is YHWH's *mišpāṭ* that serves as 'a light to the peoples', and it is YHWH's action that is the object of the nations' hope (or expectation).[58] The announcement in verse 4, which is addressed to the Israelites and refers to the time when Zion will be comforted, discourages any suggestion that the law to be promulgated will simply match the one that already exists. Regarding verse 7:

> the perspective seems to have passed to a 'realized eschatology,' as the gifts promised in vss. 4–5 appear to be already present in vss. 6–8. Whether the author has Jeremiah's 'new covenant' text in mind or not, he has given a profound meaning to *tôrâ*. Here it is something that can be possessed interiorly, undoubtedly is a well-spring for conduct, and stands in close conjunction with the gift of God's enduring salvation.[59]

These comments intersect with what we have already affirmed regarding the heart circumcision that the author of Psalm 119 seems to have benefited from[60] and the fact that '*tôrâ*' in book 5 is a broad notion.

---

[57] Ibid. 404.
[58] As in Isa. 42:4, the verb in v. 5 is the piel of *y-ḥ-l*.
[59] Jensen 1973: 23–24.
[60] See p. 129.

Conclusion: simple renewal of Sinaitic legislation not envisaged, though some continuity

What may we conclude regarding the 'law' that the new-covenant believer is expected to put into practice? There are multiple reasons that we have seen for being confident that the commandments that apply do not simply equate to the Sinaitic legislation. There is a newness here that runs in parallel with other elements of newness that are tied to the new covenant. But the 'particulars' are not given to us at this stage of biblical revelation; and we have also noted along the way that there are good reasons to expect the new body of legislation to lie in the trajectory of the law that was promulgated by Moses for the people of the old regime.

7
Summary and conclusions

In this closing chapter, I provide the conclusions to our enquiry. I will summarize the Psalter's message from the point of view of covenant relationships and specify, via twenty-eight statements, how the new covenant is new relative to the Davidic covenant. I will then evaluate our seven models in this regard, highlight some New Testament data that confirm our conclusions and end by paving the way for an exploration of some of the implications of this study.

The answer to the psalmist's perplexity

In this section, I propose to reiterate and bind together the essential points from several chapter conclusions. This will facilitate an appreciation of the broad canvas of the Psalter's unfolding message in relation to new-covenant newness.

The message of the Psalter from a covenant-relationships perspective

The introductory and programmatic Psalm 2 enabled us to appreciate that the question of how the new covenant relates to the Davidic covenant is on the agenda of this long biblical book. It seems that the Davidic covenant, which promises a perpetually established throne for David's son and seed, is encompassed and transcended by the larger schema of the (eschatological) new covenant. Yet, already, Psalms 18, 20 – 21 and 89 showcase the historical David enjoying some considerable measure of the fulfilment of promises that apply to his son and that ultimately go hand in hand with the realization of the new covenant. This strong link between the Davidic covenant and the new covenant is established by means of typology and is signalled in the original dynastic oracle of 2 Samuel 7 which speaks of David's 'house', 'kingdom' and 'throne' being established 'before [him]' (v. 16).

Once the new covenant comes to be fulfilled, this must involve fulfil-ment not only of the Davidic covenant (Pss 45 and 72) but also of the Abrahamic covenant. Indeed, it is precisely in the new-covenant king, promised according to the terms of the Davidic covenant, that the Abrahamic promise of blessing for all nations will come to be realized (Ps. 72:17b).

According to Psalm 89, nothing can stand in the way of the Davidic covenant's being fulfilled: it was established unconditionally and thus is characterized by inviolability. God would never lie! And so the psalmist is perplexed when, in the face of the Babylonian exile, the Davidic throne becomes vacant. What has happened to YHWH's covenant loyalty (ḥesed and 'ĕmûnâ)? Yet we also saw that there was a need for obedience, on the part of king and people, to Sinaitic-covenant stipulations (Pss 50 – 51; 78; 81).

We needed to let the tension stand. It is true that we caught a glimpse of the eschatological Abrahamic–Davidic solution towards the end of book 3 (Pss 84 – 87), but we still had questions. How is it that the curses of the Sinaitic covenant can square with the unconditional promise to David regarding the perpetual establishment of the Davidic throne? What is it that can make the post-exilic new-covenant solution possible? Under what conditions can it come about?

Book 4 provided the essential 'theological ammunition' by way of an answer to that perplexed calling into question of the durability of the Davidic covenant. In this 'Moses-book', the fundamental answer lies not with the Mosaic (Sinaitic) covenant but with the Abrahamic covenant. That God will not renege on his promises to Abraham implies that the means whereby those Abrahamic promises reach fulfilment have not been set aside. Therefore, ultimately, the Davidic covenant must come to be realized.

Yet it must be understood that the Davidic covenant has a conditional dimension and that the fundamental problem that needs to be resolved is not the exile but sin (Pss 90; 106). The Noahic covenant does not deal with sin, but it does provide for the stability of the creation (Ps. 104). The Abrahamic covenant will give rise to the solution, although it does not, in and of itself, equate to this solution (Pss 105 – 106). What is required is a (superior) antitype of the structures of Israel's history (Pss 93 – 100; 106): a greater mediation, exodus, city, temple, earth (cosmos) . . . and king. It appears that fulfilment of the Levitical covenant remains on the agenda

(Ps. 106), and this must also mean that the Davidic covenant will reach fulfilment (cf. Jer. 33).

Indeed, such a new-covenant scenario is in prospect on the other side of the exile. YHWH is powerful enough to bring this about (Pss 93 – 100)! People from all nations will figure among the beneficiaries of this covenant, on the basis of conversion (Pss 95 – 100; 102 – 103). It seems that the key to the covenant's realization lies with an eschatological king who will satisfy the conditions of the Sinaitic and Davidic covenants and who is also a suffering servant – the people's representative and substitute (Pss 101 – 102). Sins will be forgiven (Ps. 103).

By the end of book 4, we had travelled a long way in our enquiry, but we were on the lookout for greater clarity regarding the new-covenant scenario that needed to come about. And so we turned to the concluding book of the Psalms and also the Psalter's concluding doxology. We found not only that enhanced clarity but also a reinforcement of the message of book 4. The perplexity voiced in Psalm 89 is answered by a new-covenant regime that establishes the conditions which provide for the fulfilment of the Abrahamic and Davidic covenants. Accordingly, relative to the Davidic covenant, the new covenant is new both temporally and in its capacity to bring together, in the context of a new exodus, these two covenants that had been established previously. It is also predicated on the stability of the creation guaranteed by the Noahic covenant.

The realization of the Davidic covenant presupposes the satisfaction, achieved under the new covenant, of the conditions that were stipulated under the Sinaitic covenant; forgiveness is assured that is total in scope and permanent in efficacy. Such fulfilment rests with the eschatological son of David. This king proves also to be a righteous suffering servant as well as a permanent priest in whom the Levitical covenant finds its fulfilment within the context of a new (Melchizedekian) order. His victory and sufferings are heightened relative to those of his ancestor David.

Although the new covenant – which thus encompasses the Davidic covenant – constitutes a definitive response to the exile (there will be no further deportation!), the new exodus does not occur in an instant. The democratization of blessings won by the Messiah's victory presupposes the presence of a people at a rebuilt Zion and the final judgment of the nations. This judgment is more terrifying than what befell Pharaoh; the enemies of the people of Abraham are cursed in line with the promise of Genesis 12:3.

This new-covenant people, who will enjoy royal and priestly responsibilities not afforded to them during the Sinaitic regime, is made up of Jews and non-Jews. By raising up a 'horn . . . for David' (Ps. 132:17), YHWH also raises up a 'horn for his people' (Ps. 148:14) which includes those from among the nations who 'fear' him, fulfilling the promises to Abraham. Such beneficiaries of the solution to the sin problem, showered with privileges and blessings, will praise YHWH, along with the entire created order, 'for he is good, for his covenant faithfulness endures for ever'.

In summary: the covenant-relationships answer to the psalmist's perplexity

The answer to the psalmist's perplexity – the crisis of book 3 and notably of Psalm 89 – lies with the Abrahamic covenant which is the promise of a solution to the sin problem. This solution comes in the shape of the new covenant whose setting-up takes place on the other side of the exile and provides a full-orbed answer to that exile. Central to this new covenant is the establishment of the throne of David in the shape of the eternal rule of David's superior, righteous seed and son who is also a suffering servant. Closely allied to this is the establishment of a perpetual priesthood. New-covenant fulfilment presupposes the bedrock of the Noahic covenant, depends on the fulfilment of the Abrahamic, Davidic and Levitical covenants and involves the fulfilment of the conditionality inherent in the Sinaitic covenant.

New-covenant newness as set forth in the Psalter

Wherein lies the newness of the new covenant relative to the Davidic covenant, according to the Psalter? Here, I propose to reproduce information from chapter conclusions in order to provide an at-a-glance overview of our findings. I summarize these in twenty-eight statements and then more succinctly.

Twenty-eight statements

We have noted that:

1 the Davidic covenant is encompassed and transcended by the new covenant (Ps. 2);

2 new-covenant typology is incorporated in the Davidic covenant (Pss 18; 20 – 21): the Messiah of the new covenant is set forth within the framework of the Davidic covenant (Ps. 89);

3 fulfilment of the Davidic covenant is entailed by fulfilment of the new covenant (Pss 45; 72);

4 the Sinaitic- and Davidic-covenant conditions are to be satisfied by the eschatological king (Pss 101; 132).

A full-orbed answer, however, requires us to explain how these two covenants relate to others, for we saw that:

5 a Davidic-covenant solution is intimately connected to the Abrahamic-covenant solution (Pss 93 – 100 with Ps. 89).

The problem that the solution in question remedies is that of sin:

6 the Adamic problem is exposed (Ps. 90:3–11);

7 the need for repentance and mercy is highlighted by the conditionality of the Sinaitic covenant (Pss 50 – 51); Sinaitic conditionality is also flagged in book 3 (Pss 78 and 81);

8 the remedy for the exile will be a consequence of the remedy for Adamic sin (Ps. 90:12–17).

We noted that the Abrahamic covenant is critical in terms of providing the solution, but it is not in itself the solution:

9 the Abrahamic covenant is the basis for the exiles' prayer (Ps. 106:45–47);

10 the Abrahamic solution is to be applied to the exile (Pss 89 – 90);

11 the Abrahamic covenant per se is insufficient as a solution (Pss 105 – 106).

So what exactly is the relationship between the Abrahamic covenant and the new covenant?

12 Fulfilment of the Abrahamic covenant is entailed by fulfilment of the new covenant (Ps. 72:17b).

13 New-covenant fulfilment is the framework for fulfilment of the Abrahamic covenant (Pss 84 – 87).

14 The new-covenant people are drawn from all nations (Abrahamic covenant), on the basis of conversion, and do not include all Israelites (Pss 93 – 100); 'sons of Adam' and 'all nations' are included in the new exodus (Ps. 107).

15 New-covenant and Abrahamic-covenant fulfilment will be enabled by a suffering servant (Ps. 102).

Overall, then (and this has proven to be underlined in the Psalter), we must recognize:

16 the convergence of Abrahamic-, Davidic- and new-covenant fulfilment (Pss 103; 107; 118 and immediately preceding context; 136 and immediately preceding context; 145; 146 – 150).

But there is another covenant that plays an important part, particularly in relation to the Davidic and new covenants:

17 the Levitical covenant is associated with the Davidic covenant (Ps. 106:30–31);

18 the 'pedagogy of failure' anticipates superior mediation (Ps. 106);

19 the Levitical covenant is fulfilled by a superior priesthood – combined with kingship (Ps. 110).

Although it has not been a major theme in the Psalter, it should not be overlooked that:

20 the Noahic covenant is an indispensable part of the solution (Pss 104; 148).

We have come to appreciate the superiority of the new-covenant regime:

21 the typological structures are to be recapitulated in a new-covenant solution (Pss 93 – 100);

22 David is recapitulated in a superior antitype (Pss 108 – 110; 138 – 145): victory, judgment and suffering are intensified, and the role of king is combined with that of righteous suffering servant;

23 the priesthood is democratized (Pss 118; 134 – 135);

24 blessings are democratized (Ps. 144);

25 the new-covenant believer's ethic does not correspond to the Sinaitic legislation but does seem to lie in its trajectory (Ps. 119).

All this presupposes that:

26 Sinaitic conditionality is observed (Ps. 133).

With regard to the timing of new-covenant fulfilment, we learned that:

27 new-covenant fulfilment is not yet experienced in the post-exilic period (Ps. 107:43);
28 the new covenant is fulfilled in stages (Pss 119 – 136).

A diagram showing aspects of the interconnectedness of the covenants

I do not attempt to incorporate all twenty-eight statements into this diagram (see Fig. 7.1), but there are advantages here in terms of visualizing some aspects of the interconnectedness of the various biblical covenants. We have seen that the covenants represented by the lighter shading are unconditional and aligned with the new covenant. All five covenants converge in their fulfilment within the framework of the new regime. Conditionality is indicated by the darker shading: conditions must be satisfied under the new covenant. The overlap between the Sinaitic covenant and the Levitical and

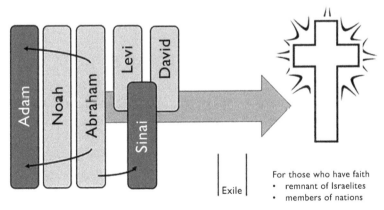

 : conditional covenant

Figure 7.1 **Interconnections between the various biblical covenants**

Davidic covenants reflects the conditional dimension of the latter two covenants. The Abrahamic covenant provides for the solution to the Adamic problem (hence the thin arrows pointing from 'Abraham' to 'Adam'). The thin arrow leading from 'Abraham' to 'Sinai' accommodates the tensions between these two covenants: for as long as the Sinaitic covenant remains in force, we are exposed to the 'pedagogy of failure' (Ps. 106) pending the recapitulation of Sinaitic-covenant types. Yet the Abrahamic covenant will, in time, on the other side of the exile, give rise to the new covenant (hence the thick arrow leading to the cross). The new-covenant antitypes are more glorious than any prior covenant provisions (hence the 'radiance' surrounding the cross in the diagram). They apply to the converted – to those who 'fear YHWH', who have faith in him.

Two key summarizing phrases

The newness of the new covenant relative to the Davidic covenant may be summarized by means of two phrases of two words each: (1) 'eschatological satisfaction' and (2) 'transcendent inauguration'. On the one hand (1), the conditions that provide for the fulfilment of the Davidic covenant are satisfied, following the exile, thanks to the convergence of several covenants in their fulfilment. On the other hand (2), a glorious new regime is inaugurated, transcending the provisions of the Davidic covenant, in which blessings originally promised to Abraham flow to people of all nations, on the basis of conversion.

Evaluation of the seven models

The time has come for us to return to the seven models we presented in chapter 2 (see Fig. 7.2, which is a repetition of Fig. 2.1). At the end of that chapter, I listed several issues raised by a comparison of these models. Where are the models in line with the Psalter's perspective on new-covenant newness, and where are they out of step with the data of the Psalms? Where should we position ourselves on the covenant-relationships spectrum, according to the Psalter? I refer to chapter 2 (this may be the best time for some to read it!), as well as to the twenty-eight statements above, in the discussion that follows.[1]

---

[1] We restrict our comments on model 5 to the specific question of the law (cf. our discussion of this model in chapter 2).

1	2	3	4	5	6	7
Westminster covenant-alism	Reformed Baptist covenant theology	1689 federalism	progressive covenant-alism	new covenant theology	progressive dispensa-tionalism	classical dispensa-tionalism

Figure 7.2 **Evangelical models of covenant relationships viewed on a spectrum (revisited)**

Covenant partner and beneficiary

There are changes evident between the Davidic and new covenants at the fundamental level of the covenant partners and beneficiaries involved. The earlier covenant has as partner David, son of Jesse, even if the people as a whole are indirect beneficiaries, and even if this covenant cannot be dissociated from the Abrahamic and Sinaitic covenants whose partner is Israel.[2] The new-covenant partner is every worshipper of YHWH, all who 'fear' him,[3] Jew or non-Jew (see statements 7 and 14 above).

There are, however, difficulties that we should not avoid in relation to how the new covenant is understood at both ends of the spectrum. Robertson (representing model 1) is ultimately right to speak of the new-covenant people of God as an antitype of Israel[4] – one that incorporates believing Jews. But there is no suggestion in the Psalter that the new-covenant *partner* and the new-covenant *beneficiary* are at variance with each other. If the partner and the beneficiary are one and the same (those who fear YHWH), that creates difficulties for the idea, found within classical Presbyterianism (model 1), that the infants of believing parents may be 'participants in the covenant'.[5] At the other end of the spectrum (classical dispensationalism, model 7), there is, again, an illegitimate disjunction between the partner (Israel) and the beneficiary of the new covenant (which can include believing non-Jews). This disjunction also exists in model 6 (progressive dispensationalism), although it is less marked.

---

[2] For the partner of the Abrahamic covenant, see p. 75 n. 48.

[3] See e.g. p. 122. We have had occasion to note this 'fear' theme in relation to Pss 85; 103; 115 – 118; 135; 145; 147 – 148.

[4] Even if his leaning on Jer. 31 in this regard may be exegetically questionable. See Hely Hutchinson 2022: 189–190.

[5] Although model 2 (the version of covenant theology espoused by Reformed Baptists) is close to model 1, it departs from Westminster at this point: new-covenant members and beneficiaries are those who are regenerate.

Typology and the 'transcendence' implied by the new covenant

The importance of typology in general has been underlined by our study of the Psalter (see statements 2, 18, 19, 21, 22 and 25 above). We have seen that one of the functions of the Davidic covenant is to provide a type of the new-covenant king. We have even been impelled to speak of new-covenant fulfilment in David himself, although this needs to be understood within the framework of David's role as a type. I have commented on the ways in which the notions of exodus, city, king and priest in particular are recapitulated, escalated and reconfigured.

Typology plays an important part in models 1–6. In principle, it is more important in model 3 than in models 1 and 2, for 1689 federalism views the Davidic covenant as a 'typological covenant': we noted that '[e]very single part' of it is considered typologically to reveal the new covenant. In practice, though, we also noted the considerable significance of typology for our representative of model 1. Model 6 (progressive dispensationalism) proposes an unsatisfactory flattening of the type–antitype relationship with its contention that the Melchizedekian priesthood forms part of the Davidic covenant. Expectations regarding 'national, territorial Israel' in this model also undermine the grandiose character of the antitypical structures that the Psalter associates with the new covenant. Model 6 does, however, recognize the superiority of the new-covenant king relative to David. Model 7's literalist hermeneutic militates against its benefiting from the function of typological structures in pointing up the glorious nature of the antitype (in chapter 2, we mentioned the physical temple structure that is understood by classical dispensationalists to form part of a future Israelite kingdom).

I use the adjective 'transcendent' to describe the new-covenant structures in order to highlight the dimension of glory involved in connection with the superiority of the new covenant. It is not simply a matter of 'difference' relative to previous structures. 'Difference' does, however, play a part. For this criterion, one may assume that the more one moves to the right of the spectrum, the more one observes a conception of new covenant that is discontinuous with covenants set up beforehand. In this regard, the first two models exhibit the weakness of flattening the contours of redemptive history owing to their conception of a single covenant. As 1689 federalism (model 3) puts it, it is not a matter of 'more of the same' on a greater scale: there is qualitative, substantive difference in the new covenant.

Combination of kingship and priesthood

A key feature of the new covenant is its combining of the antitype of Davidic kingship and the antitype of Aaronic priesthood in a single figure within the context of a reconfigured (Melchizedekian) order (see statements 19 and 22 above). The democratization of these two functions[6] also forms part of this new order (see statement 23). The 'regime change' that all this entails implies considerable discontinuity relative to what precedes the new covenant. Other things being equal, this tends to move us away from the Westminster-covenantalism pole of the spectrum, although this first model does speak of a change of 'administration'. The Levitical covenant is undervalued in the literature, though given extensive treatment in model 4 (progressive covenantalism). Its close proximity to the Davidic covenant has been an important observation for us (see statements 17 and 19).

Discontinuity with the Sinaitic covenant and distinctions between covenants

The new covenant stands in contrast to the Sinaitic covenant whose demands prove to be too exacting for all except the eschatological, Davidic king (see statements 4, 7 and 26 above). In this regard – discontinuity between the Sinaitic and new covenants – we find ourselves out of step with models 1–3 and lined up with models 4–6. Calvin's speaking of the Abrahamic covenant as being the same as the Sinaitic covenant and the same as the new covenant does not square with our findings. At the other end of the spectrum, model 7 recognizes the Sinaitic conditionality but does not consider this covenant to play a major role in God's plan. Between these two poles, Reformed Baptist covenant theology (model 2) and 1689 federalism (model 3) affirm the conditional dimension of the Sinaitic covenant, though without this constituting a major phenomenon; the idea in model 3 that the Abrahamic covenant might be conditional – since this would be an entailment of its being 'controlled' by the Mosaic covenant – needs to be rejected[7] (see statements 9 and 10 and much of chapter 4).

---

[6] The democratization of *kingship* has not been a major feature, but see p. 146 (Ps. 149).

[7] Although cf. Hely Hutchinson 2022: 90–99 for a discussion of conditionality within the original presentation of the Abrahamic covenant.

Relative to the Davidic covenant, blessings are democratized under the new covenant (statement 24),[8] and the blessing of all nations – promised to Abraham and a major theme in the Psalter (statement 14) – clearly fetches up in the new covenant and leaves model 7 wanting in this respect. Given my hesitation regarding Kaiser's reading of 2 Samuel 7:19b ('the charter for humanity')[9] and my conviction that the Davidic covenant does not itself provide for the blessing of the nations, I lean towards model 6 with regard to the distinctions that need to be maintained between the Abrahamic and Davidic covenants. But I have acknowledged that, in some respects, the Davidic covenant emerges from Abrahamic soil.[10] Further, if model 4 is right to speak of the Davidic covenant as a 'subset of the old covenant', we have not seen this in the Psalter, although it is certainly the case that 'the Davidic king was under Torah' (cf. statement 4). A relationship of 'overlap' seems preferable (cf. Fig. 7.1 showing aspects of interconnectedness between covenants). Again, to suggest that 'the Mosaic covenant controls' the Davidic covenant (model 3) does not fit with what we have seen, except inasmuch as the Sinaitic conditionality needs to be observed. We should not downplay the unconditional promises of the Davidic covenant (cf. Ps. 89!).

The twenty-eight statements above allow us to recognize important distinctions between covenants. It is not appropriate to designate the Abrahamic, Mosaic and Davidic covenants together as forming 'the old covenant' (models 1 and 3); nor, similarly, should we view all covenants prior to the new covenant as being 'incorporated' in the Mosaic covenant (model 2). Model 4 serves us well on this score, recognizing not only the 'organic relationships' between the Davidic and other covenants but also that there is a contrast between the new covenant and the old (Sinaitic) which the new replaces.[11] Model 7 downplays these organic relationships and attributes a significance to the Transjordanian ('Palestinian') covenant that far surpasses its role according to our analysis in chapter 4.[12]

In general, the Psalter speaks more than the various models do of the need for conditions to be satisfied (statements 4, 6, 7, 8, 26). The righteous king (notably of Pss 2; 18; 45; 72; 101 and book 5) is able to satisfy the Sinaitic conditionality, and the people assembled at the new Zion,

---

[8] See also pp. 31–32 and 35.

[9] See p. 32.

[10] See p. 44.

[11] Cf. Jer. 31:32; 2 Cor. 3:14; Heb. 8:13.

[12] See p. 72.

circumcised of heart,[13] are ultimately characterized by obedience: no further exile[14] needs to be envisaged.

Quality of newness

The various models have in common the idea that a *new* regime is inaugurated, but this notion varies between a new administration of the same covenant (model 1) and the establishment of an Israelite kingdom (models 6 and 7). We need to be in the middle of the spectrum on this matter.

Temporality of newness

Our study has enabled us to appreciate the clear dimension of newness at the temporal level (see statements 8, 9 and 10). The new covenant is established after the Babylonian exile and constitutes a response to that catastrophe, which occurred four centuries after the setting-up of the Davidic covenant. All models recognize temporal newness inasmuch as they aim to be sensitive to the unfolding of redemptive history. But the importance of being on the other side of the exile, highlighted by the Psalter, is not majored on in the literature.

Climax, timing and mode of fulfilment

The response to the exile provided by the new covenant is definitive. To be sure, fulfilment occurs in stages (not in a punctiliar fashion: see statements 27 and 28). But the new covenant represents the terminus and climax (see statements 4, 12, 16, 18, 19, 21, 22, 26). No further covenants are required! Model 4 articulates this well in speaking of the new covenant as being the '*fulfillment, telos, and terminus of the biblical covenants*'. There are no suggestions in the Psalter, contra models 6 and 7, that we should await a stage of fulfilment in the millennium that is centred on national Israel.

New-covenant integration

The Davidic covenant comes to be integrated into the new covenant (statement 1). Model 7 falls far short of the revelation of the Psalter in its assertion that the new covenant develops *one aspect* of the Abrahamic covenant. We have seen that the Abrahamic covenant is the basis of the exiles' prayer and thus that it ultimately gives rise to the new covenant[15] (cf. statements 9–13).

---

[13] See p. 129.
[14] See p. 144.
[15] Cf. Gal. 3:8.

Model 6 (progressive dispensationalism) is strikingly clear on this point. But its classical counterpart (model 7) clearly diminishes the stature of the new covenant. It considers the Davidic covenant to develop one aspect of the Abrahamic covenant in an analogous way to the new covenant's developing another aspect, whereas it should be stressed that the new-covenant framework encompasses both the Abrahamic covenant and the Davidic covenant (cf. statements 1, 3, 5, 12–13, 16).

Convergence in fulfilment

The notion of fulfilment features all across the board and is given particular prominence in the middle of the spectrum, in models 3 and 4. The fulfilment of the Davidic covenant depends on the convergence of several other covenants in their fulfilment (statements 3, 12, 13, 15, 16, 19, 20, 26). In one respect, this leads us to acknowledge the ultimately high degree of continuity between the covenants that sits most readily with model 1. Yet even models 6 and 7 recognize the convergence of the Davidic and new covenants in their fulfilment.

Models 4 and 6 may be appreciated for the way in which they express the relationship between the Abrahamic and Davidic covenants in their fulfilment: the Davidic king mediates the Abrahamic covenant blessings (cf. Fig. 3.2[16] and in line with statements 5 and 16).

Tension

We saw fit to square the 'conditionality' and 'unconditionality' strands of the Davidic covenant in a different manner from the scholarly consensus, allowing the tension to remain until it is reconciled by the new-covenant king, YHWH's 'stand-in', who honours the conditions and thus guarantees the promise (see statements 2, 4, 22, 26). In general, such tension is an appreciable hallmark of model 4. This phenomenon of tension should be distinguished from the more general notion of progressive revelation whose importance also features in models 1, 2 and 3.

Law

The law of Moses is no longer in force under the new covenant, not only with regard to its condemning function but also with regard to its regulatory function. This observation fits with models 4–7. The Psalter

---

[16] See p. 45.

will not allow us to affirm, with Robertson (model 1), that the law written on the heart is 'essentially the same' as that of the old covenant. The new law that regulates the new-covenant believer's ethical life does, however, exhibit considerable continuity with the Mosaic code (statement 25). That said, it is not possible, on the basis of the data that we have considered, to adjudicate between models 4 and 5 on the question of whether the Mosaic law should fulfil any function as an indirect guide for the believer's ethic.

Concluding comments regarding the spectrum

It transpires from the above evaluation that I believe the Psalter's perspective to sit most comfortably with model 4 (progressive covenantalism). The other side of the coin is that, as we veer towards either pole, one feels growing discomfort.

But, for two reasons, we should not set too much store by the spectrum. First, in each model, regeneration, faith and the forgiveness of sins are recognized as applying to new-covenant beneficiaries. Second, although the spectrum helps us to evaluate degrees of continuity and discontinuity, it does not cater for all of the specific features of the individual models. This is an important point to highlight, for each model has its strengths. For example, I have already pinpointed the emphasis on typology in model 1. The second model underscores many important aspects of the superiority of the new covenant. Advocates of the third model rightly insist on the qualitatively different character of the new covenant. Progressive dispensationalism (model 6) draws attention to 'three key covenants' (Abrahamic, Davidic, new) and the convergence of these covenants in their fulfilment; this is exactly what we found in books 4 and 5 of the Psalter (see statement 16). Dwight Pentecost (arguing for model 7) emphasizes the fundamental importance of the Abrahamic covenant.

So it is not just a matter of placing oneself – or the Psalter – on the spectrum but also of appropriating the valid insights of each model and eschewing their respective deficiencies.

This brings us back to an important point made in the opening chapter: the debate addressed by this book takes place among those who are seeking to submit to Scripture – among friends (indeed, brothers and sisters) who are fellow partners and beneficiaries of the new covenant. May it be pursued in an irenic atmosphere. May 'iron sharpen iron' (cf. Prov. 27:17). In my experience, many believers have convictions located at a variety of points on the spectrum,[17] and we should be slow to pigeonhole people as we engage in discussion. We are all looking to grow in 'grace and knowledge' (cf. 2 Pet. 3:18).

Covenant relationships elsewhere in Scripture

Other biblical books or corpora?

A residual question needs to be addressed: what if our conclusions are valid only for the Psalter? I am convinced that the type of study we have undertaken in this book could usefully be conducted in other parts of Scripture such as the twelve Minor Prophets (as a group), Chronicles, Luke's Gospel and Hebrews. At no point have I claimed that the Psalter provides a complete answer to every aspect of every covenant-relationships model we considered in chapter 2. May the work of listening attentively to every part of Scripture continue.

That said, having done some of the work on much of the rest of Scripture,[18] I am convinced that our findings in the Psalter line up with biblical revelation in general. Some of the key data from the New Testament are as follows.

The perspective of the New Testament

1. The kinship between the Adamic and Sinaitic covenants (both conditional) emerges clearly from the New Testament. The curses entailed by these covenants are in store (respectively) for humanity in general and the Israelites in particular. Whether it be transgression of the law written on the heart or that of the Mosaic code, the 'whole world' stands guilty before God (Rom. 1:18 – 3:20; 5:12–21; 7:7ff.; 1 Cor. 15:22; Gal. 4:3, 9).

2. Jesus Christ meets the requirements of the conditional covenants. He is the 'last Adam' and the true Israel who succeeds where Adam and Israel failed (John 15:1 [cf. Ps. 80; Isa. 5]; Matt. 2:15 [cf. Exod. 4:22; Hos. 11:1]; 3:15; Luke 3:23–38; 4:1–12; Rom. 5:19; 1 Cor. 15:22; Heb. 2:5–8; 10:5–10

---

[17] If I may speak anachronistically, Martin Luther was associated with model 1 as far as baptism was concerned but perhaps model 5 as far as the law was concerned!
[18] Hely Hutchinson 2022.

[cf. Ps. 40:6–8 (MT 40:7–9)]). The dimension of conditionality featuring in the Davidic and Levitical covenants is also honoured by Christ.

3. The old covenant (that of Sinai) is at odds with the Abrahamic covenant inasmuch as its conditionality – which the Israelite/Jewish people are unable to fulfil – gives rise to cursing (Gal. 3). The law was 'ordained through angels by the agency of a mediator' (Gal. 3:19 NASB), that law covenant being inferior to the Abrahamic covenant;[19] to be under that regime means being in slavery (Gal. 4:21 – 5:1).[20] The new covenant is 'superior' relative to the old (Heb. 7:22; 8:6; cf. Acts 13:38–39): in place of partial and temporary removal of God's wrath brought about by the ministry of sinful mediators, it provides for intercession that is total in its scope, permanent in its effectiveness and sin-free in its administration (Heb. 7 – 10).

4. The promises of the Abrahamic covenant were made to Christ, and, under the new covenant, all those who are united to Christ benefit from them (Gal. 3:6 – 4:7): all who have faith are children of Abraham (Gal. 3:7; Rom. 4:16–19). However, unbelieving Jews are under condemnation (Matt. 21:33–44; cf. 1 Thess. 2:15–16).

5. The Abrahamic and Davidic covenants stand in clear continuity with each other, Jesus being the long-awaited seed of Abraham and David (Matt. 1:1, 17;[21] Luke 1:67–79; John 7:42; Acts 3:25–26; 13:16–37). The 'Psalm 2 king' – the new/eschatological David – is greater than the immediate son of Jesse and also greater than Solomon (Mark 12:35–37; Luke 1:30–33; 11:31; Acts 13:33; Rom. 1:3–4; Col. 1:15–19; Rev. 19:16). The Levitical covenant also finds fulfilment in Christ, even if the priesthood in question undergoes transposition: this Melchizedekian priesthood is indissolubly tied to Christ's kingship (Heb. 1:5; 5:5–6).

---

[19] Cf. Schreiner 2010: 243.

[20] The Hagar–Sarah comparison speaks of 'two covenants' (Gal. 4:24). The covenant that is contrasted with Sinai is not specified. The Abrahamic covenant features in the preceding context (Gal. 3:8, 15–16). It may be, however, that we should understand that the contrast is made with the new covenant (the quoting of Isa. 54 in v. 27 may be cited in favour of this view). Either way, Gal. 3:8 has already made it clear that the Abrahamic covenant gives rise to the new covenant.

[21] The structure of redemptive history, according to Matt. 1, moves from Abraham to David, thence to the exile, and thence to Christ.

6. Hebrews 8:1 – 10:18 elucidates extensively the relationships between the old and new covenants in the area of typology. The author focuses on these two covenants to the extent of calling Sinai the 'first' covenant (8:7, 13; 9:1, 18) and the new covenant 'a second' (8:7). The old covenant must give way to the new (8:7, 13). The superiority of the latter, already noted (8:6), is underlined by means of a range of terms that evoke the contrast between the Sinaitic regime and the fulfilment in Christ (cf. 9:9, 11; 10:1). What we find in the old covenant is a 'copy' (8:5; cf. 9:23), a 'shadow' (8:5; 10:1), a 'parable' (9:9), 'regulations for the body imposed until the time of reformation' (9:10), 'holy places made with hands, which are copies of the true things' (Heb. 9:24 ESV).

7. '[W]hen there is a change in the priesthood, there is necessarily a change in the law as well' (Heb. 7:12 ESV). Under the new covenant, the believer's life is regulated not by Sinai but by the ethic of the 'kingdom of heaven' (Matt. 5 – 7) or the 'law of Christ' (1 Cor. 9:21; Gal. 6:2), which is the new-covenant antitype of the law of Moses (Matt. 5:17ff., 48; 7:12; 22:36–40; Gal. 5:14).

8. The Abrahamic covenant is 'the gospel proclaimed in advance' (Gal. 3:8). But the gospel *itself* is the covenant that the Abrahamic covenant gives rise to, namely the new covenant. This new covenant can be realized only when the Abrahamic covenant comes to be fulfilled alongside other covenants. New-covenant fulfilment occurs in stages. It would not have been possible to know from Psalm 2 that there would be a delay between Christ's resurrection (v. 7; cf. Acts 13:33) and his coming to judge the nations (v. 9; cf. Rev. 19:15). Yet our treatment of book 5 did indicate that the new-exodus journey would be spread over a period of some length.[22] This may be understood as beginning with the cross (which is an *exodos*, 'exodus' [Luke 9:31]) and ending with the setting-up of the new heaven and new earth (Rev. 21 – 22).

9. Thus, our current period is one of tension. The rule of the eschatological king has already come (Matt. 4:17; 12:28; 28:18; Mark 1:14–15; Luke 4:17–22; 11:20; 1 Cor. 10:11; 2 Cor. 5:17; Heb. 6:4) but is also a future concept (Matt. 6:10; Luke 11:2; 22:15–16; 1 Cor. 6:9–10). To be sure, we live

---

[22] See pp. 129–130.

during the 'last days' (Acts 2:17; 2 Pet. 3:3; Heb. 1:2) – even the 'last hour' (1 John 2:18) – but the day of judgment awaits the end of this world (Matt. 13:39–40, 49–50), when Christ returns (Matt. 25:31–32).

10. So we may usefully consider new-covenant fulfilment as occurring in three stages.[23] First (stage 1), the new covenant is inaugurated by the death of Christ (Luke 22:20; 1 Cor. 11:25). It is on the cross that Christ is enthroned (John 12:27–33), that he suffers as God's servant (Acts 8:30–36), that he defeats Satan (Col. 2:14–15) and that he obtains the forgiveness of sins and the blessings of the Abrahamic covenant on behalf of his people (Gal. 3:13–14; 1 Pet. 2:22–24). Christ's coming was welcomed as the end of the exile (Luke 2 – 4).

11. Stage 2 corresponds to the period during which we currently live. Under the new covenant, believers are circumcised of heart by the Spirit (Rom. 2:29; 2 Cor. 3:7–18), but sin, suffering and persecution have yet to be eradicated (we live in the era of frustration – Rom. 8:18–25 – and the new-exodus journey is still continuing). To be sure, everything that Christ has procured for us is already ours in the heavenly realms, by faith (Eph. 1:3–14; 2:6). We have arrived at our terminus: we have come to Zion – to 'Jesus, the mediator of a new covenant' (Heb. 12:22–24 ESV). At the same time, 'here we have no lasting city, but we seek the city that is to come' (Heb. 13:14 ESV). We are 'sojourners and exiles' (1 Pet. 2:11 ESV) in this world (1 Pet. 1–2; Heb. 11:13). The Spirit is the guarantee of our heavenly inheritance (2 Cor. 1:21–22; 2 Cor. 5:5; Eph. 1:14). [If the parousia seems to be long in coming, we do well to remind ourselves that the resurrection of Christ is inextricably tied to the judgment/end (Acts 17:31; 1 Cor. 15) as is also justification to glorification (Rom. 5:9–10; 8:30). We may groan, though not without hope (Rom. 8:23–24)!]

12. Stage 3 lies in the future. The full realization of the new covenant must await the time when we obey God perfectly in a new cosmos, with sin and its effects no longer present (2 Pet. 3:13; Rev. 21:3–4, 27; 22:3). Although it evokes the circumstances that prevailed before the fall (Rev. 22:1–5), this definitive new-covenant fulfilment will not amount to a simple return to the garden of Eden, for a vast community of the redeemed, drawn from

---

[23] Cf. Goldsworthy 1991: 261–305.

all nations, will serve God and the Lamb (Davidic king) for all eternity (Rev. 7; 21 – 22).

Implications

I have elsewhere explored the implications of one's stance on covenant relationships.[24] We may usefully conclude by pointing the way for some of these implications.

At the level of our appreciation of the gospel

A right understanding of new-covenant newness is important inasmuch as precision and accuracy in our grasp of biblical revelation in general is important. The quest for accuracy applies particularly to those of us who have the responsibility of teaching God's Word to others (2 Tim. 2:15). Scripture's message is the gospel message. When we take the Lord's Supper, we want to understand what our Lord meant by the words 'This cup is the new covenant in my blood' (Luke 22:20; cf. 1 Cor. 11:25). We want others to understand too. The meaning of the death of Jesus Christ is at issue. We are at the heart of the glorious gospel.

On the Emmaus road, Cleopas and his companion had the privilege of being taught biblical theology by the Master himself (Luke 24). A little later, reflecting on this experience, '[t]hey said to each other, "Did not our hearts burn within us while he talked to us on the road, while he opened to us the Scriptures?"' (v. 32 ESV). Is it not fair to suggest that this should be the experience of all healthy believers? Gospel-induced joy hinges in considerable measure on an ability rightly to grasp the contours of redemptive history.[25] Tension, typology, progressive revelation and new-covenant climax all play their part. According to 2 Corinthians 3:7–18, as we gaze on the glory of the new-covenant king from the standpoint of biblical theology, we are transformed 'from one degree of glory to another' (v. 18 ESV).

By contrast, if we are positioned at model 7, our focus could readily be elsewhere – on geopolitical developments in the Middle East, and with the expectation that a physical temple will be erected in Jerusalem and sacrifices offered there.

---

[24] Hely Hutchinson 2022: 161–181.
[25] Cf. Hely Hutchinson 2015b.

At a practical-theological level

If the findings of this book are correct, the Psalter draws a clear distinction between the old (Sinaitic) and new covenants, and there is significant discontinuity between the two. If, however, we line ourselves up with model 1, we are required, in practice, to choose between giving pride of place to old-covenant theology or to new-covenant theology. Most interpreters at that point on the spectrum 'flatten the contours' in favour of the new covenant. But what if one privileges the old covenant? Some, who hold to justification by faith alone in principle, nonetheless apply the theology of the Sinaitic covenant to us new-covenant believers in such a way as to make salvation conditional on performance.[26] Consider these words:

> The covenant is no automatic guarantee of salvation, for it is a working relationship. The salvation of covenant children is endangered when they become lax and slack, for the devil always lies waiting at the door. Our sinful and weak nature continues to bother us. Therefore we have to give our utmost in the Lord's service.[27]

The pastoral stakes here are high: the consequences in terms of depriving believers of the assurance of their salvation can be disastrous! It is the performance of our perfect new-covenant king – and not our own – that is the basis on which we may know that new-covenant blessings apply to us who have faith.

At a practical level

An example of a directly practical implication of model 1 relates to evangelism.[28] There are no commandments in the law of Moses that call upon the Israelites to evangelize the nations. Israel was required to be 'a kingdom of priests and a holy nation' for the benefit of the surrounding nations (Exod. 19:5–6). The dynamic that was meant to be at work here is centripetal (converging on the centre [Deut. 4:5–8]). We see this dynamic operating for the benefit of Jethro, Rahab and Naaman (among others), but, in essence, the Israelites failed to live up to their calling.

---

26 Cf. Hely Hutchinson 2022: 166–168.
27 Stam 1999: 147.
28 For a fuller treatment of this theme, see Hely Hutchinson 2021b.

They are replaced by the suffering servant of Isaiah 42 – 61 (unlike Israel, he will fulfil his mission as a priest; for example, 'he will sprinkle many nations' [Isa. 52:15 NIV]). But with the advent of the servant, the regime changes, and so does the dynamic of mission. Thanks to the servant, salvation is to 'reach to the ends of the earth' (Isa. 49:6). How does this happen in practice? He makes his new-covenant partners priests (Isa. 61:6; Acts 13:47). The dynamic has become fundamentally centrifugal (moving away from the centre), and we believers are caught up in it.

If one considers that there is only one covenant, one is liable to apply an old-covenant model of evangelism to our new-covenant era, as some Presbyterian authors do.[29] Under this scenario, the idea is that godly behaviour within the local church should attract unbelievers. There is, of course, a place for this dynamic under the new covenant (cf. 1 Cor. 14:23–25), but the major thrust is centrifugal (Matt. 28:18–20; 1 Pet. 2:9).

Even if one flattens the contours in the other direction, the motivation for evangelism is impaired. On this scenario, in which a new-covenant model is attributed to the Israelites, there is no distinction between our evangelistic activity and that of the Israelites: in both covenants, the call is to move outward in order to proclaim the message. If this is what we believe, we fail to appreciate the *privilege* that centrifugal mission constitutes when we view it from the perspective of redemptive history and, in particular, in the light of its *contrast* with the old-covenant (centripetal) dynamic.

At the other end of the spectrum, it can be considered important under model 7 to promote the return of Jewish people to the land of modern-day Israel. An example of this may be found in the activities and exhortations of the organization Ebenezer Operation Exodus.[30] In its statement of faith, we read: 'God has a prophetic, spiritual purpose for the return of the Jewish people to The Land He promised them.' Accordingly, this organization's 'work involves helping as many Jewish people as possible to immigrate to Israel'. The vision statement declares that part of the aim is 'to proclaim God's kingdom purposes for [the Jews'] return'.

The Psalter's perspective points in a different direction: the typological structures of the old covenant are recapitulated (statement 21).

---

[29] Cf. Hely Hutchinson 2022: 171–173.
[30] <https://ebenezer-oe.org/about-us> (accessed 31 December 2022).

Closing doxology

I give the last words to New Testament authors, with the prayer that they may provide a particular impetus for us to give glory to God for the wonder of the new-covenant newness set forth in the Psalter:

> But Jesus answered [John the Baptist], 'Let it be so now, for thus it is fitting for us to fulfil all righteousness.'
> (Matt. 3:15 ESV)

> Praise be to the Lord, the God of Israel,
>   because he has come to his people and redeemed them.
> He has raised up a horn of salvation for us
>   in the house of his servant David
> (as he said through his holy prophets of long ago),
> salvation from our enemies
>   and from the hand of all who hate us –
> to show mercy to our ancestors
>   and to remember his holy covenant,
>   the oath he swore to our father Abraham:
> to rescue us from the hand of our enemies,
>   and to enable us to serve him without fear
>   in holiness and righteousness before him all our days.
> (Luke 1:68–75 NIV)

> We tell you the good news: what God promised our ancestors he has fulfilled for us, their children, by raising up Jesus. As it is written in the second Psalm:

> 'You are my son;
>   today I have become your father.'
> (Acts 13:32–33 NIV)

> In the same way, Christ did not take on himself the glory of becoming a high priest. But God said to him,

> 'You are my Son;
>   today I have become your Father.'

And he says in another place,

> 'You are a priest for ever,
>> in the order of Melchizedek.'
> (Heb. 5:5–6 NIV)

The former regulation is set aside because it was weak and useless (for the law made nothing perfect), and a better hope is introduced, by which we draw near to God. And it was not without an oath! Others became priests without any oath, but he became a priest with an oath when God said to him:

> 'The Lord has sworn
>> and will not change his mind:
>> "You are a priest for ever."'

Because of this oath, Jesus has become the guarantor of a better covenant.
(Heb. 7:18–22 NIV)

When He said, 'A new *covenant*,' He has made the first obsolete. But whatever is becoming obsolete and growing old is ready to disappear.
(Heb. 8:13 NASB)

And they sing the song of Moses, the servant of God, and the song of the Lamb, saying,

> 'Great and amazing are your deeds,
>> O Lord God the Almighty!
> Just and true are your ways,
>> O King of the nations!
> Who will not fear, O Lord,
>> and glorify your name?
> For you alone are holy.
>> All nations will come
>> and worship you,
> for your righteous acts have been revealed.'
> (Rev. 15:3–4 ESV)

Appendix 1
Hierarchy[1] of key indicators
of Psalter shape/shaping

1 Psalm 72:20 (explanatory note)
2 Psalm 89:52 [MT 89:53] (closing doxology necessarily more tied to book 3 than to the psalm)
3 The five-book division
4 Psalms 146 – 150 ('Final Hallel')
5 Psalms 120 – 134 (Songs of Ascents)
6 Chain-linking ('concatenation') across Psalms 134, 135 and 136
7 Psalms 105 – 106 ('twins')
8 Psalms 103 – 107
9 Psalms 96 – 99
10 Psalms 93 – 100
11 Psalms 25; 34 (acrostics whose irregularities are similar)
12 Psalms 111 – 112 ('twin' acrostics)
13 Psalms 9 – 10; 32 – 33
14 Entire first book explicitly Davidic (once links in item 13 assumed)
15 Psalms 1 – 2 as introduction
16 Psalms 42 – 43; 70 – 71 (which links imply an absence of 'orphan psalms'[2] in book 2)
17 Predominance of the historical David in book 2
18 Book 1 republications in book 2: Psalms 14 and 53; Psalms 40:13–17 [MT 40:14–18] and 70

---

[1] The hierarchy proper applies to the first fifteen indicators; thereafter I simply follow Psalter order.
[2] Psalms lacking a title.

19 Extremities of book 3 – the theme of crisis:
- turnaround in Psalm 73 mirrored by turnaround in Psalm 89
- complementary perspectives of psalms adjacent to extremities (Pss 74 and 88)
- the role of the Babylonian exile in giving rise to the crisis

20 The same anguished questioning in the middle of book 3
21 The rhetorical effect of the end of Psalm 89
22 The change of tone in the last two books
23 Book 4 as 'Moses-book'
24 The sin–wrath–intercession frame of book 4, and the links between Psalms 90 and 103
25 The structure of book 5 (several groupings)
26 Composite psalms in book 5 (notably Pss 108; 144)
27 The conclusion of Psalm 144 (double 'Amen'; cf. Pss 1 – 2)

Appendix 2
Second example of ambiguity between YHWH and his king in a prophecy concerning the new covenant

We read in Zechariah 11:10: 'And I took my staff Favour, and I broke it, annulling the covenant that I had made with all the peoples' (ESV). Thomas McComiskey expresses the exegetical difficulty as follows: 'The reference to "my covenant" within a series of first-person suffixes referring to the prophet is unusual. We cannot refer this suffix to him, for only Yahweh could exercise control over the nations.'[1] Here is a possible solution: 'The reference to the covenant "that *I* had made" . . . shows the immediacy of the divine presence in the prophet's consciousness, for he can move easily from his words to those of Yahweh.'[2]

But Paul Lamarche's structural analysis may hold the key to a more satisfying explanation.[3] He identifies four sections which describe 'the successive phases of the efforts made by the king or the pastor to save the people of Israel'[4] (9:9–10; 11:4–17; 12:10 – 13:1; 13:7–9).[5] In other words, the figure that the prophet symbolizes in 11:4ff. has already been evoked in 9:9–10: it is the shepherd-king, who is intimately tied to YHWH. This king had made a covenant with 'all the peoples'[6] (11:10). But the link

---

[1] McComiskey 1998: 1197.

[2] Ibid. 1200–1201; emphasis original.

[3] Inasmuch as the solution may be discerned within the book, pending the brighter light of the NT.

[4] Lamarche 1961: 110.

[5] For examples of the influence of Lamarche's structure, see Baldwin 1972: 74–81; K. L. Barker 1985: 600; *Bible d'étude Semeur 2000* 2001: 1369.

[6] This is probably a reference to the totality of Israelites, drawn from Judah and Israel (see Petterson 2015: 248; Hely Hutchinson 2022: 222).

between YHWH and this king is such that the wages that the king receives (v. 12) correspond – at least according to the most natural reading of the syntax of verse 13 – to the 'price at which [YHWH] was valued' (NASB). Whose wages: YHWH's or the king's? Who is the 'I' of verse 10? That this case of ambiguity between YHWH and his king occurs in the context of new-covenant prophecy is particularly clear in the last of Lamarche's 'messiah' sections (see Zech. 13:9).

Appendix 3
Second possible explanation of the relationship between Psalm 106 and 1 Chronicles 16

While I do not believe that Psalm 106 quotes 1 Chronicles 16, it is unclear whether the explanation for the overlap between the two passages is that of independent sourcing (which we mention in chapter 4) or the following explanation.

It is possible that the Chronicler cites Psalm 106. If this is the case, he does so highly selectively, drawing on only three verses of the psalm, consciously omitting (*inter alia*) the latter's reference to the exile ('those holding them captive' [Ps. 106:46]) and reworking the material in a way that is appropriate to another context.[1] The other two psalms that correspond to 1 Chronicles 16:8–36 (Pss 96; 105), likewise, do not feature in their entirety. This would again suggest that, if there is dependence in one or other direction, it is the Chronicler who does the quoting and not the psalmist.

If one compares the whole passage of 1 Chronicles 16:8–36 with the three parallel psalms,[2] additional reasons emerge that point to the Chronicler's use of the psalms and not the reverse. First, where Psalm 105:6 addresses the 'seed of Abraham' (*zera' 'abrāhām*), we find in 1 Chronicles 16:13 'seed of Israel' (*zera' yiśrā'ēl*), in keeping with the Chronicler's emphasis on the theme of 'all Israel'.[3] Second, the cohesion of 1 Chronicles 16:8–36 as a unit[4] would be less clear if the first word of verse 35,

---

[1] The prayer of v. 35 would presuppose the dispersion of prisoners of war long before the time of the exile. Cf. Keil, cited by Payne (1988: 392).

[2] Cf. Auffret 1995: 307; Wallace 1999: 269–271.

[3] Cf. H. G. M. Williamson 1982: 129; Pratt 1998: 15–16.

[4] Cf. Becker 1986: 72.

wĕ'imrû ('and say [plural imperative]'), were absent. Significantly, this word is indeed absent from the Psalm 106 parallel: Delitzsch goes so far as to say that it is 'an indispensable brace in the fitting together of cvi. 1 (cvii. 1) and cvi. 47. The device of which the historian, who connects various passages together as in a mosaic, makes use is patent.'[5]

There is a second place where a plural imperative in the Chronicles passage is found where the Psalter uses a perfective (a phenomenon which is not found in reverse):[6] in 1 Chronicles 16:15, the people are instructed to remember (*zikrû*) the Abrahamic covenant, whereas in Psalm 105:8 it is YHWH who remembers it. In addition, another case of second person in place of third person features four verses later (a pronominal suffix: 'when you were' [*bihyôtĕkem* (1 Chr. 16:19), as opposed to 'when they were' [*bihyôtām* (Ps. 105:12)]).

These differences between 1 Chronicles 16:8–36 and its Psalter parallels readily square with the Chronicler's overall aim, which Brevard Childs summarizes as follows: 'to interpret to the restored community in Jerusalem the history of Israel as an eternal covenant between God and David which demanded an obedient response to the divine law'.[7] With regard to chapter 16 in particular, Hugh Williamson remarks:

> [I]t is probable that [the Chronicler] would be inviting [his contemporaries] to renew their faith in the God who, having answered the prayers and aspirations expressed in these verses so abundantly in the days of David and Solomon, could be relied upon to do so again despite all appearances in a later day.[8]

This would explain the Chronicler's preference for imperatives: his concern is to exhort his readers to celebrate YHWH's faithfulness to his promises. The absence in Chronicles of Psalm 105's lengthy recounting of the history of the Israelites would be explained by the Chronicler's emphasis, in the immediate context, on the arrival of the ark in Jerusalem.[9] Again, the concern in Psalm 106 to highlight the inveterate sinfulness of

---

[5] Delitzsch 1889: 133.
[6] Although there are imperatives in Ps. 96:10 and Ps. 106:48 where the Chronicler has, respectively, a jussive and an infinitive absolute (the latter functioning as an imperative).
[7] Childs 1979: 644.
[8] H. G. M. Williamson 1982: 128. Cf. Pratt 1998: 144.
[9] Cf. Japhet 1993: 317.

the people is not that of the Chronicler, hence his drawing on only the beginning and end of the psalm.[10]

We may summarize this view in Leslie Allen's words:

> In verses 8–36 the Chronicler gives three samples of praise in an anthology derived from the Book of Psalms . . . He adduces them as appropriate expressions of praise at this juncture in Israel's history. In so doing, he has to adapt his material slightly . . . The chief merit of these particular extracts for the Chronicler is that they served to reflect, as in a mirror, his dominant concerns in this overall section and bridged the gap between ancient history and contemporary worship in the Chronicler's day.[11]

We should stress that should this account of the relationship between Psalms and Chronicles be correct, it would not undermine the latter's historical authenticity. As Derek Kidner rightly states, '1 Chronicles 16 does not claim that these were necessarily the very words that were sung on that occasion': verse 7 'leaves the exact relation of the psalms to the narrative undefined'.[12] If it is right to consider 1 Chronicles 16:8–36 to be the *ipsissima vox* and not the *ipsissima verba* of the Levites (their voice, as opposed to their precise words), historicity remains intact ('historical reportage is often more akin to painting than photography').[13]

---

[10] Pratt 1998: 144.
[11] Allen 1987: 116.
[12] Kidner 1975: 347, incl. n. 1.
[13] Long 1994: 85.

Appendix 4
Meaning of 'Of David'
after Psalm 72:20

The Psalter reader has to reckon with the difficult question of the meaning of 'Of David' (*lĕdāwid*) when it occurs after what an editor–compiler has told us is the last of David's prayers (Ps. 72:20).

We submit that the key to the answer lies with its first occurrence, in Psalm 86, and in particular with noting, with Brevard Childs, that 'almost every line [of Psalm 86] has picked up a phrase from another portion of Scripture and fashioned it into a poem'.[1] It is, asserts Kirkpatrick, 'the composition of some pious soul whose mind was steeped with the scriptures already in existence, and who recast reminiscences of them into a prayer to suit his own particular needs'.[2] There is no reason, in our view (and contra Kirkpatrick), why this 'pious soul' could not have (in practice) been David, (immediate) son of Jesse, himself; but that is not the matter at hand, for Kirkpatrick is right that we are to see here 'an imitation' of David's prayers[3] – or, better, a recapitulation. For this recasting of prior material has a particular Psalter context – one in which David's final prayer has already been uttered (Ps. 72:20) and in which there is no Davidic throne. '[P]erhaps [Psalm 86] is a timely reminder, at a time of exile, that all the old truths of the anointed king and his covenant God are as relevant now – when there is no king – as they ever were.'[4] This squares with our earlier discussion of how Psalm 86 functions to presage new-covenant realities.[5]

What, then, is the meaning of 'Of David' in a post-book 2 setting? In Christopher Seitz's words, '[n]ot David the man, but David the

---

[1] Childs 1979: 514; cf. also Harman 1998: 293.
[2] Kirkpatrick 1895: 515.
[3] Ibid.
[4] Ash 2018: 177.
[5] See pp. 55–56.

paradigmatic ruler, will now be the focus of interest'.[6] In sum, it seems appropriate to interpret *lĕdāwid* as 'relating to a recapitulated (/new/ eschatological) David'. The number of other post-Psalm 72 'David' psalms that are composites (drawing on earlier psalms) – discussed in relation to book 5[7] – supports this understanding of the phrase.

[6] Seitz 1998: 159.
[7] See chapter 5, pp. 134ff., including nn. 76 and 77.

Appendix 5
Referent of the first-person plural in Psalm 117:2

In Psalm 117:2, we read that YHWH's *ḥesed* 'is strong towards us'. Is it possible to identify the referent of the first-person plural – the 'us' of 'towards us' (*ʿālênû*)?

As is the case for the equivalent pronominal suffix in Psalm 100:3 (*ʿāśānû*) and the independent personal pronoun 'we' (*ʾănaḥnû*) in that same verse, already discussed,[1] many commentators neglect to analyse this or to adopt a stance on the question; for others, the exegetical choice seems arbitrary. 'The psalm almost appears to tease its listeners with the question of who the "us" is in verse 2,' declares Craig Broyles.[2] According to the consensus view among those who express an opinion on the matter, the first-person plural refers to the people of Israel. On this understanding, the meaning would be that the nations should praise YHWH for his faithfulness towards the Jews.

This majority position is compatible with our insistence on the fact that the nations are on view in the phrase 'those who fear YHWH' in Psalm 118:4. Thus Kirkpatrick asserts: '[the] invitation to all nations to join in praising Jehovah for His goodness to Israel is virtually a recognition that the ultimate object of Israel's calling was the salvation of the world.'[3] This stance has the advantage of being of a piece with the Genesis texts that speak of the nations as indirect beneficiaries[4] of the Abrahamic promises rather than immediate covenant partners.[5]

---

[1] See p. 100.

[2] Broyles 1999: 437.

[3] Kirkpatrick 1901: 691.

[4] Although the blessing of all nations is the climactic, even principal, purpose of the Abrahamic covenant (cf. Hely Hutchinson 2022: 86–88).

[5] The partner being the three patriarchs and their 'seed' (*zeraʿ* [Gen. 12:7; 13:15; 17:7; 24:7; 26:2–4; 28:13–14; 35:12]). Cf. also Lev. 26:42–45 and chapter 4, n. 48.

There are, however, scholars who are open to the possibility that the first-person plural includes non-Jews.[6] Alec Motyer is decisive in this regard. For him, 'us' corresponds to 'a "world-Israel", the whole family of the children of Abraham'.[7] Our reading of book 5 allows us to line up with Motyer[8] and to offer reasons in favour of this position that emerge from the data of the Psalter itself.

First, although Psalm 117:2 may appear to provide only *general* reasons why the nations should praise God, as Walter Brueggemann vigorously maintains,[9] its content, as constrained by the literary context of the Egyptian Hallel (Pss 113 – 118), is specific.[10] As we saw in chapter 5, the (*ḥesed*) and loyalty (*'ĕmet*) in question (Ps. 117:2) refer to these attributes of YHWH not in a general sense but in relation to his delivering of his people from the Babylonian exile. We have demonstrated that, from the standpoint of book 5, members of the nations participate in this new exodus.

Second, the idea that YHWH's *ḥesed* is 'strong' (*gābar*) has already featured in Psalm 103:11.[11] Since we do not find this collocation elsewhere in Scripture, we do well to consider what intertextual dialogue may be operating here. In chapter 4, I discussed the Abrahamic hue of Psalm 103 and considered that the phrase 'those who fear [YHWH]' can accommodate non-Jews.[12] In chapter 5, we again understood this phrase in Psalms 115 and 118 to encompass non-Jews and noted that the context of the occurrences of the phrase places the burden of proof on those who would restrict the referent to Jews.[13]

Third, Jacquet is no doubt right to suggest that in Psalm 117:2 the psalmist 'condenses the thought of the so-called royal Psalms 96 – 100,

---

[6] Kidner 1975: 412; Broyles 1999: 437; Schaefer 2001: 287–288; Eaton 2003: 402; Bullock 2017: 345.

[7] Motyer 1994: 564.

[8] Although I would prefer not to use his phrase 'world-Israel': the people of God is redefined across the Psalter, but the distinctions between Israelites and the nations are not left aside.

[9] Brueggemann 1984: 159. Here, though, he is writing before the rise of editorial criticism and his landmark 1991 article.

[10] It is interesting to note that, some seventy years ago, long before the rise of canonical exegesis, Edward Kissane could be influenced by Ps. 117's placement (he mentions the adjacent psalms) in concluding that the 'fidelity' of v. 2 refers to the election of the people and their settlement in the land (1954: 215). In his view, however, the people in question are the Israelites and the settlement which took place in Canaan following the *first* exodus, whereas I argue for a recapitulation of Israel's history.

[11] As noted, implicitly or explicitly, by several commentators, including Beaucamp (1979: 215, citing inadvertently Ps. 113:11).

[12] See pp. 107–109.

[13] See pp. 122–123.

giving it a more incisive, even more triumphant expression'.[14] There can be no doubting that, in the final form of the Psalter, Psalm 117 echoes Psalm 100. Our interpretation of the suffix in Psalm 117:2 squares with the reading we provided for that similar case in Psalm 100:3.[15]

---

[14] Jacquet 1978: 297.
[15] Our interpretation certainly fits well with Paul's point as he cites Ps. 117 in Rom. 15:11.

Bibliography

Allen, L. C. (1976), *The Books of Joel, Obadiah, Jonah, and Micah*, NICOT, Grand Rapids: Eerdmans.

—— (1983), *Psalms 101–150*, WBC 21, Waco: Word.

—— (1987), *1, 2 Chronicles*, Communicator's Commentary, Dallas: Word.

—— (2002), *Psalms 101–150*, WBC 21, 2nd edn, Nashville: Thomas Nelson.

Amsler, S. (1992), 'Amos', in E. Jacob, C.-A. Keller, S. Amsler, *Osée, Joël, Abdias, Jonas, Amos*, Commentaire de l'Ancien Testament XIa, 3rd edn, Geneva: Labor et Fides, 159–247.

Anderson, A. A. (1972a), *The Book of Psalms, vol. 1: Introduction and Psalms 1–72*, NCBC, London: Marshall, Morgan & Scott.

—— (1972b), *The Book of Psalms, vol. 2: Psalms 73–150*, NCBC, London: Marshall, Morgan & Scott.

—— (1989), *2 Samuel*, WBC 11, Dallas: Word.

Anderson, R. D. (1994), 'The Division and Order of the Psalms', *WTJ* 56: 219–241.

Ash, C. (2018), *Teaching Psalms: From Text to Message, vol. 2: A Christian Introduction to Each Psalm*, Fearn: Christian Focus; London: PT Resources.

Auffret, P. (1982), *La Sagesse a bâti sa maison: Études de structures littéraires dans l'Ancien Testament et spécialement dans les Psaumes*, Orbis Biblicus et Orientalis 49, Fribourg: Editions Universitaires; Göttingen: Vandenhoeck & Ruprecht, 409–438.

—— (1995), *Merveilles à nos yeux: Étude structurelle de vingt psaumes dont celui de 1Ch 16,8–36*, BZAW 235, Berlin: De Gruyter.

Auwers, J.-M. (1996), 'Le Psaume 132 parmi les graduels', *RB* 103: 546–560.

—— (2000), *La Composition littéraire du Psautier: Un état de la question*, CRB 46, Paris: Gabalda.

—— (2003), 'Les Voies de l'exégèse canonique du Psautier', in J.-M. Auwers and H. J. de Jonge (eds.), *The Biblical Canons*, BETL 163, Leuven: Leuven University Press, 5–26.

Baldwin, J. G. (1972), *Haggai, Zechariah, Malachi: An Introduction and Commentary*, TOTC, Leicester: Inter-Varsity Press; Downers Grove: InterVarsity Press.

Barbiero, G. (2014), 'Messianismus und Theokratie: Die Verbindung der Psalmen 144 und 145 und ihre Bedeutung für die Komposition des Psalters', *OTE* 27: 41–52.

Barcellos, R. C. (2001), *In Defense of the Decalogue: A Critique of New Covenant Theology*, Enumclaw: Winepress.

Barker, D. G. (1986), 'The Waters of the Earth: An Exegetical Study of Psalm 104:1–9', *Grace Theological Journal* 7: 57–80.

Barker, K. L. (1985), 'Zechariah', in Frank E. Gaebelein (ed.), EBC 7, Grand Rapids: Zondervan, 595–697.

Beaucamp, E. (1976), *Le Psautier: Ps 1–72*, Paris: Gabalda.

—— (1979), *Le Psautier: Ps 73–150*, Paris: Gabalda.

Becker, J. (1986), *1 Chronik*, Die Neue Echter Bibel 18, Würzburg: Echter Verlag.

Beckwith, R. T. (1985), *The Old Testament Canon of the New Testament Church and Its Background in Early Judaism*, London: SPCK.

—— (1995), 'The Early History of the Psalter', *TynBul* 46: 1–28.

Berder, M. (1996), *'La Pierre rejetée par les bâtisseurs': Psaume 118,22–23 et son emploi dans les traditions juives et dans le Nouveau Testament*, Études Bibliques nouvelle série 31, Paris: Gabalda.

Berthoud, P. (2001), 'L'Appel à la justice et à l'amour de Dieu: Réflexions sur les psaumes imprécatoires', unpublished lecture delivered on the occasion of the opening ceremony of the Faculté Libre de Théologie Evangélique de Vaux-sur-Seine (via cassette).

Bible d'étude Semeur 2000 (2001), Cléon d'Andran: Excelsis.

Blackburn, E. M. (2013), 'Covenant Theology Simplified', in E. M. Blackburn (ed.), *Covenant Theology: A Baptist Distinctive*, Birmingham: Solid Ground, 17–62.

Blaising, C. A. (1993), in C. A. Blaising and D. L. Bock (eds.), *Progressive Dispensationalism*, Grand Rapids: Baker, chs. 5–6, 128–211.

Blocher, H. A. G. (1988), *Révélation des origines: Le début de la Genèse*, rev. and expanded edn, Lausanne: Presses Bibliques Universitaires.

—— (2000), *La Doctrine du péché et de la rédemption*, Collection Didaskalia, Vaux-sur-Seine: Edifac.

—— (2002), *La Doctrine du Christ*, Collection Didaskalia, Vaux-sur-Seine: Edifac.

Block, D. I. (2003), 'My Servant David: Ancient Israel's Vision of the Messiah', in R. S. Hess and M. D. Carroll R. (eds.), *Israel's Messiah in the Bible and the Dead Sea Scrolls*, Grand Rapids: Baker Academic, 17–56.

—— (2012), *Deuteronomy*, NIVAC, Grand Rapids: Zondervan.

—— (2021), *Covenant: The Framework of God's Grand Plan of Redemption*, Grand Rapids: Baker Academic.

Bock, D. L. (2022), 'Progressive Dispensationalism', in B. E. Parker and R. J. Lucas (eds.), *Covenantal and Dispensational Theologies: Four Views on the Continuity of Scripture*, Spectrum Multiview, Downers Grove: IVP Academic, 112–146.

Boice, J. M. (1996), *Psalms: An Expositional Commentary, vol. 2: Psalms 42–106*, Grand Rapids: Baker.

Briggs, C. A., and E. G. Briggs (1907), *A Critical and Exegetical Commentary on the Book of Psalms*, vol. 1, Edinburgh: T&T Clark.

Brown, W. P. (2002), *Seeing the Psalms: A Theology of Metaphor*, Louisville: Westminster John Knox.

Broyles, C. C. (1999), *Psalms*, NIBC 11, Peabody: Hendrickson; Carlisle: Paternoster.

Brueggemann, W. (1984), *The Message of the Psalms: A Theological Commentary*, Minneapolis: Augsburg.

—— (1988), *Israel's Praise: Doxology against Idolatry and Ideology*, Philadelphia: Fortress.

—— (1991), 'Bounded by Obedience and Praise: The Psalms as Canon', *JSOT* 50: 63–92.

Buis, P. (1968), 'La Nouvelle Alliance', *VT* 18: 1–15.

—— (1976), *La Notion d'alliance dans l'Ancien Testament*, Lectio Divina 88, Paris: Cerf.

Bullock, C. H. (2001), *Encountering the Book of Psalms: A Literary and Theological Introduction*, Encountering Biblical Studies, Grand Rapids: Baker.

—— (2017), *Psalms, vol. 2: Psalms 73–150*, Teach the Text, Grand Rapids: Baker.

Butler, T. C. (1978), 'A Forgotten Passage from a Forgotten Era', *VT* 28: 142–150.

Calvin, J. (1859), *Commentaires sur le livre des Pseaumes, vol. I: Pss 1–68*, Paris: Ch. Meyrueis (translation available at <https://biblehub.com/commentaries/calvin/psalms/1.htm> accessed 26 February 2023).

—— (1960), *Institutes of the Christian Religion*, ed. J. T. McNeill, tr. F. L. Battles, 2 vols., Philadelphia: Westminster.

Chantry, W. J. (2013), 'Baptism and Covenant Theology', in E. M. Blackburn (ed.), *Covenant Theology: A Baptist Distinctive*, Birmingham: Solid Ground, 125–135.

Childs, B. S. (1962), *Memory and Tradition in Israel*, SBT 37, Naperville: Alec R. Allenson.

—— (1979), *Introduction to the Old Testament as Scripture*, Philadelphia: Fortress.

Clemens, D. M. (1994), 'The Law of Sin and Death: Ecclesiastes and Genesis 1–3', *Themelios* 19: 5–8.

Clifford, R. J. (2000), 'What Does the Psalmist Ask For in Psalms 39:5 and 90:12?', *JBL* 119: 59–66.

Clines, D. J. A. (1997), *The Theme of the Pentateuch*, JSOTSup 10, 2nd edn, Sheffield: Sheffield Academic Press.

Coppens, J. (1955), *La Portée messianique du Psaume CX*, ALBO 3/1, Leuven: Publications Universitaires de Louvain; Bruges: Desclée de Brouwer.

Craigie, P. C. (1976), *The Book of Deuteronomy*, NICOT, Grand Rapids: Eerdmans.

—— (1983), *Psalms 1–50*, WBC 19, Waco: Word.

Creach, J. F. D. (1996), *Yahweh as Refuge and the Editing of the Hebrew Psalter*, JSOTSup 217, Sheffield: Sheffield Academic Press.

—— (1998), 'The Shape of Book Four of the Psalter and the Shape of Second Isaiah', *JSOT* 80: 63–76.

Dahood, M. (1970), *Psalms III: 101–150*, ABC 17A, New York: Doubleday.

Davis, D. R. (1999), *2 Samuel: Out of Every Adversity*, Focus on the Bible, Fearn: Christian Focus.

—— (2002), *The Wisdom and the Folly: An Exposition of the Book of First Kings*, Focus on the Bible, Fearn: Christian Focus.

deClaissé-Walford, N. L. (1997), *Reading from the Beginning: The Shaping of the Hebrew Psalter*, Macon: Mercer University Press.

—— (2014), 'The Canonical Approach to Scripture and *The Editing of the Hebrew Psalter*', in N. L. deClaissé-Walford (ed.), *The Shape and Shaping of the Book of Psalms: The Current State of Scholarship*, Ancient Israel and Its Literature, Atlanta: SBL Press, 1–11.

deClaissé-Walford, N. L., R. A. Jacobson and B. L. Tanner (2014), *The Book of Psalms*, NICOT, Grand Rapids and Cambridge: Eerdmans.

Deissler, A. (1955), *Psalm 119 (118) und seine Theologie: Ein Beitrag zur Erforschung der anthologischen Stilgattung im Alten Testament*, Münchener Theologische Studien 1/11, Munich: Karl Zink.

—— (1993), *Die Psalmen*, 7th edn, Düsseldorf: Patmos.

Delitzsch, F. (1888), *Biblical Commentary on the Psalms, vol. 2: Psalms 36–89*, tr. D. Eaton, London: Hodder & Stoughton (4th rev. German edn 1883).

—— (1889), *Biblical Commentary on the Psalms, vol. 3: Psalms 90–150*, tr. D. Eaton, London: Hodder & Stoughton (4th rev. German edn 1883).

—— (1894), *Biblical Commentary on the Psalms, vol. 1: Psalms 1–35*, tr. D. Eaton, London: Hodder & Stoughton (4th rev. German edn 1883).

Dempsey, C. J. (2015), 'Poems, Prayers and Promises: The Psalms and Israel's Three Covenants', in R. J. Bautch and G. N. Knoppers (eds.), *Covenant in the Persian Period: From Genesis to Chronicles*, Winona Lake: Eisenbrauns, 331–338.

Dempster, S. G. (2003), *Dominion and Dynasty: A Biblical Theology of the Hebrew Bible*, NSBT 15, Leicester: Apollos; Downers Grove: InterVarsity Press.

Denault, P. (2014), 'By Farther Steps: A Seventeenth-Century Particular Baptist Covenant Theology', in R. C. Barcellos (ed.), *Recovering a Covenantal Heritage: Essays in Baptist Covenant Theology*, Palmdale: RBAP, 71–107.

—— (2017), *The Distinctiveness of Baptist Covenant Theology: A Comparison between Seventeenth-Century Particular Baptist and Paedobaptist Federalism*, 2nd edn, Birmingham: Solid Ground.

Driver, S. (1915), *Studies in the Psalms*, London: Hodder & Stoughton.

Dumbrell, W. J. (1980), 'The Davidic Covenant', *Reformed Theological Review* 39: 40–47.

—— (1984), *Covenant and Creation: An Old Testament Covenantal Theology*, Exeter: Paternoster; Flemington Markets: Lancer.

—— (2002), *The Faith of Israel: A Theological Survey of the Old Testament*, 2nd edn, Grand Rapids: Baker.

Dumortier, J.-B. (1972), 'Un rituel d'intronisation: Le Ps. LXXXIX 2–38', *VT* 22: 176–196.

Eaton, J. H. (2003), *The Psalms: A Historical and Spiritual Commentary with an Introduction and New Translation*, London: T&T Clark.

Ellison, S. D. (2021), 'Old Testament Hope: Psalm 4, the Psalter, and the Anointed One', *Themelios* 46: 534–545.

Emadi, M. H. (2022), *The Royal Priest: Psalm 110 in Biblical Theology*, NSBT 60, London: Apollos; Downers Grove: InterVarsity Press.

Emerton, J. A. (2000), 'The Problem of Psalm LXXXVII', *VT* 50: 183–199.

Eslinger, L. (1994), *House of God or House of David: The Rhetoric of 2 Samuel 7*, JSOTSup 164, Sheffield: Sheffield Academic Press.

Estes, D. J. (2019), *Psalms 73–150*, NAC 13, Nashville: B&H.

Even-Shoshan, A. (1989), *A New Concordance of the Bible: Thesaurus of the Language of the Bible. Hebrew and Aramaic Roots, Words, Proper Names, Phrases and Synonyms*, 2nd edn, Jerusalem: Kiryat-Sefer.

Eveson, P. (2014), *Psalms: From Suffering to Glory, vol. 1: Psalms 1–72, The Servant King*, Darlington: EP Books.

—— (2015), *Psalms: From Suffering to Glory, vol. 2: Psalms 73–150, God's Manual of Spirituality*, Welwyn: EP Books.

Ferry, B. C. (2009), 'Works in the Mosaic Covenant: A Reformed Taxonomy', in B. D. Estelle, J. V. Fesko and D. VanDrunen, *The Law Is Not of Faith: Essays on Works and Grace in the Mosaic Covenant*, Phillipsburg: P&R, 76–103.

Fesko, J. V. (2016), *The Trinity and the Covenant of Redemption*, Mentor, Fearn: Christian Focus.

Feuillet, A. (1975), 'Les Psaumes eschatologiques du règne de Yahvé', *Études d'exégèse et de théologie biblique: Ancien Testament*, Paris: Gabalda, 363–394.

Firth, D. G. (2005), 'Speech Acts and Covenant in 2 Samuel 7:1–17', in J. A. Grant and A. I. Wilson (eds.), *The God of Covenant: Biblical, Theological and Contemporary Perspectives*, Leicester: Apollos, 79–99.

Floyd, M. H. (1992), 'Psalm LXXXIX: A Prophetic Complaint about the Fulfillment of an Oracle', *VT* 42: 442–457.

Freedman, D. N. (1985), 'Who Asks (or Tells) God to Repent?', *Bible Review* 1.4, 56–59.

—— (1999), *Psalm 119: The Exaltation of Torah*, Biblical and Judaic Studies from the University of California, San Diego 6, Winona Lake: Eisenbrauns.

Freedman, D. N., and D. Miano (2003), 'People of the New Covenant', in S. E. Porter and J. C. R. de Roo (eds.), *The Concept of the Covenant in the Second Temple Period*, Supplements to the Journal for the Study of Judaism 71, Leiden: Brill, 7–26.

Frey, R. (2022), *Introduction à la théologie de la nouvelle alliance*, Trois-Rivières: Publications Chrétiennes.

Gentry, P. J., and S. J. Wellum (2018), *Kingdom through Covenant: A Biblical-Theological Understanding of the Covenants*, 2nd edn, Wheaton: Crossway.

Gerstenberger, E. H. (2001), *Psalms, Part 2, and Lamentations*, FOTL 15, Grand Rapids and Cambridge: Eerdmans.

Gese, H. (1974), 'Die Entstehung der Büchereinteilung des Psalters', in *Vom Sinai zum Sion: Alttestamentliche Beiträge zur biblischen Theologie*, Beiträge zur Evangelischen Theologie 64, Munich: Chr. Kaiser Verlag, 159–167.

Gibson, J. C. L. (1994), *Davidson's Introductory Hebrew Grammar – Syntax*, Edinburgh: T&T Clark.

Gileadi, A. (1988), 'The Davidic Covenant: A Theological Basis for Corporate Protection', in A. Gileadi (ed.), *Israel's Apostasy and Restoration*, FS R. K. Harrison, Grand Rapids: Baker, 157–163.

Girard, M. (1994a), *Les Psaumes redécouverts: De la structure au sens, vol. 2: Psaumes 51–100*, Quebec: Bellarmin.

—— (1994b), *Les Psaumes redécouverts: De la structure au sens, vol. 3: Psaumes 101–150*, Quebec: Bellarmin.

——(1996), *Les Psaumes redécouverts: De la structure au sens, vol. 1: Psaumes 1–50* (*Les Psaumes: Analyse structurelle et interprétation*, 1984), 2nd edn, Quebec: Bellarmin.

Goldingay, J. (2006), *Psalms, vol. 1: Psalms 1–41*, BCOT, Grand Rapids: Baker Academic.

—— (2007), *Psalms, vol. 2: Psalms 42–89*, BCOT, Grand Rapids: Baker Academic.

—— (2008), *Psalms, vol. 3: Psalms 90–150*, BCOT, Grand Rapids: Baker Academic.

Goldsworthy, G. L. (1991), *According to Plan: The Unfolding Revelation of God in the Bible*, Leicester: Inter-Varsity Press; Homebush West: Lancer.

Gordon, R. P. (1984), *1 & 2 Samuel*, OTG 2, Sheffield: JSOT Press.

—— (1986), *1 & 2 Samuel: A Commentary*, Exeter: Paternoster.

Gosse, B. (1998), 'L'Alliance avec Abraham et les relectures de l'histoire d'Israël en Ne 9, Ps 105–106, 135–136 et 1 Ch 16', *Transeuphratène* 15, Mélanges J. Briend 2, 1998, 123–135.

—— (2002), 'Ex 15, Ps 120–134 et le livre d'Isaïe, le salut d'Israël et celui du Psalmiste (II)', *Bibbia e Oriente* 44: 193–206.

Goswell, G. (2020), 'The Portrait of David in the Psalter', in A. T. Abernethy and G. Goswell (eds.), *God's Messiah in the Old Testament: Expectations of a Coming King*, Grand Rapids: Baker Academic, 182–196.

Goulder, M. D. (1975), 'The Fourth Book of the Psalter', *JTS* 26: 269–289.

—— (1982), *The Psalms of the Sons of Korah*, JSOTSup 20, Sheffield: JSOT Press.

—— (1998), *The Psalms of the Return (Book V, Psalms 107–150)*, JSOTSup 258, Sheffield: Sheffield Academic Press.

Grelot, P. (1962), *Sens chrétien de l'Ancien Testament: Esquisse d'un traité dogmatique*, Tournai: Desclée.

Grisanti, M. (1999), 'The Davidic Covenant', *The Master's Seminary Journal* 10: 233–250.

Grogan, G. W. (2008), *Psalms*, Two Horizons Old Testament Commentary, Grand Rapids and Cambridge: Eerdmans.

Gundersen, D. A. (2015), 'Davidic Hope in Book IV of the Psalter', PhD diss., Southern Baptist Theological Seminary.

Hamilton Jr, J. M. (2021a), 'Did the New Testament Authors Read the Psalter as a Book?', *Southern Baptist Journal of Theology* 25.5: 9–34.

—— (2021b), *Psalms, vol. 1: Psalms 1–72*, EBTC, Bellingham: Lexham Academic.

—— (2021c), *Psalms, vol. 2: Psalms 73–150*, EBTC, Bellingham: Lexham Academic.

Haney, R. G. (2002), *Text and Concept Analysis in Royal Psalms*, SBL 30, New York: Peter Lang.

Harman, A. M. (1995), 'The Continuity of the Covenant Curses in the Imprecations of the Psalter', *Reformed Theological Review* 54: 65–72.

—— (1998), *Commentary on the Psalms*, Mentor, Fearn: Christian Focus.

—— (2010), 'The Abrahamic Covenant in the Psalter', FS W. J. Dumbrell, Supplement to the *Reformed Theological Review* 4, 83–99.

Harmon, M. S. (2020), *The Servant of the Lord and His Servant People: Tracing a Biblical Theme through the Canon*, NSBT 54, London: Apollos; Downers Grove: InterVarsity Press.

Hayes, E. (1999), 'The Unity of the Egyptian Hallel: Psalms 113–118', *BBR* 9, 145–156.

Hely Hutchinson, J. (2005a), 'A New-Covenant Slogan in the Old Testament', in J. A. Grant and A. I. Wilson (eds.), *The God of Covenant: Biblical, Theological and Contemporary Perspectives*, Leicester: Apollos, 100–121.

—— (2005b), 'The Psalms and Praise', in P. S. Johnston and D. G. Firth (eds.), *Interpreting the Psalms*, Leicester: Inter-Varsity Press, 85–100.

—— (2006), 'Alliance davidique et nouveauté de l'alliance nouvelle dans la perspective du psautier hébraïque', Vaux-sur-Seine, France: Faculté Libre de Théologie Évangélique, unpublished doctoral dissertation.

—— (2013a), 'Psalms', in *NIV Proclamation Bible: Correctly Handling the Word of Truth*, London: Hodder & Stoughton, 577–579.

—— (2013b), 'The Psalter as a Book', in A. G. Shead (ed.), *Stirred by a Noble Theme: The Book of Psalms in the Life of the Church*, Nottingham: Apollos, 23–45.

—— (2015a), 'Le Messianisme dans le livre des Psaumes', *Redécouvrir les Psaumes*, Interprétation, Vaux-sur-Seine: Edifac; Charols: Excelsis, chs. 5–6, 105–150.

—— (2015b), 'La Théologie biblique: Pourquoi est-elle importante est passionnante?', *Le Maillon,* Spring: 5–9, <www.institutbiblique.be/article?x=la-theologie-biblique-pourquoi-est-elle-importante-et-passionnante> (accessed 7 December 2022).

—— (2021a), 'Le Jour que le Seigneur a fait (Psaumes 118.24)', in S. Perez (ed.), *Hors contexte: Redécouvrez 17 versets connus mais mal compris*, Lyons: Clé, 67–73.

—— (2021b), 'La Motivation la plus performante qui soit pour l'évangélisation?', *Le Maillon*, Winter–Spring: 17–21, <www.institutbiblique.be/article?x=la-motivation-la-plus-performante-qui-soit-pour-l-evangelisation&p=2> (accessed 31 December 2022).

—— (2022), *La Nouveauté de la nouvelle alliance*, Charols: Excelsis.

Hengstenberg, E. W. (1851), *Commentary on the Psalms*, vol. 1, tr. Patrick Fairbairn and John Thomson, 3rd edn, Edinburgh: T&T Clark.

—— (1854), *Commentary on the Psalms,* vol. 3, tr. Patrick Fairbairn and John Thomson, 2nd edn, Edinburgh: T&T Clark.

Hensley, A. D. (2018), *Covenant Relationships and the Editing of the Hebrew Psalter*, LHBOTS (formerly JSOTSup) 666, London: Bloomsbury T&T Clark.

—— (2021), 'David, Once and Future King? A Closer Look at the Postscript of Psalm 72.20', *JSOT* 46: 24–43.

Hoftijzer, J. (1956), *Die Verheissungen an die drei Erzväter*, Leiden: Brill.

Horton, M. S. (2022), 'Covenant Theology', in B. E. Parker and R. J. Lucas (eds.), *Covenantal and Dispensational Theologies: Four Views on the Continuity of Scripture*, Spectrum Multiview, Downers Grove: IVP Academic, 35–73.

Hossfeld, F.-L. (2002), 'Ps 89 und das vierte Psalmenbuch (Ps 90–106)', in E. Otto and E. Zenger (eds.), *'Mein Sohn bist du' (Ps 2,7): Studien zu den Königspsalmen*, Stuttgart: Katholisches Bibelwerk, 173–183.

Hossfeld, F.-L., and E. Zenger (1993), *Die Psalmen I: Psalm 1–50*, Die Neue Echter Bibel, Würzburg: Echter Verlag.

—— (2012), *Die Psalmen III: Psalm 101–150*, Die Neue Echter Bibel, Würzburg: Echter Verlag.

House, P. R. (1998), *Old Testament Theology*, Downers Grove: InterVarsity Press.

Howard Jr, D. M. (1993), 'A Contextual Reading of Psalms 90–94', in J. C. McCann Jr (ed.), *The Shape and Shaping of the Psalter*, JSOTSup 159, Sheffield: Sheffield Academic Press, 108–123.

—— (1997), *The Structure of Psalms 93–100*, Biblical and Judaic Studies from the University of California, San Diego, 5, Winona Lake: Eisenbrauns.

Jacquet, L. (1975), *Les Psaumes et le coeur de l'Homme: Étude textuelle, littéraire et doctrinale. Introduction et Premier Livre du Psautier: Psaumes 1 à 41*, Gembloux: Duculot.

—— (1977), *Les Psaumes et le coeur de l'Homme: Étude textuelle, littéraire et doctrinale. Introduction et Premier Livre du Psautier: Psaumes 42 à 100*, Gembloux: Duculot.

—— (1978), *Les Psaumes et le coeur de l'Homme: Étude textuelle, littéraire et doctrinale. Psaumes 101 à 150*, Gembloux: Duculot.

Japhet, S. (1993), *I & II Chronicles: A Commentary*, OTL, London: SCM Press.

Jean-Nesmy, C. (ed.) (1973), *La Tradition médite le Psautier: Psaumes 1 à 71*, Paris: Téqui.

Jenkins, S. G. (2020), 'The Antiquity of Psalter Shape Efforts', *TynBul* 71: 161–180.

—— (2022), *Imprecations in the Psalms: Love for Enemies in Hard Places*, Eugene: Wipf & Stock.

Jensen, J. (1973), *The Use of tôrâ by Isaiah: His Debate with the Wisdom Tradition*, CBQMS 3, Washington: Catholic Biblical Association of America.

Johnson, J. D. (2014), 'The Fatal Flaw of Infant Baptism: The Dichotomous Nature of the Abrahamic Covenant', in R. C. Barcellos (ed.), *Recovering a Covenantal Heritage: Essays in Baptist Covenant Theology*, Palmdale: RBAP, 223–256.

Johnson, T. L. (2003), 'Restoring Psalm Singing to Our Worship', in P. G. Ryken, D. W. H. Thomas and J. L. Duncan (eds.), *Give Praise to God: A Vision for Reforming Worship*, FS J. M. Boice, Phillipsburg: P&R, 257–286.

Jones, G. H. (1965), 'The Decree of Yahweh (Ps II 7)', *VT* 15: 336–344.

Kaiser Jr, W. C. (1972), 'The Old Promise and the New Covenant: Jeremiah 31:31–34', *JETS* 15: 11–23.

—— (1974), 'The Blessing of David: The Charter for Humanity', in J. H. Skilton (ed.), *The Law and the Prophets: Old Testament Studies Prepared in Honor of Oswald Thompson Allis*, Nutley: Presbyterian and Reformed, 298–318.

—— (1978), *Toward an Old Testament Theology*, Grand Rapids: Zondervan.

—— (1996a), 'The Law as God's Guidance for the Promotion of Holiness', in W. G. Strickland (ed.), *Five Views on Law and Gospel* (*The Law, the Gospel and the Modern Christian*, 1993), Grand Rapids: Zondervan, 177–199.

—— (1996b), 'Response to Douglas Moo', in W. G. Strickland (ed.), *Five Views on Law and Gospel* (*The Law, the Gospel and the Modern Christian*, 1993), Grand Rapids: Zondervan, 393–400.

—— (1996c), 'Response to Wayne G. Strickland', in W. G. Strickland (ed.), *Five Views on Law and Gospel* (*The Law, the Gospel and the Modern Christian*, 1993), Grand Rapids: Zondervan, 302–308.

Kidner, F. D. (1973), *Psalms 1–72: An Introduction and Commentary on Books I and II of the Psalms*, TOTC, Leicester: Inter-Varsity Press; Downers Grove: InterVarsity Press.

—— (1975), *Psalms 73–150: A Commentary on Books III to V of the Psalms*, TOTC, Leicester: Inter-Varsity Press; Downers Grove: InterVarsity Press.

Kim, J. (1989), *Psalm 89: Its Biblical-Theological Contribution to the Presence of Law within the Unconditional Covenant*, Ann Arbor: University Microfilms International.

Kirkpatrick, A. F. (1891), *The Book of Psalms (I—XLI)*, Cambridge Bible for Schools and Colleges, Cambridge: Cambridge University Press.

—— (1895), *The Book of Psalms (XLII–LXXXIX)*, Cambridge Bible for Schools and Colleges, Cambridge: Cambridge University Press.

—— (1901), *The Book of Psalms (XC—CL)*, Cambridge Bible for Schools and Colleges, Cambridge: Cambridge University Press.

Kissane, E. J. (1954), *The Book of Psalms, Translated from a Critically Revised Hebrew Text, with a Commentary, vol. 2: Psalms 73–150*, Dublin: Browne & Nolan.

Koorevaar, H. (2010), 'The Psalter as a Structured Theological Story with the Aid of Subscripts and Superscripts', in E. Zenger (ed.), *The Composition of the Book of Psalms*, BETL 238, Leuven: Peeters, 579–592.

Kraus, H.-J. (2003), *Psalmen 60–150*, Biblischer Kommentar Altes Testament 15/2, 7th edn, Neukirchen-Vluyn: Neukirchener Verlag.

Lam, J. (2014), 'Psalm 2 and the Disinheritance of Earthly Rulers: New Light from the Ugaritic Legal Text RS 94.2168', *VT* 64: 34–64.

Lamarche, P. (1961), *Zacharie IX–XIV: Structure littéraire et messianisme*, Paris: Gabalda.

Leow, W.-P. (2017), 'Form and Experience Dwelling in Unity', *TynBul* 68: 185–202.

Levenson, J. D. (1987), 'The Sources of Torah: Psalm 119 and the Modes of Revelation in Second Temple Judaism', in P. D. Miller Jr, P. D. Hanson and S. D. McBride (eds.), *Ancient Israelite Religion*, FS F. M. Cross, Philadelphia: Fortress, 559–574.

Lohfink, N. (1990), 'Die Universalisierung der "Bundesformel" in Ps 100,3', *Theologie und Philosophie* 65: 172–183.

Long, V. P. (1994), *The Art of Biblical History*, Foundations of Contemporary Interpretation 5, Grand Rapids: Zondervan.

Longman III, T. (2014), *Psalms*, TOTC 15–16, Nottingham: Inter-Varsity Press; Downers Grove: InterVarsity Press.

Lucas, E. C. (2003), *Exploring the Old Testament, vol. 3: A Guide to the Psalms and Wisdom Literature*, Downers Grove: InterVarsity Press.

McCann Jr, J. C. (1993), *A Theological Introduction to the Book of Psalms*, Nashville: Abingdon.

McComiskey, T. E. (1985a), *The Covenants of Promise: A Theology of the Old Testament Covenants*, Grand Rapids: Baker.

—— (1985b), 'Micah', in F. E. Gaebelein (ed.), EBC 7, Grand Rapids: Zondervan, 395–445.

—— (1998), 'Zechariah', in T. McComiskey (ed.), *The Minor Prophets: An Exegetical and Expository Commentary, vol. 3: Zephaniah–Malachi*, Grand Rapids: Baker, 1003–1244.

McConville, J. G. (2002a), *Deuteronomy*, AOTC 5, Leicester: Apollos; Downers Grove: InterVarsity Press.

—— (2002b), *Exploring the Old Testament, vol. 4: A Guide to the Prophets*, Downers Grove: InterVarsity Press.

McFall, L. (2000), 'The Evidence for a Logical Arrangement of the Psalter', *WTJ* 62: 223–256.

McKelvey, M. G. (2010) (repr. 2014), *Moses, David and the High Kingship of Yahweh: A Canonical Study of Book IV of the Psalter*, Gorgias Dissertations 55, Piscataway: Gorgias Press.

Maclaren, A. (1903), *The Psalms, vol. 3: Psalms 90–150*, 5th edn, London: Hodder & Stoughton.

Malone, A. S. (2017), *God's Mediators: A Biblical Theology of Priesthood*, NSBT 43, London: Apollos; Downers Grove: InterVarsity Press.

Martin-Achard, R. (1989), 'Quelques remarques sur la nouvelle alliance chez Jérémie (Jérémie 31,31–34)', in C. Brekelmans, *Questions disputées d'Ancien Testament: Méthode et théologie*, rev. M. Vervenne, BETL 33, Leuven: Leuven University Press, 1989, 140–164.

Mays, J. L. (1994), *Psalms*, Interpretation, Louisville: John Knox.

Meyer, J. C. (2016), 'The Mosaic Law, Theological Systems, and the Glory of Christ', in S. J. Wellum and B. E. Parker (eds.), *Progressive Covenantalism: Charting a Course between Dispensational and Covenant Theologies*, Nashville: B&H Academic, 69–99.

Michaud, R. (1993), *Les Psaumes: Adaptation de l'oeuvre en trois volumes de Gianfranco Ravasi*, Montreal: Editions Paulines; Paris: Médiaspaul.

Milgrom, J. (2001), *Leviticus 23–27: A New Translation with Introduction and Commentary*, ABC 3B, New York: Doubleday.

Mitchell, D. C. (1997), *The Message of the Psalter: An Eschatological Programme in the Book of Psalms*, JSOTSup 252, Sheffield: Sheffield Academic Press.

Motyer, J. A. (1993), *The Prophecy of Isaiah: An Introduction and Commentary*, Downers Grove: InterVarsity Press.

—— (1994), 'The Psalms', in D. A. Carson, R. T. France, J. A. Motyer and G. J. Wenham (eds.), *New Bible Commentary*, 4th edn, Leicester: Inter-Varsity Press; Downers Grove: InterVarsity Press, 485–583.

Nelson, R. D. (2002), *Deuteronomy: A Commentary*, OTL, Louisville and London: Westminster John Knox.

Ngoda, S. S. (2014), 'Revisiting the Theocratic Agenda of Book 4 of the Psalter for Interpretive Premise', in N. L. deClaissé-Walford (ed.), *The Shape and Shaping of the Book of Psalms: The Current State of Scholarship*, Ancient Israel and Its Literature, Atlanta: SBL Press, 147–159.

Nichols, A. H. (1996), *Mirror of the Soul: 40 Studies on the Psalms for Lent and Other Times*, Sydney: Anglican Press Australia.

Nicole, É. (1996), 'L'Ancien Testament comme pédagogie de Dieu pour le lecteur', *Fac-Réflexion* 34: 4–14.

—— (2004), 'Atonement in the Pentateuch', in C. E. Hill and F. A. James (eds.), *The Glory of the Atonement: Biblical, Theological and Practical Perspectives*, FS R. Nicole, Downers Grove: InterVarsity Press, 35–50.

Nielsen, K. (2002), 'Why Not Plough with an Ox and an Ass Together? Or: Why Not Read Ps 119 Together with Pss 120–134?', *SJOT* 14: 56–66.

Olson, D. T. (1994), *Deuteronomy and the Death of Moses: A Theological Reading*, Overtures to Biblical Theology, Minneapolis: Augsburg Fortress.

Oswalt, J. N. (1998), *The Book of Isaiah: Chapters 40–66*, NICOT, Grand Rapids and Cambridge: Eerdmans.

Parker, B. E., and R. J. Lucas (eds.) (2022), *Covenantal and Dispensational Theologies: Four Views on the Continuity of Scripture*, Spectrum Multiview, Downers Grove: IVP Academic.

Payne, J. B. (1988), *1, 2 Chronicles*, EBC 4, Grand Rapids: Zondervan.

Pentecost, J. D. (1958/1964), *Things to Come: A Study in Biblical Eschatology*, Grand Rapids: Zondervan.

Petterson, A. R. (2015), *Haggai, Zechariah & Malachi*, AOTC 25, Nottingham: Apollos; Downers Grove: InterVarsity Press.

Pratt, R. L. (1998), *1 and 2 Chronicles*, Mentor, Fearn: Christian Focus.

Prinsloo, G. T. M. (2005), 'The Role of Space in the שירי המעלות (Psalms 120–134)', *Biblica* 86: 457–477.

—— (2006), 'Še'ôl → Yerûšālayim ← Šāmayim: spatial orientation in the Egyptian Hallel (Psalms 113–118)', *OTE* 19: 739–760.

Renaud, B. (1989), 'De la bénédiction du roi à la bénédiction de Dieu (Ps 72)', *Biblica* 70: 305–326.

—— (1997), 'Un oracle prophétique (2 S 7) invalidé? Une approche du Psaume 89', in J.-G. Heintz (ed.), *Oracles et prophéties dans l'antiquité: Actes du Colloque de Strasbourg, 15–17 juin 1995*, Travaux du Centre de Recherche sur le Proche-Orient et la Grèce Antiques 15, Paris: De Boccard, 215–229.

Renihan, M., and S. Renihan (2014), 'Reformed Baptist Covenant Theology and Biblical Theology', in Richard C. Barcellos (ed.), *Recovering a Covenantal Heritage: Essays in Baptist Covenant Theology*, Palmdale: RBAP, 475–506.

Richardson, N. H. (1987), 'Psalm 106: Yahweh's Succoring Love Saves from the Death of a Broken Covenant', in J. H. Marks and R. M. Good (eds.), *Love and Death in the Ancient Near East*, FS M. H. Pope, Guilford: Four Quarters, 191–203.

Robertson, O. P. (1980), *The Christ of the Covenants*, Phillipsburg: Presbyterian and Reformed.

—— (2000), *The Israel of God: Yesterday, Today, and Tomorrow*, Phillipsburg: P&R.

—— (2015), *The Flow of the Psalms: Discovering their Structure and Theology*, Phillipsburg: P&R.

Roffey, J. W. (1997), 'Beyond Reality: Poetic Discourse and Psalm 107', in E. E. Carpenter (ed.), *A Biblical Itinerary: In Search of Method, Form and Content, Essays in Honor of George W. Coats*, JSOTSup 240, Sheffield: Sheffield Academic Press, 60–76.

Rogerson, J. W., and J. W. McKay (1977), *Psalms 101–150*, Cambridge Bible Commentary on the New English Bible, Cambridge: Cambridge University Press.

Romerowski, S. (2016), *Manuel pour le cours sur les prophètes, troisième partie* [*Nahoum–Sophonie– Habaquq–Jérémie– Lamentations*], Nogent-sur-Marne (unpublished, quoted with permission).

Ross, A. P. (2011), *A Commentary on the Psalms, vol. 1: Psalms 1–41*, KEL, Grand Rapids: Kregel.

—— (2013), *A Commentary on the Psalms, vol. 2: Psalms 42–89*, KEL, Grand Rapids: Kregel.

—— (2016), *A Commentary on the Psalms, vol. 3: Psalms 90–150*, KEL, Grand Rapids: Kregel.

Sailhamer, J. H. (1992), *The Pentateuch as Narrative: A Biblical-Theological Commentary*, Library of Biblical Interpretation, Grand Rapids: Zondervan.

Sakenfeld, K. D. (1978), *The Meaning of hesed (sic) in the Hebrew Bible: A New Enquiry*, HSM 17, Missoula: Scholars Press.

Schaefer, K. (2001), *Psalms*, Berit Olam, Collegeville: Liturgical Press.

Schibler, D. (1989), *Le Livre de Michée*, CEB, Vaux-sur-Seine: Edifac.

Schmutzer, A. J., and R. X. Gauthier (2009), "The Identity of "Horn" in Psalm 148:14a: An Exegetical Investigation in the MT and LXX Versions', *BBR* 19: 161–183.

Schreiner, T. R. (2010), *Galatians*, Zondervan Exegetical Commentary on the New Testament, Grand Rapids: Zondervan.

—— (2017), *Covenant and God's Purpose for the World*, Short Studies in Biblical Theology, Wheaton: Crossway.

Schröten, J. (1995), *Entstehung, Komposition und Wirkungsgeschichte des 118. Psalms*, Bonner Biblische Beiträge 95, Weinheim: Beltz Athenäum.

Seitz, C. R. (1998), 'Royal Promises in the Canonical Books of Isaiah and the Psalms', in *Word without End: The Old Testament as Abiding Theological Witness*, Grand Rapids and Cambridge: Eerdmans, 150–167.

Shead, A. G. (2012), *A Mouth Full of Fire: The Word of God in the Words of Jeremiah*, NSBT 29, Nottingham; Apollos; Downers Grove: InterVarsity Press.

Sheppard, G. T. (1992), 'Theology and the Book of Psalms', *Interpretation* 46: 143–155.

Ska, J.-L. (2000), *Introduction à la lecture du Pentateuque: Clés pour l'interprétation des cinq premiers livres de la Bible*, tr. F. Vermorel, Brussels: Lessius.

Smith, G. V. (2001), *Hosea, Amos, Micah*, NIVAC, Grand Rapids: Zondervan.

Snearly, M. K. (2016), *The Return of the King: Messianic Expectation in Book V of the Psalter*, LHBOTS (formerly JSOTSup) 624, London: Bloomsbury T&T Clark.

Snoeberger, M. A. (2022), 'Traditional Dispensationalism', in B. E. Parker and R. J. Lucas (eds.), *Covenantal and Dispensational*

Theologies: Four Views on the Continuity of Scripture, Spectrum Multiview, Downers Grove: IVP Academic, 147–182.

Stam, C. (1999), *The Covenant of Love: Exploring Our Relationship with God*, Winnipeg: Premier.

Stuart, D. K. (1998), 'Malachi', in T. E. McComiskey (ed.), *The Minor Prophets: An Exegetical and Expository Commentary, vol. 3: Zephaniah–Malachi*, Grand Rapids: Baker, 1245–1396.

—— (2006), *Exodus*, NAC 2, Nashville: B&H.

Sumpter, P. (2013), 'The Coherence of Psalms 15–24', *Biblica* 94: 186–209.

Sweeney, M. (2000), *The Twelve Prophets, vol. 2: Micah–Malachi*, Berit Olam, Collegeville: Liturgical Press.

Tate, M. E. (1990), *Psalms 51–100*, WBC 20, Dallas: Word.

Terrien, S. L. (2003), *The Psalms: Strophic Structure and Theological Commentary*, Eerdmans Critical Commentary, Grand Rapids and Cambridge: Eerdmans.

Tournay, R. J. (1984), 'Le Psaume CXLIV: Structure et interprétation', *RB* 91: 520–530.

—— (1988), *Voir et entendre Dieu avec les Psaumes, ou la liturgie prophétique du second temple à Jérusalem*, CRB 24, Paris: Gabalda.

Tov, E. (1972), 'L'Incidence de la critique textuelle sur la critique littéraire dans le livre de Jérémie', *RB* 79: 189–199.

Tucker, W. D., and J. A. Grant (2018), *Psalms: Volume 2*, NIVAC, Grand Rapids: Zondervan.

Van Groningen, G. (1997), *Messianic Revelation in the Old Testament*, 2 vols., Eugene: Wipf & Stock.

Van Pelt, M. V. (ed.) (2016), *A Biblical-Theological Introduction to the Old Testament: The Gospel Promised*, Wheaton: Crossway.

Van Winkle, D. W. (1985), 'The Relationship of the Nations to Yahweh and to Israel in Isaiah XL–LV', *VT* 35: 446–458.

Vang, C. (1995), 'Ps 2,11–12 – A New Look at an Old Crux Interpretum', *SJOT* 9: 163–184.

VanGemeren, W. A. (2008), *Psalms*, EBC 5, ed. T. Longman III and D. E. Garland, rev. edn, Grand Rapids: Zondervan.

Veijola, T. (1982), *Verheissung in der Krise, Studien zur Literatur und Theologie der Exilszeit anhand des 89. Psalms*, Annales Academiae Scientiarum Fennicae B 220, Helsinki: Suomalainen Tiedeakatemia.

Verhoef, P. (1987), *The Books of Haggai and Malachi*, NICOT, Grand Rapids: Eerdmans.

Vesco, J.-L. (2008a), *Le Psautier de David traduit et commenté*, vol. 1, LD, Paris: Cerf.

—— (2008b), *Le Psautier de David traduit et commenté*, vol. 2, LD, Paris: Cerf.

Von Rad, G. (1957), *Theologie des Alten Testaments, vol. I: Die Theologie des geschichtlichen Überlieferungen Israels*, Munich: Chr. Kaiser Verlag.

Wallace, H. N. (1999), 'What Chronicles Has to Say about Psalms', in M. P. Graham and S. L. McKenzie (eds.), *The Chronicler as Author: Studies in Text and Texture*, JSOTSup 263, Sheffield: Sheffield Academic Press, 267–291.

Waltke, B. K. (1988), 'The Phenomenon of Conditionality within Unconditional Covenants', in A. Gileadi (ed.), *Israel's Apostasy and Restoration*, FS R. K. Harrison, Grand Rapids: Baker, 123–139.

—— (1993), 'Micah', in T. E. McComiskey (ed.), *The Minor Prophets: An Exegetical and Expositional Commentary, vol. 2: Obadiah–Habakkuk*, Grand Rapids: Baker, 591–764.

Waltke, B. K., and M. O'Connor (1990), *An Introduction to Biblical Hebrew Syntax*, Winona Lake: Eisenbrauns.

Walton, J. H. (1991), 'Psalms: A Cantata about the Davidic Covenant', *JETS* 34: 21–31.

—— (1994), *Covenant: God's Purpose, God's Plan*, Grand Rapids: Zondervan.

Watts, R. E. (2003), 'Exodus', in T. D. Alexander and D. W. Baker (eds.), *Dictionary of the Old Testament: Pentateuch*, Leicester: Inter-Varsity Press; Downers Grove: InterVarsity Press, 482–484.

Webb, B. G. (1996), *The Message of Isaiah: On Eagles' Wings*, BST, Leicester: Inter-Varsity Press.

Weber, B. (2001), *Werkbuch Psalmen I: Die Psalmen 1 bis 72*, Stuttgart: Kohlhammer.

—— (2003), *Werkbuch Psalmen II: Die Psalmen 73 bis 150*, Stuttgart: Kohlhammer.

Weiser, A. (1962), *The Psalms: A Commentary*, OTL, Philadelphia: Westminster (5th German edn 1959).

Wells, T., and F. Zaspel (2002), *New Covenant Theology: Description, Definition, Defense*, Frederick: New Covenant Media.

Wellum, S. J., and B. E. Parker (eds.) (2016), *Progressive Covenantalism: Charting a Course between Dispensational and Covenant Theologies*, Nashville: B&H Academic.

Wenham, G. J. (1981), *Numbers: An Introduction and Commentary*, TOTC, Leicester: Inter-Varsity Press; Downers Grove: InterVarsity Press.

—— (2001), 'Rejoice the Lord Is King: Psalms 90–106 (Book 4)', in C. Bartholomew and A. West (eds.), *Praying by the Book: Reading the Psalms*, Carlisle: Paternoster, 89–120.

—— (2005), 'The Ethics of the Psalms', in P. S. Johnston and D. G. Firth (eds.), *Interpreting the Psalms*, Leicester: Inter-Varsity Press, 175–194.

—— (2012), *Psalms as Torah: Reading Biblical Song Ethically*, Studies in Theological Interpretation, Grand Rapids: Baker Academic.

White, A. B. (2008), *The Newness of the New Covenant*, Frederick: New Covenant Media.

——(2012), *What Is New Covenant Theology? An Introduction*, Frederick: New Covenant Media.

Whiting, M. J. (2013), 'Psalms 1 and 2 as a Hermeneutical Lens for Reading the Psalter', *EvQ* 85: 246–262.

Wilcock, M. (2001a), *The Message of Psalms 1–72: Songs for the People of God*, BST, Leicester: Inter-Varsity Press.

—— (2001b), *The Message of Psalms 73–150: Songs for the People of God*, BST, Leicester: Inter-Varsity Press.

Willgren, D. (2016), *The Formation of the 'Book' of Psalms*, Forschungen zum Alten Testament 2, Reihe 88, Tübingen: Mohr Siebeck.

Williams, D. (1986), *Psalms 1–72*, Mastering the Old Testament 13 (Communicator's Commentary Series, Old Testament), Dallas: Word.

—— (1987), *Psalms 73–150*, Mastering the Old Testament 14 (Communicator's Commentary Series, Old Testament), Dallas: Word.

Williamson, H. G. M. (1982), *1 and 2 Chronicles*, NCBC, Grand Rapids: Eerdmans; London: Marshall, Morgan & Scott.

—— (1998), *Variations on a Theme: King, Messiah and Servant in the Book of Isaiah*, Didsbury Lectures 1997, Carlisle: Paternoster.

Williamson, P. R. (2000a), 'Covenant', in T. D. Alexander and B. S. Rosner (eds.), *New Dictionary of Biblical Theology: Exploring the Unity and Diversity of Scripture*, Leicester: Inter-Varsity Press; Downers Grove: InterVarsity Press, 419–429.

—— (2000b), 'Promise and Fulfilment: The Territorial Inheritance', in P. S. Johnston and P. W. L. Walker (eds.), *The Land of Promise: Biblical, Theological and Contemporary Perspectives*, Leicester: Apollos; Downers Grove: InterVarsity Press, 15–34.

—— (2003), 'Covenant', in T. D. Alexander and D. W. Baker (eds.), *Dictionary of the Old Testament: Pentateuch*, Leicester: Inter-Varsity Press; Downers Grove: InterVarsity Press, 139–155.

—— (2007), *Sealed with an Oath: Covenant in God's Unfolding Purpose*, NSBT 23, Nottingham: Apollos; Downers Grove: InterVarsity Press.

Wilson, G. H. (1985), *The Editing of the Hebrew Psalter*, SBL Dissertation Series 76, Chico: Scholars Press.

—— (1986), 'The Use of Royal Psalms at the "Seams" of the Hebrew Psalter', *JSOT* 35: 85–94.

—— (2002a), *Psalms, vol. 1: From Biblical Text to Contemporary Life*, NIVAC, Grand Rapids: Zondervan.

—— (2002b), 'Psalms and Psalter: Paradigm for Biblical Theology', in S. J. Hafemann (ed.), *Biblical Theology: Retrospect and Prospect*, Leicester: Apollos; Downers Grove: InterVarsity Press, 100–110.

Witt, A. (2012), 'Hearing Psalm 102 within the Context of the Hebrew Psalter', *VT* 62: 582–606.

Würthwein, E. (1980), *The Text of the Old Testament: An Introduction to the Biblia Hebraica*, London: SCM Press.

Zenger, E. (1994), 'Das Weltenkönigtum des Gottes Israels (Ps 90–106)', in N. Lohfink and E. Zenger (eds.), *Der Gott Israels und die Völker: Untersuchungen zum Jesajabuch und zu den Psalmen*, Stuttgarter Bibelstudien 154, Stuttgart: Verlag Katholisches Bibelwerk, 151–178.

—— (1996), 'Komposition und Theologie des 5. Psalmenbuchs 107–145', *Biblische Notizen* 82: 97–116.

—— (1997a), '"Daß alles Fleisch den Namen seiner Heiligung segne" (Ps 145,21): Die Komposition Ps 145–150 als Anstoß zu einer christlich-jüdischen Psalmenhermeneutik', *Biblische Zeitschrift* 41: 1–27.

—— (1997b), *Die Nacht wird leuchten wie der Tag: Psalmenauslegungen*, Herder: Freiburg im Breisgau.

—— (1999), 'Der Psalter als Heiligtum', in B. Ego, A. Lange and P. Pilhofer (eds.), *Gemeinde ohne Tempel: Zur Substituierung und Transformation des Jerusalemer Tempels und seines Kults im Alten Testament, antiken Judentum und frühen Christentum*, WUNT 118, Tübingen: Mohr Siebeck, 115–130.

Ziegler, J. (1973), 'Ps 144.14', in H. Gese and H. P. Ruge (eds.), *Wort und Geschichte*, FS K. Elliger, Alter Orient und Altes Testament 18, Kevelaer: Butzon & Bercker; Neukirchen-Vluyn: Neukirchener Verlag, 191–197.

Zimmerli, W. (1960), 'Le Nouvel "Exode" dans le message des deux grands prophètes de l'exil', in D. Lys with J. Cadier (eds.), *Maqqél shâqédh: la branche d'amandier*, FS W. Vischer, Montpellier: Causse Graille Castelnau, 216–227.

—— (1972), 'Zwillingspsalmen', in J. Schreiner (ed.), *Wort, Lied und Gottesspruch: Beiträge zu Psalmen und Propheten*, FS J. Ziegler, Würzburg: Echter Verlag, 105–113.

Index of authors

Index of biblical covenants

Index of Scripture references

Titles in this series:

An index of Scripture references for all the volumes may be found at http://www.thegospelcoalition.org/resources/nsbt.